IMAGES
of America

LIVINGSTON

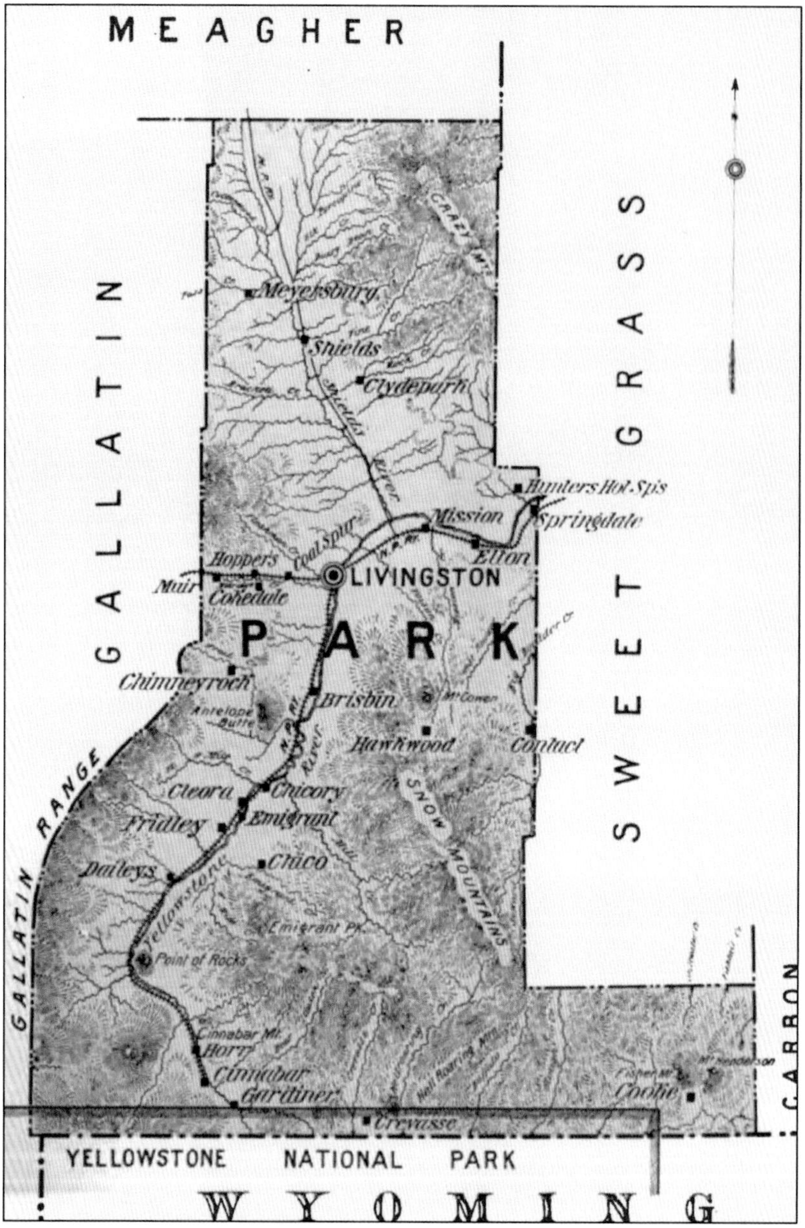

Carved out of Gallatin County in 1887, Park County was created with Livingston as its county seat. Located in south-central Montana and framed by the Gallatin Range to the west, Crazy Mountains to the north, Absaroka Mountains (Snow Mountains) to the east, and Yellowstone National Park to the south, Livingston's scenic locale charmed residents and tourists alike from its earliest day. (Department of the Interior.)

ON THE COVER: Originally built of brick or stone to provide engine service facilities, the roundhouse embodied the hub of railroad activities during the era of the steam locomotive. Hostlers, such as these men in this *c.* 1891 image, moved and serviced iron horses in the roundhouse in much the same manner as the older definition of the term, when men moved and tended horses in barns of early-day hostelries. (Yellowstone Gateway Museum.)

IMAGES
of America

LIVINGSTON

Elizabeth A. Watry and
Robert V. Goss

ARCADIA
PUBLISHING

ISBN 978-0-7385-7044-0

Published by Arcadia Publishing
Charleston, South Carolina

Printed in the United States of America

Library of Congress Control Number: 2009921922

For all general information contact Arcadia Publishing at:
Telephone 843-853-2070
Fax 843-853-0044
E-mail sales@arcadiapublishing.com
For customer service and orders:
Toll-Free 1-888-313-2665

Visit us on the Internet at www.arcadiapublishing.com

This book is dedicated to Doris Whithorn, Park County's self-appointed ambassador of local history. Her faithful devotion to chronicling community annals has been an inspiration to us all.

Contents

ACKNOWLEDGMENTS

Past, present, and future historians researching Montana's vast history owe a huge debt of gratitude to Bill and Doris Whithorn. This husband-and-wife team created an invaluable historical legacy for Montana with the compilation of photographs, newspapers, and documents of Livingston's past as well as other neighboring communities. Thank you, Doris, for leaving us your treasure trove! And thank you Yellowstone Gateway Museum for preserving and sharing this outstanding collection.

The authors would also like to thank a generous private collector who wishes to remain unnamed for a wonderful collection of photographs that have increased the importance of this book immeasurably. And thank you to the Pioneer Museum and various private collectors for granting us permission to publish images from their repositories.

INTRODUCTION

Long before white men traversed the high desert plateau of the Yellowstone River valley, Native Americans lived and camped in this region. Prior to the 1804–1806 Lewis and Clark expedition survey of the territory acquired by the Louisiana Purchase, the area surrounding Livingston, Montana, served as a favorite way point for the Crow as well as other transient Native American tribes. Upon their return trip to St. Louis from the Pacific coast, Captains Meriwether Lewis and William Clark chose to take separate routes through the area that was later established as the state of Montana. In an effort to expand their explorations, Lewis took a northern route to investigate the Marias River and Clark took a southern route to survey the Yellowstone River. On July 15, 1806, Clark and his party, including Sacajawea and her son, Pomp, stopped to rest and graze their horses on a bend of the Yellowstone just east of present-day Livingston. Within the next 80 years, this area of the Yellowstone River valley would be transformed from a mere intersection of Native American trails to an important cultural crossroad of the American West.

Fur trappers, relatively few in number, were the first to follow in the footsteps of Lewis and Clark. They plied their trade in relative peace within this long-established Native American territory for more than 30 years after Clark's trek along the Yellowstone River. But the discovery of gold in 1863 near Bannack, Montana, spawned a rush of prospectors and fortune seekers. South of present-day Livingston, the mining town of Yellowstone City, located at the mouth of Emigrant Gulch, grew up within months of the 1864 gold strike. After 1865, the lands west of the Mississippi seemed to offer the promise of a better life to a great many Americans that had become disheartened by the prolonged American Civil War. With the completion of the transcontinental railroad in 1869, expanding ribbons of steel rail lines soon eclipsed well-worn moccasin trails traversing the plains of the West.

Prior to the iron horse charging into the frontier region of the Upper Yellowstone River valley, a few primitive settlements had developed. Hostilities caused by white encroachment on Crow lands prompted government intervention. Forcing the Crow to reduce their land holdings and to be confined on a reservation near Mission Creek, Montana, in 1868, the government set up Fort Parker and Crow Agency. The fort's mission to teach the Crow farming failed miserably because of the combination of poor climate and adverse environmental conditions. In 1875, the government abandoned the Mission Creek site and moved Crow Agency farther east to Rosebud Creek near Absarokee, Montana. By 1884, the agency had moved to its present location near Hardin, Montana.

Supplies for Fort Parker's personnel and this early agricultural experiment as well as annuities for the Indians initiated the founding of a ferry operation on the Yellowstone River in 1869. By 1882, this early ferry-based settlement known as Benson's Landing, located a scant 3 miles east of the yet-to-be established city of Livingston, had become an early Yellowstone River transportation hub for the growing influx of gold miners and settlers to the Upper Yellowstone Valley.

In July 1882, a supply train of 30 freight wagons, loaded with 140,000 pounds of merchandise to equip the advancing Northern Pacific Railroad (NPRR) construction crews, passed through the Yellowstone River valley en route to a site just upriver from Benson's Landing. This site was named Clark City in honor of Herman Clark, the principal contractor for the NPRR. As the population swelled, in part by the relocation of the residents of Benson's Landing, log structures began to appear. With a population of 500 souls by late November 1882, Clark City had given rise to 2 hotels, 1 hardware store, 2 restaurants, 2 watchmakers, 3 blacksmiths, 2 wholesale liquor dealers, 2 meat markets, 6 general merchandise stores, 2 drugstores, and 30 saloons.

Upon the formal arrival of the NPRR in December 1882, railroad officials surveyed and platted a site just northwest of Clark City for their new rail line hub. Christening the town Livingston, they set about planning vast railroad shops needed to supply the NPRR main line route as well as the proposed Yellowstone Park Branch Line. An early 1883 *Northwest Magazine* advertisement for Livingston claimed that the railroad "had reserved over 300 acres for the requirements of the future machine shops, roundhouse, stockyards, and manufacturing establishments." Within the next year, Livingston's future prospects materialized with the construction of a major railroad facility, a significant commercial district, and a considerable residential neighborhood.

At the turn of the 20th century, NPRR operations continued to expand, mining and ranching interests multiplied, tourism to Yellowstone National Park escalated, and Livingston assumed an air of activity that abounded throughout the town. The establishment of cigar factories, brickyards, breweries and beverage bottling works, sawmills and lumber yards, slaughterhouses and meat-packing facilities, newspapers, a flour mill, an overall manufacturing plant—as well as a courthouse and a city hall, a Carnegie Library, two hospitals, seven schools, a golf course and racetrack, a rodeo arena, several theaters, and hundreds of residences—physically displayed the enterprising character of Livingston that advanced the city's evolution from frontier town into progressive city well into the 20th century.

Centrally located along the Northern Pacific corridor, Livingston, Montana, became an Eden of progress almost overnight. Images of America: *Livingston* offers a photographic memory of a city that swiftly became a western place of importance beginning in the early 1880s. With the building of the NPRR's huge locomotive repair complex, the development of the mineral region surrounding it, the agricultural and ranching potential of the contiguous valleys, and the supplying of the burgeoning tourist trade, Livingston grew to be a principal center of commerce and retained that eminent distinction through the 1950s. Designed thematically to reveal and illuminate the notable and resonant history of Livingston, Montana, this book and its authors invite you to embark on a vivid visual journey through the golden days of this western town that still boasts its long and rich heritage of being the original entrance to Yellowstone, America's first national park. All aboard!

One

The Early Days

Following the Fort Laramie treaty of 1868, the establishment of the Crow Indian agency known as Fort Parker and the ferry community of Benson's Landing represented the earliest settlements in the Yellowstone River valley. Not far from Fort Parker, Dr. Andrew Jackson Hunter in the 1870s built his home and developed a hotel with hot spring baths that later became the well-known resort that bore his name, Hunter's Hot Springs. These establishments and a few scattered ranches constituted the sparse elements of human habitation in the Yellowstone River valley before 1882.

With the arrival of the Northern Pacific Railroad in December 1882, general mercantile stores, livery and feed stores, liquor stores, and hotels sprouted up as quickly as the sagebrush that covered the plains. Obtaining prominent locations along the railroad right-of-way, some of Livingston's earliest businessmen, which included Billy Miles, Billy Mitchell, George Carver, I. Orschel, and Mentor Wetzstein, made great strides in swiftly setting up businesses early in 1883. Evidenced by an 1883 bird's-eye map, hundreds of other entrepreneurs during that year apparently followed suit, hoping to capitalize on the potential of the NPRR's promising new city in the West, Livingston, Montana.

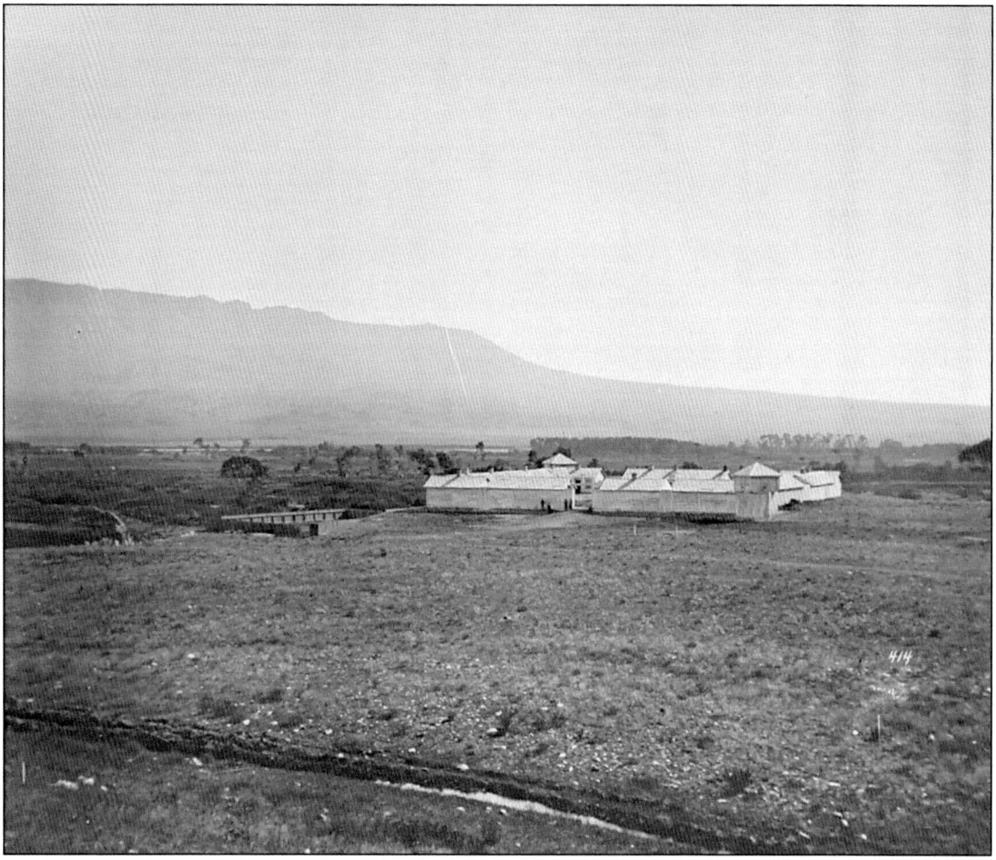

In 1868, Crow Indian leader Sits in the Middle of the Land signed a treaty with the U.S. government, which led to the establishment of Fort Parker in 1869. The original fort buildings captured in this 1871 William Henry Jackson image were constructed of square-hewn logs. A fire in the fall of 1872 consumed all the fort's buildings, which were quickly replaced with shoddy adobe structures. (Library of Congress.)

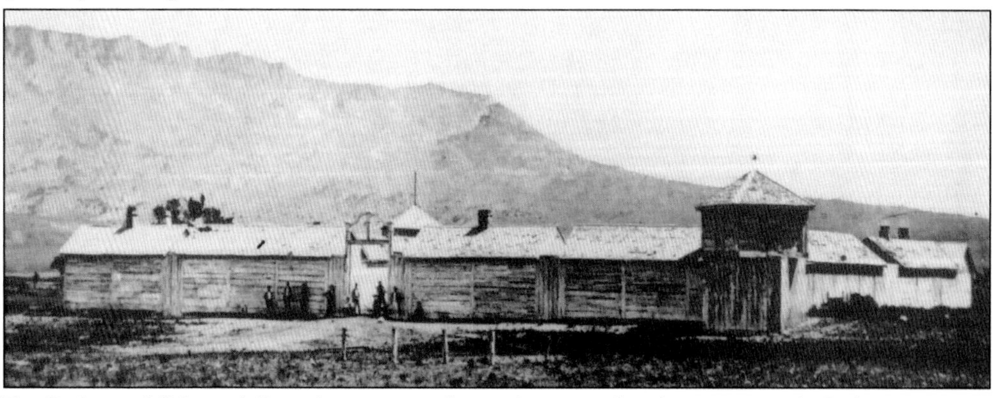

Fort Parker and (Mission) Crow Agency served as trading post, distribution center for Indian annuities, and experimental agricultural site to teach the Crow farming. Poor growing conditions contributed to the abandonment of Fort Parker and the relocation of Mission Agency to Rosebud Creek, near Absarokee, Montana, in 1875. An early superintendent of farming at Crow Agency at Fort Parker was Z. H. Daniels. (Library of Congress.)

Zadok H. Daniels counted among the earliest Park County residents and figured predominately in establishing the mines in Cooke City in the early 1870s. As scout for Gen. Alfred H. Terry, Daniels participated in several Indian campaigns before becoming post sutler at Fort Ellis and Fort Pease. A Montana resident for 40 years, Daniels served as deputy sheriff and assessor for Park County before his death in 1910. (*Livingston Souvenir.*)

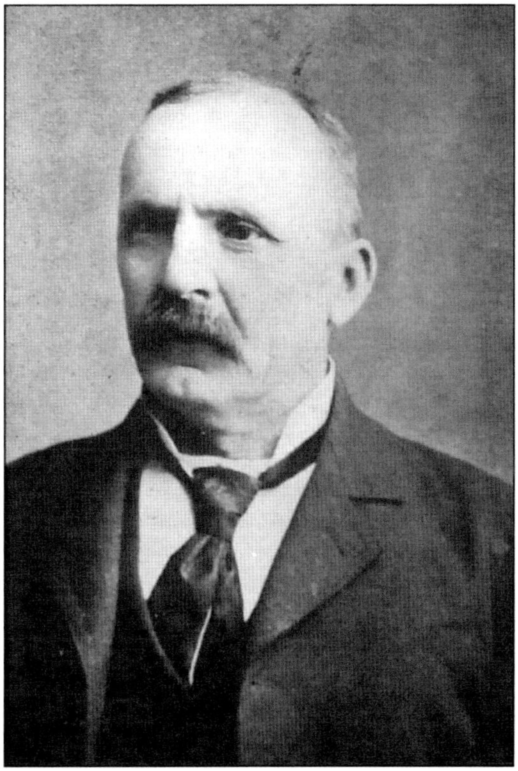

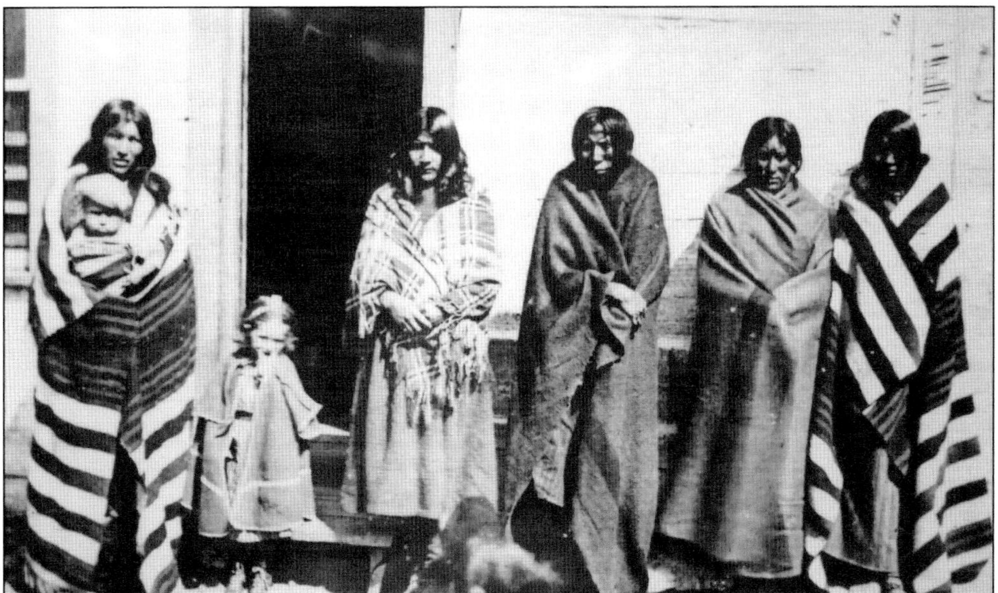

Deprived of their traditional livelihood of hunting bison on the Montana plains and restricted to reservation life by 1869, these Crow women wrapped in army-issued blankets struggled for existence on meager rations of food and clothing supplied by the government at Fort Parker. This 1871 W. H. Jackson photograph represented the beginning of a dependency lifestyle that became the bane of existence for the Crow. (Library of Congress.)

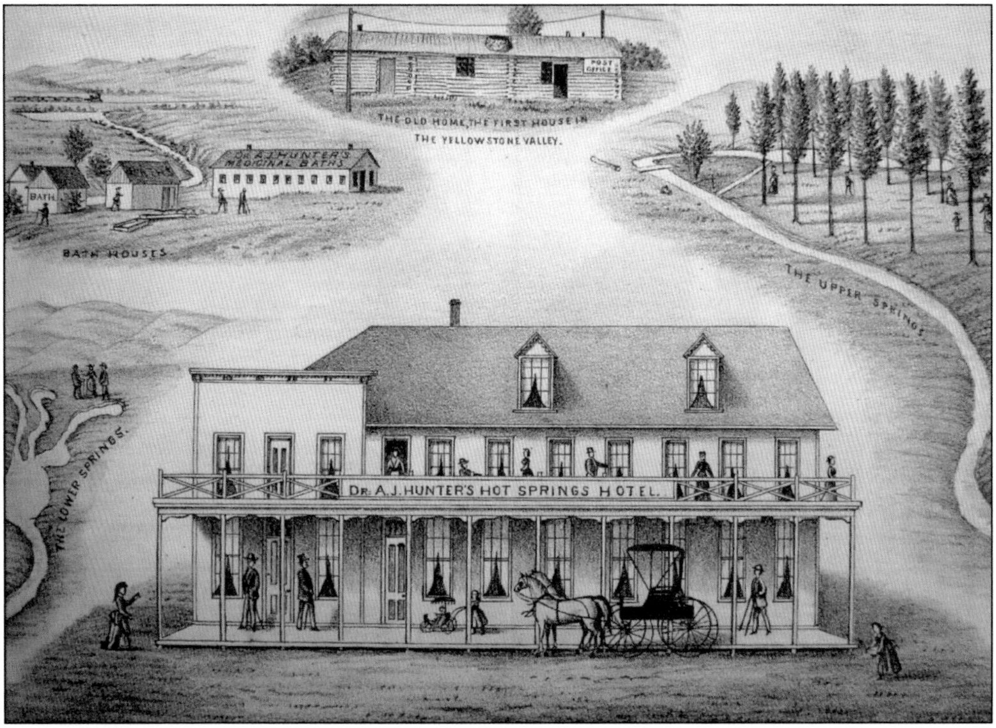

This delightful sketch of Hunter's Hot Springs, in Michael A. Leeson's 1885 *History of Montana*, illustrated the refined and sophisticated atmosphere of Dr. A. J. Hunter's health resort. While Hunter staked a claim at the hot springs in 1869 and moved his family there in 1870, the simple two-story hotel and several bathhouses did not appear until 1883. (Leeson.)

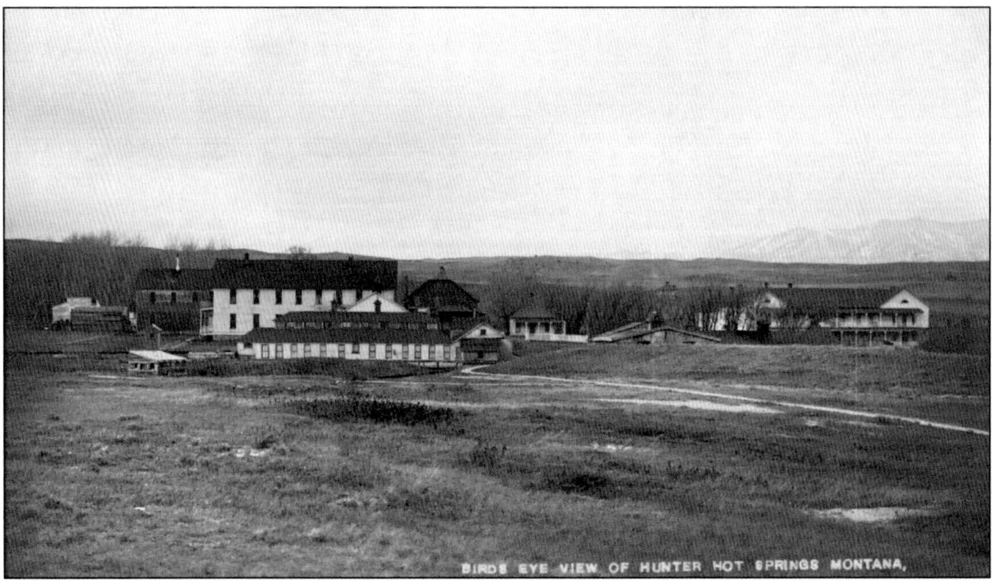

Hunter's initial "discovery" of the springs occurred when he came upon an encampment of Crow Indians bathing in the natural hot water. Observing that the people soaking in the steaming waters were mostly sick and elderly, Hunter recognized the commercial potential of the medicinal waters. With the 1882 arrival of the railroad, that prospect became a reality. (Goss Collection.)

George J. Allen participated in the Montana gold rush, working claims near Virginia City and Helena in the mid-1860s. In 1880, Allen homesteaded 8 miles south of Livingston on the west side of the Yellowstone River. Becoming one of the area's pioneer ranchers, Allen ran cattle and raised horses on his 3,200-acre ranch and started the first apple orchard in the valley. (Leeson.)

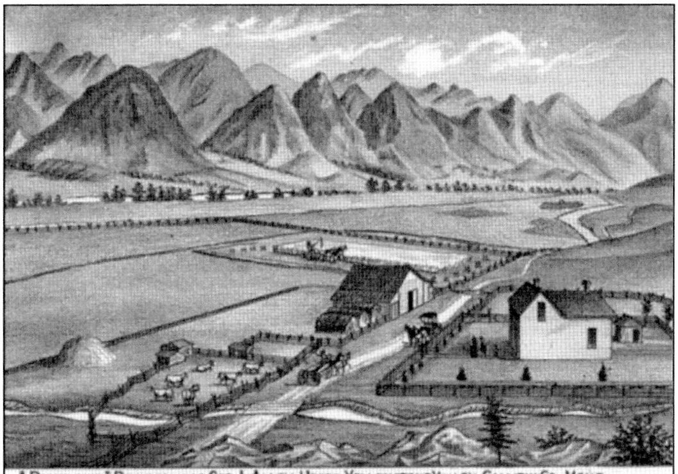

"RICHLAND," RESIDENCE OF GEO. J. ALLEN, UPPER YELLOWSTONE VALLEY, GALLATIN CO. MONT.

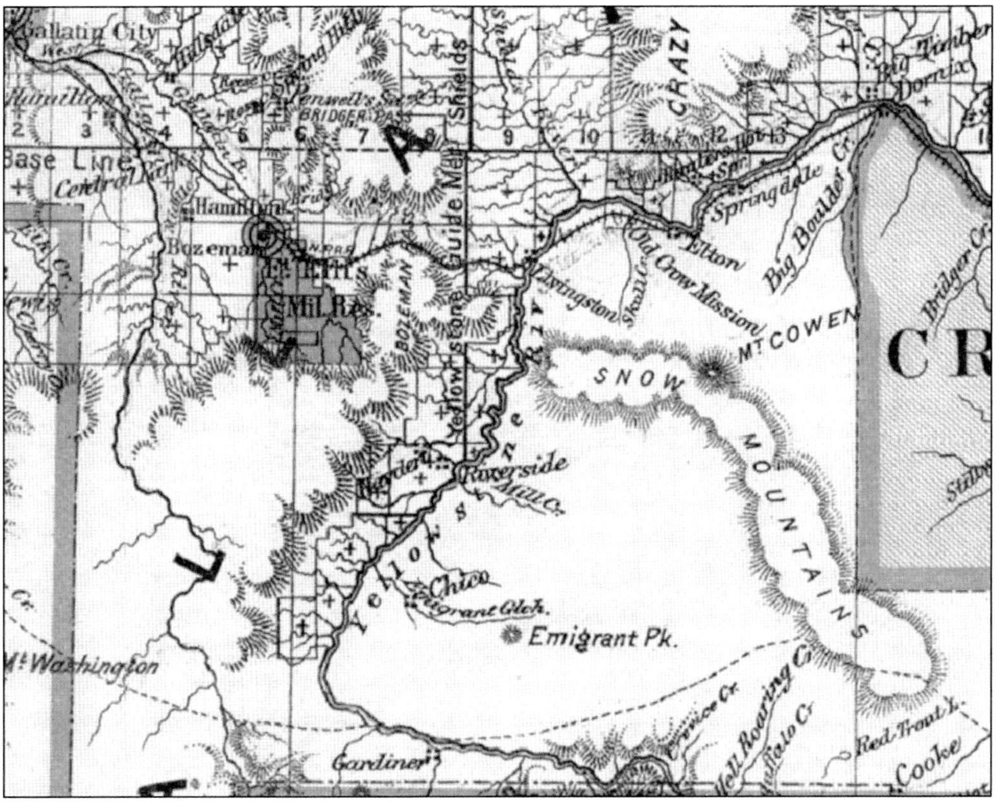

This 1883 General Land Office map clearly delineates the NPRR's progress westward. The tracks come into view from the east, making their way past Springdale, the stopping point for Hunter's Hot Springs, the old Crow Mission Agency, and through Livingston. The map reveals the tracks completed only to Bozeman, and the proposed tracks south to Gardiner had not yet appeared on the landscape. (Department of the Interior.)

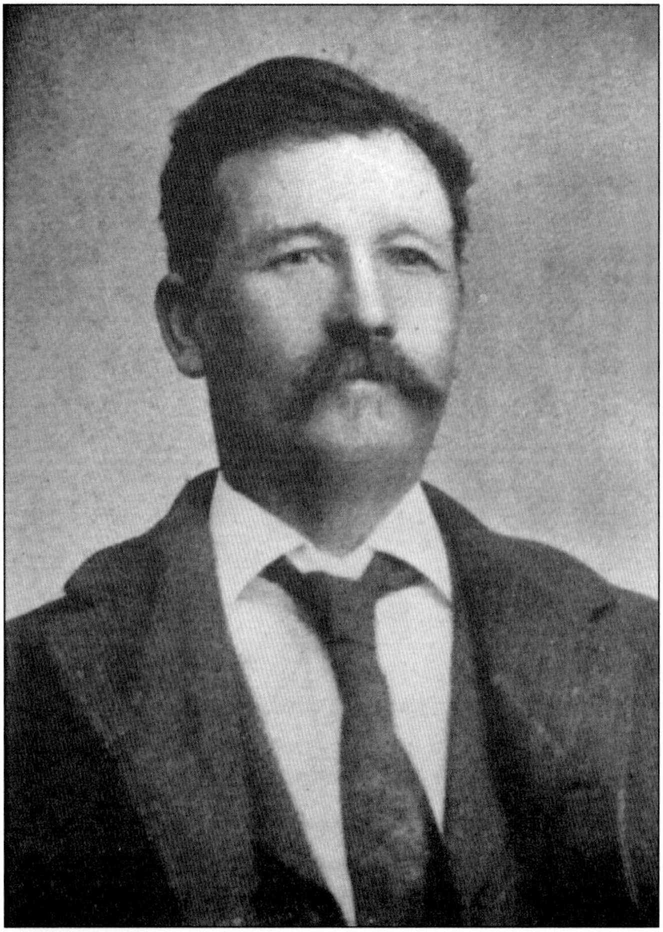

One of the earliest and most prominent businessmen in Livingston, Billy Miles landed in Clark City in 1882. One story claimed that during a stage trip to Bozeman, Miles's drunken behavior caused him to be deposited in Clark City. He remained in Livingston until his death in 1929, and was reported to be the largest property holder and the leading taxpayer in Park County. (*Livingston Souvenir.*)

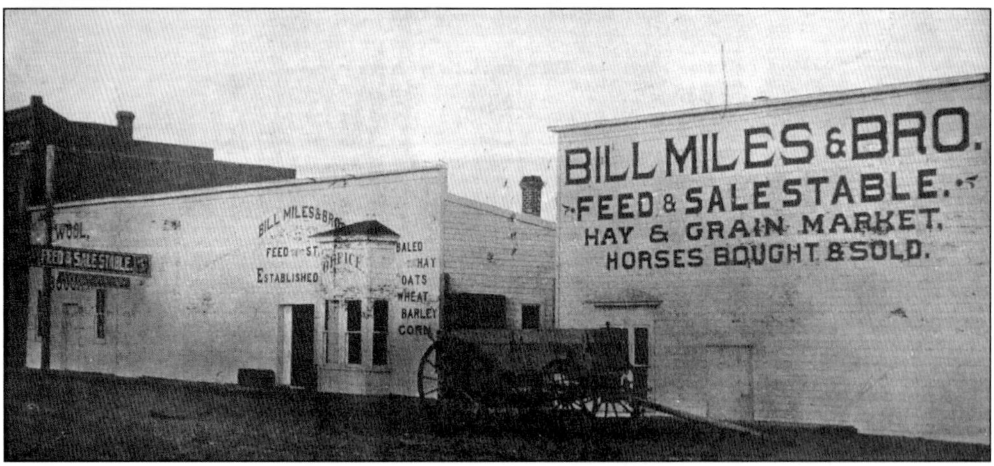

Billy Miles, along with brothers Tommy and Boyd, established the Miles Brothers Feed & Sale Stable in the fall of 1882 on lower Main Street near the bridge. They provided services to the Northern Pacific Railroad, Yellowstone Park, and county residents. Billy and Tommy continued in business together throughout their lives and owned many Main Street properties. They were well known for their "square-shooting" as well as community charity. (*Livingston Souvenir.*)

William "Billy" Mitchell decided at age 16 that farming in Wisconsin was not his future aspiration. Working his way west, Mitchell found employment in logging camps, cutting firewood for steamboats, and hunting animals for the hide trade. Mitchell followed the NPRR route westward and arrived in 1879 to the area that became Livingston. Mitchell died in 1939 at age 84, ten years after sitting for this portrait. (Private collection.)

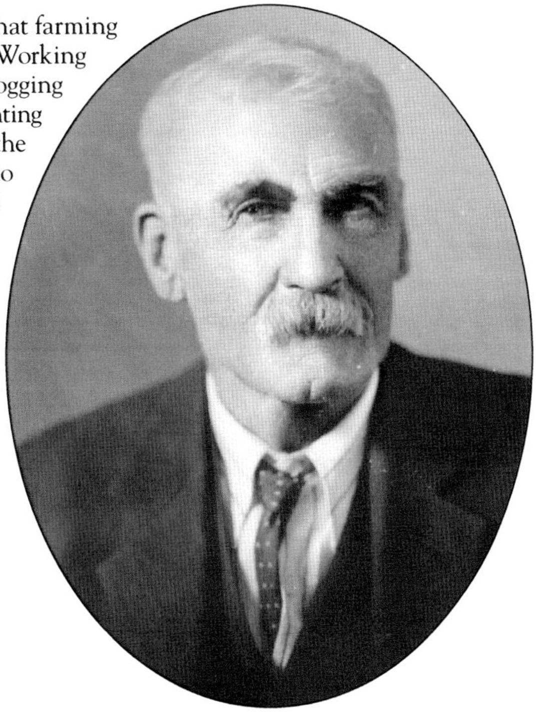

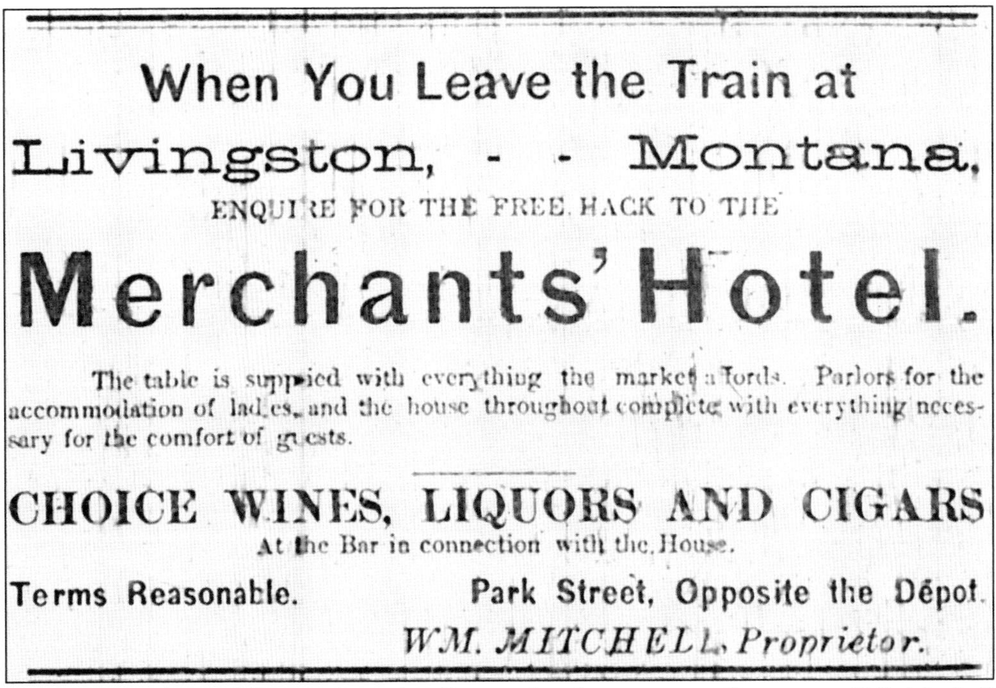

In the winter of 1882, following the railroad's arrival to the town site of Livingston, Billy Mitchell began construction of the town's first hotel, the Merchants' Hotel. Married in 1879, Mitchell and his wife, Kate, operated the popular hotel well into the 1900s and entertained American public figures as well as European dignitaries. Mitchell served as deputy sheriff for nine years in addition to other civic duties. (*Livingston Enterprise.*)

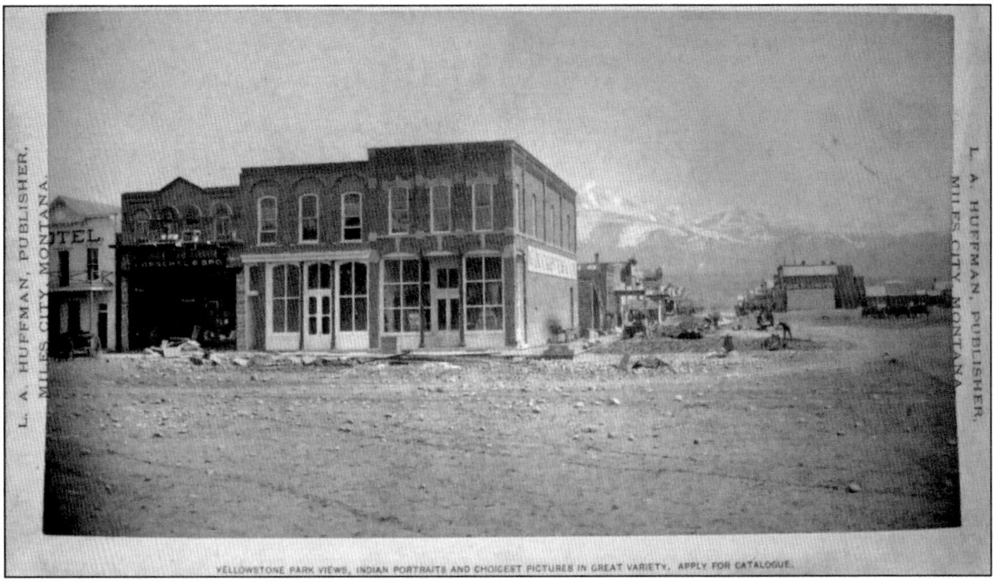

This rare *c.* 1883 L. A. Huffman cabinet card view captured Livingston's early days of building construction. The Merchants' Hotel stands at far left, while the I. Orschel and G. L. Carver buildings in the middle are nearing completion. While this photograph has been published in several local histories of Livingston, the signature border of L. A. Huffman cardstock was cropped and credit to Huffman has not been previously acknowledged. (Private collection.)

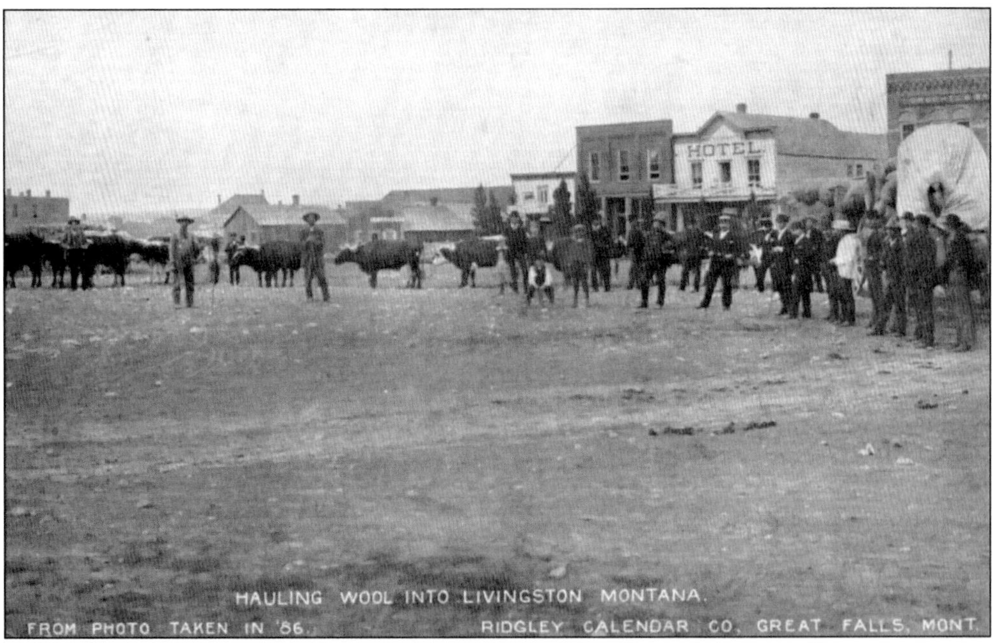

Livingston businesses in the early 1880s ranged from cigar manufacturing to hauling wool, as this Ridgley Calendar postcard view of East Park Street in 1886 portrays. The clothing worn by the gentlemen photographed in front of the Merchants' Hotel depicts everything from suits and top hats to suspendered denim trousers and Stetsons, and the image gives the appearance that the character of Livingston's population was equally as diverse. (Goss Collection.)

Among the earliest enterprises in Livingston, the Wetzstein & Company liquor business was located on Park Street between Main and 2nd Streets. Mentor Wetzstein opened his store in early July 1883 and catered to the retail trade along with wholesale accounts that included Yellowstone Park. He merchandized liquors, beer, wine, tobacco products, bar and billiard equipment, and gambling supplies. By 1900, his cigar vault could stockpile 100,000 cigars. (Private collection.)

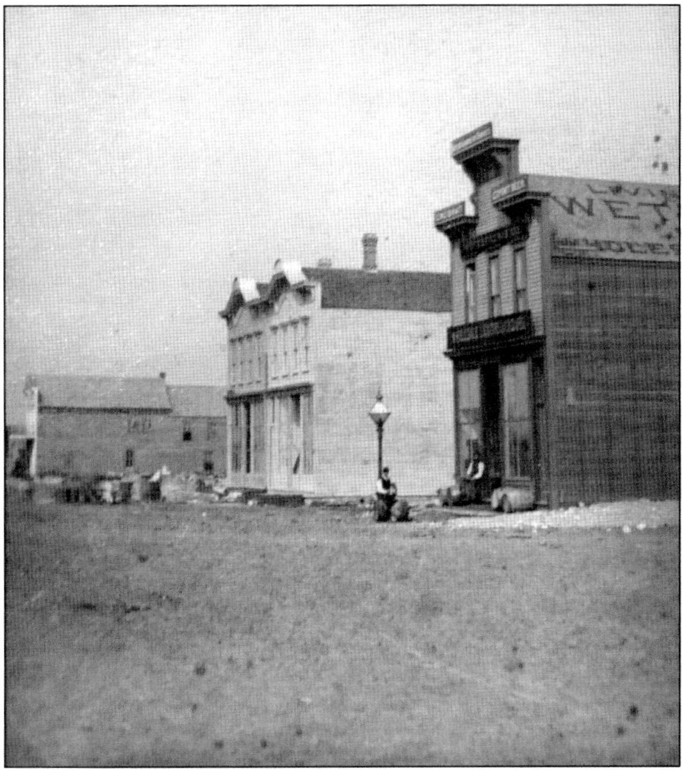

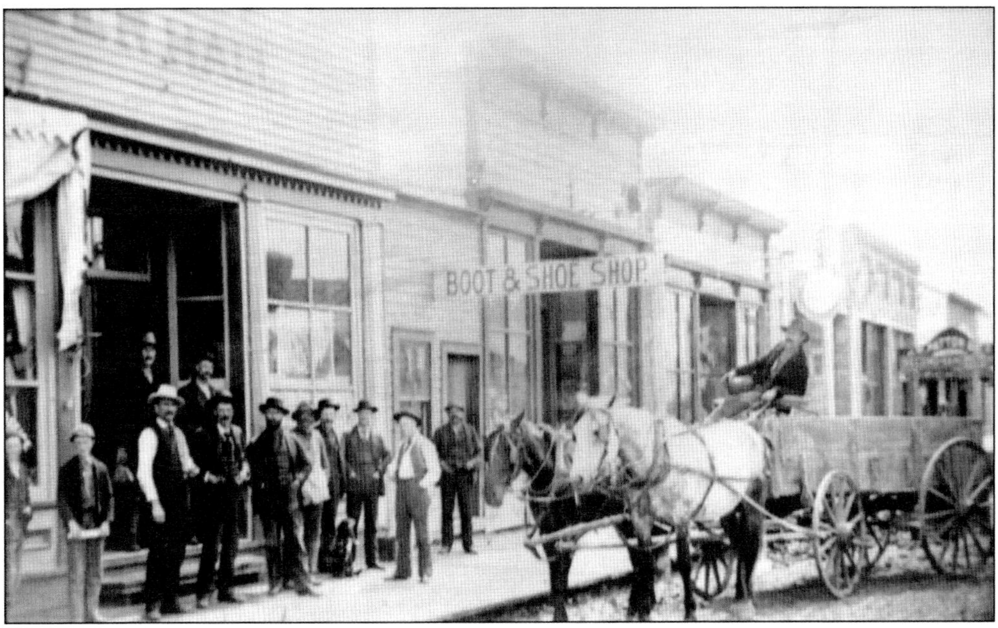

The reverse of this early photograph of a beer hall merely stated, "Beer hall on Main Street." Research has revealed that this was most likely the German Beer Hall at 101 South Main Street. Several period photographs portrayed this building at that location through the early 1900s. In 1907, Sheriff Harry McCue arrested four men playing craps at the German Beer Hall for violating the newly enacted Griffin anti-gambling law. (Private collection.)

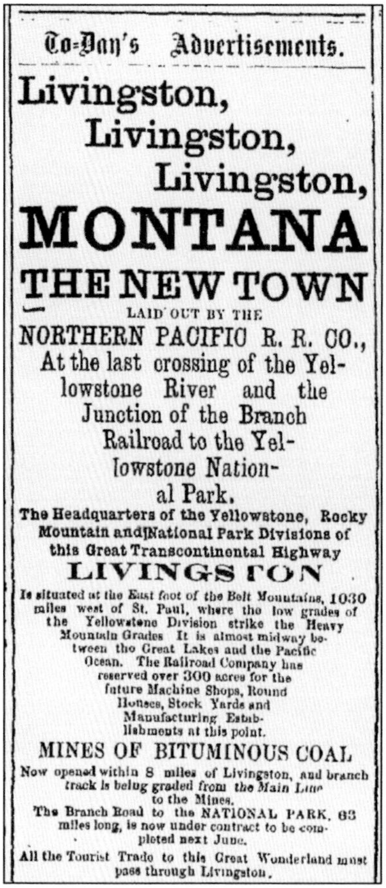

To-Day's Advertisements.

Livingston,
Livingston,
Livingston,
MONTANA
THE NEW TOWN
LAID OUT BY THE
NORTHERN PACIFIC R. R. CO.,
At the last crossing of the Yellowstone River and the Junction of the Branch Railroad to the Yellowstone National Park.
The Headquarters of the Yellowstone, Rocky Mountain and National Park Divisions of this Great Transcontinental Highway
LIVINGSTON
Is situated at the East foot of the Belt Mountains, 1030 miles west of St. Paul, where the low grades of the Yellowstone Division strike the Heavy Mountain Grades It is almost midway between the Great Lakes and the Pacific Ocean. The Railroad Company has reserved over 300 acres for the future Machine Shops, Round Houses, Stock Yards and Manufacturing Establishments at this point.
MINES OF BITUMINOUS COAL
Now opened within 8 miles of Livingston, and branch track is being graded from the Main Line to the Mines.
The Branch Road to the NATIONAL PARK, 63 miles long, is now under contract to be completed next June.
All the Tourist Trade to this Great Wonderland must pass through Livingston.

"Livingston, Livingston, Livingston, Montana," trumpeted the Winona (Minnesota) *Daily Republican* in January 1883, announcing the availability of lots in the "future Great City of the Yellowstone." Counting on the availability of coal, limestone, gold, and silver, the NPRR banked heavily on Livingston becoming an important center for manufacturing and commercial trading as well as the center of tourist trade to Yellowstone.

Bird's-eye-view maps became a popular technique of cartography in the late 1800s. This panoramic illustrated map exhibited an artistic vision of an urban landscape amid Montana's mountainous topography. Published and copyrighted in 1884 by J. J. Stoner of Madison, Wisconsin, this 1883 lithograph listed commercial establishments that were operating in Livingston by that time. (Goss Collection.)

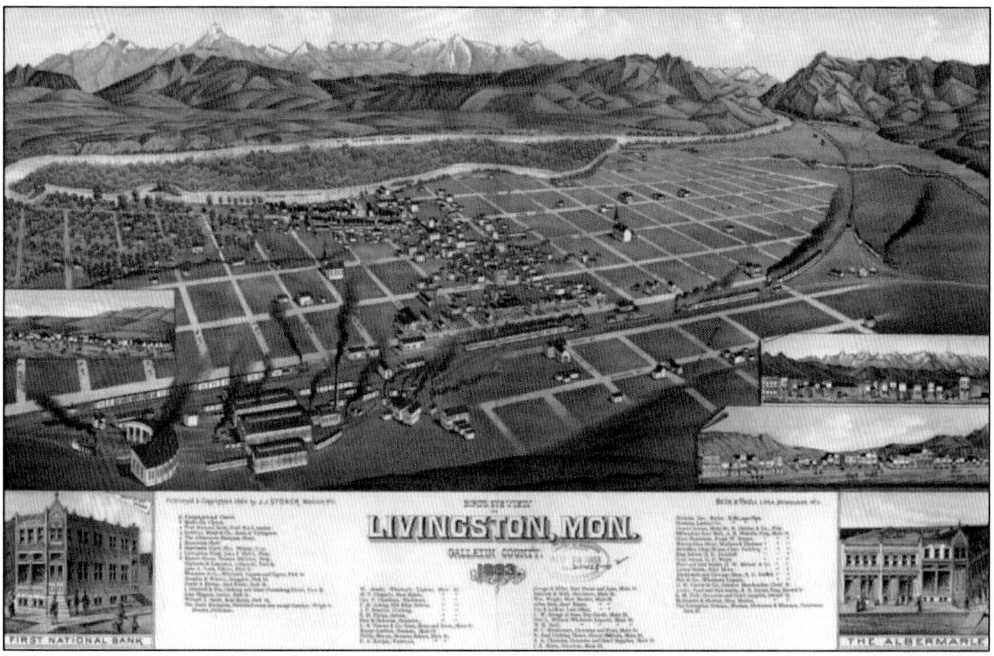

Two

Laying Tracks to Wonderland

With the arrival of the Northern Pacific Railroad (NPRR) in December 1882, Livingston began to develop without delay. The proposed building of railroad shops in Livingston provided the largest opportunity for the city's expansion. In November 1882, the *Helena Independent* newspaper announced, "The railway company has decided to build extensive repair and manufacturing shops in Livingstone [*sic*], and from these promises they reasonably anticipate that their town will be one of the great cities of Montana." Construction of the railroad shops commenced early summer 1883, and by 1884, the railroad claimed the shops employed 600 to 800 men.

The shops as well as the city continued to grow, and by 1900, the *Livingston Enterprise Souvenir* maintained that NPRR had invested half a million dollars into its machine and repair shop complex. The city's newspaper proudly touted that its prominent railroad facility included a machine shop, engine house, boiler house, blacksmith shop, and 15-stall roundhouse with a 54-foot turntable as well as storerooms and offices. The railroad operation finally reached its pinnacle of success when the *Livingston Enterprise* declared in 1917 that Livingston possessed the largest shops west of the Mississippi and the finest depot on the line.

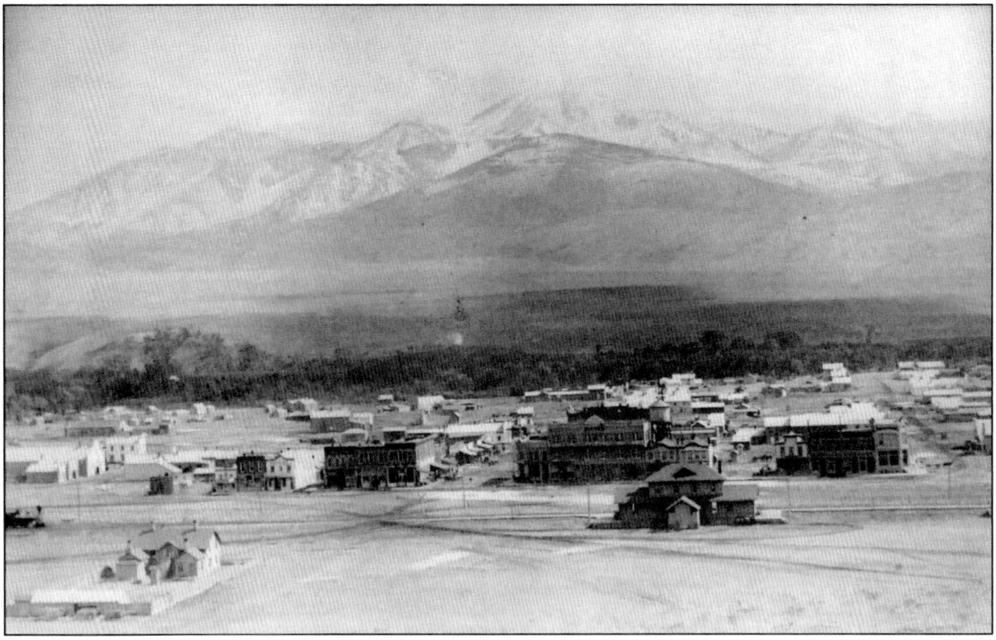

Built in 1882, Livingston's first NPRR depot sat on the south side of the railroad tracks. Wind and drifting snow made this location undesirable and necessitated moving the depot in 1885 to the north side of the tracks. This *c.* 1886 view of the developing town and the back side of the wooden two-story depot is one of the few known photographs of this early period. (Private collection.)

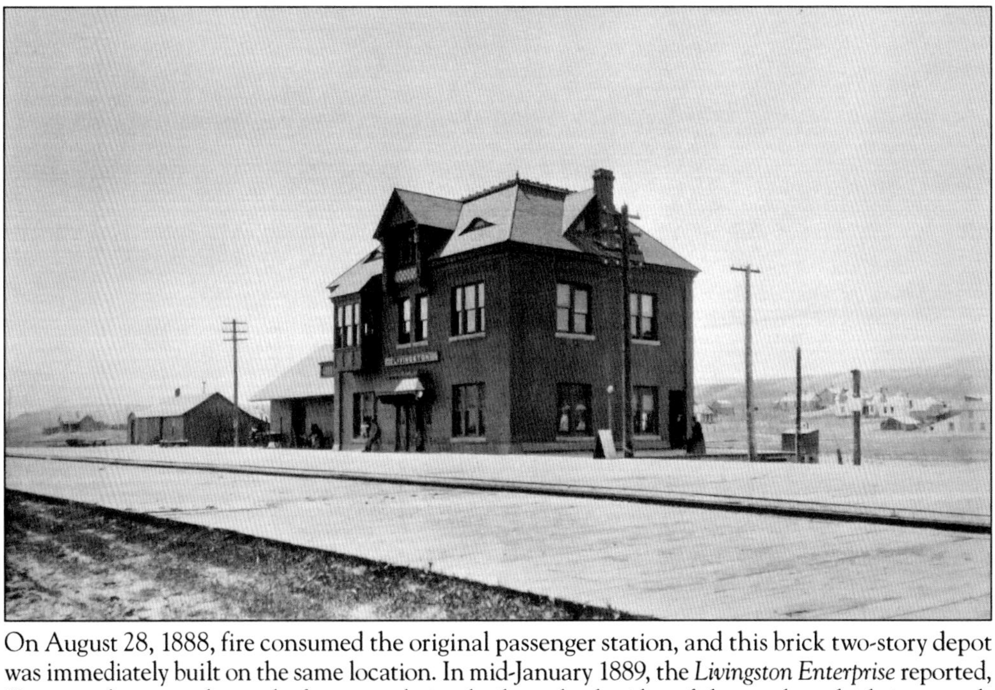

On August 28, 1888, fire consumed the original passenger station, and this brick two-story depot was immediately built on the same location. In mid-January 1889, the *Livingston Enterprise* reported, "Long and commodious platforms are being built on both sides of the tracks, which is a much needed step in the right direction." Only five months after the fire, the new depot was ready for occupancy on January 26, 1889. (Watry Collection.)

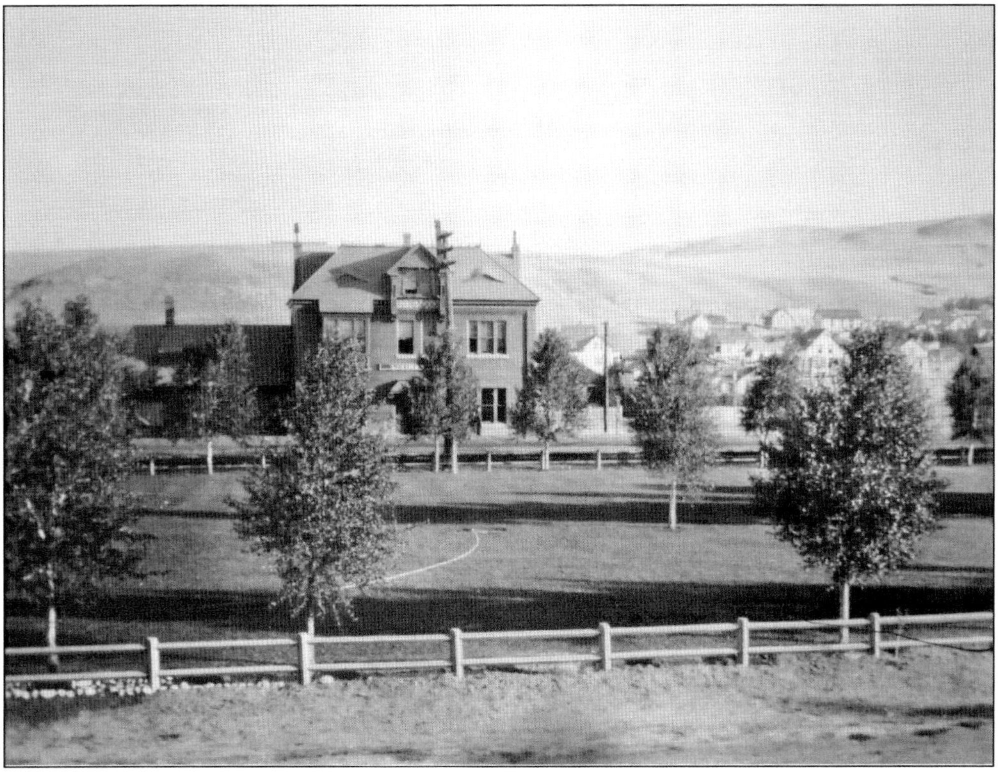

The main depot building in this *c.* 1895 photograph stood two and one-half stories high with men's and women's waiting rooms, ticket office, and telegraph offices on the lower floor, and offices for the dispatcher, superintendent, and others on the second floor. A one-story building on the west side provided baggage services. With no expense spared, this $12,000 structure was considered one of the finest between Bismarck and Helena. (Private collection.)

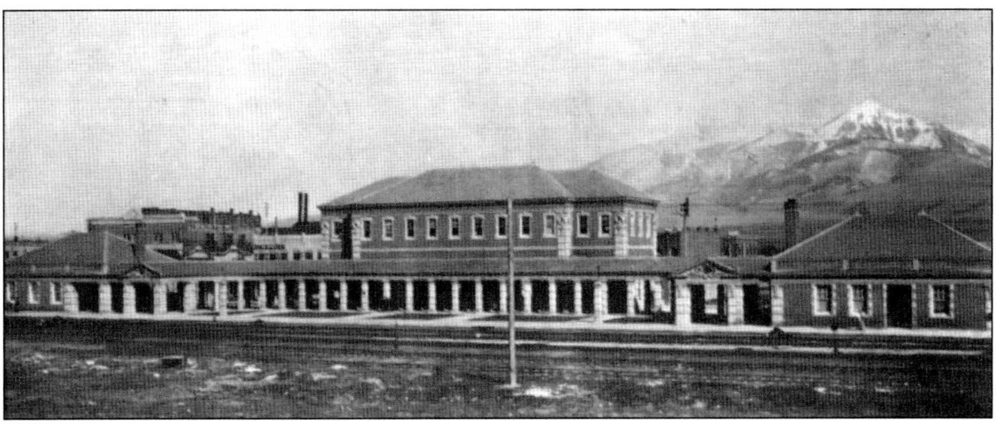

Increased passenger traffic created a need for a larger depot by 1901. In keeping with its traditional grand-style structures, the NPRR chose an impressive Italianate design that consisted of three buildings connected by two curved colonnades, which made them appear as one building. Built in 1902 on the south side of the tracks, this magnificent two-story edifice became the centerpiece of Livingston. (Goss Collection.)

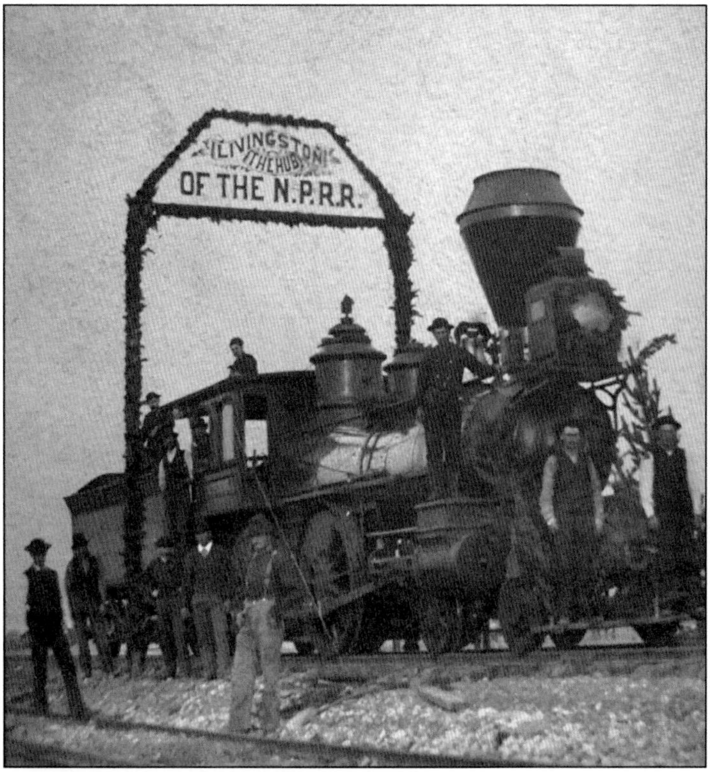

Centered between NPRR headquarters in Brainard, Minnesota, and its terminus in Portland, Oregon, Livingston became the hub of the NPRR in 1883. To navigate Bozeman Pass 10 miles west of Livingston, the NPRR designed a switchback and used helper engines stored in Livingston to assist with this steep ascent. In December 1883, the completion of the Bozeman tunnel eliminated the switchback, but helper engines remained in service. (Private collection.)

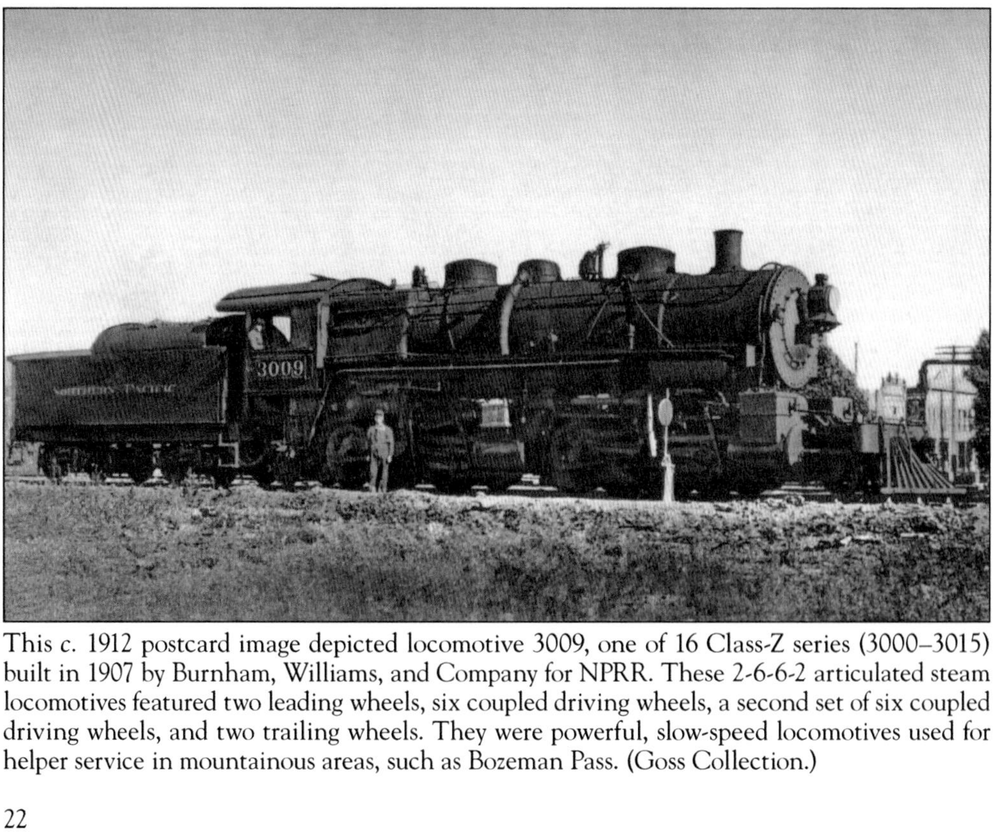

This *c.* 1912 postcard image depicted locomotive 3009, one of 16 Class-Z series (3000–3015) built in 1907 by Burnham, Williams, and Company for NPRR. These 2-6-6-2 articulated steam locomotives featured two leading wheels, six coupled driving wheels, a second set of six coupled driving wheels, and two trailing wheels. They were powerful, slow-speed locomotives used for helper service in mountainous areas, such as Bozeman Pass. (Goss Collection.)

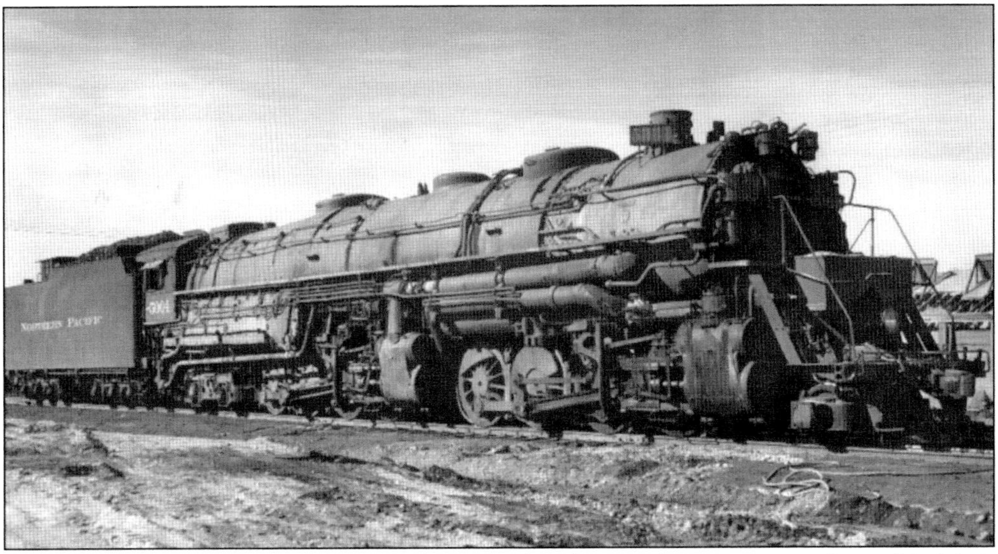

Locomotive 5004 was a Class Z-5 Mallet articulated steam locomotive configured 2-8-8-4, which indicated two leading wheels, two sets of eight driving wheels, and a four-wheel trailing truck. Baldwin Locomotive Works built 12 of these locomotives (5000–5011) for NPRR in 1930, designating them "Yellowstone" locomotives. (Goss Collection.)

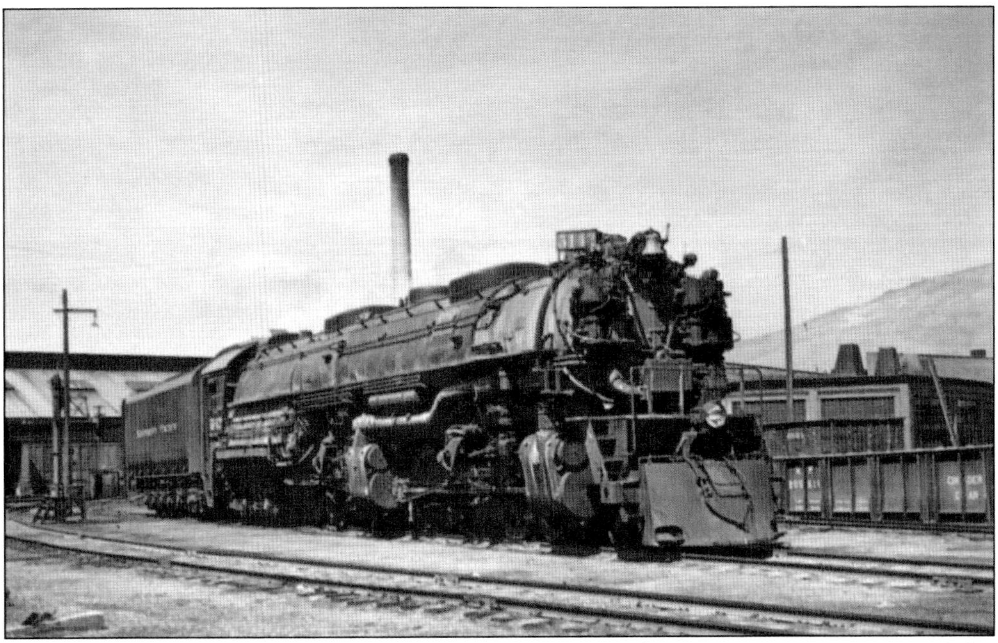

This articulated steam locomotive in front of the NPRR shops in Livingston was a 4-6-6-4 configuration, indicating four leading wheels followed by six coupled driving wheels, a second set of six driving wheels, and four trailing wheels. Numbered 5142, this Class Z-8 locomotive was one of 20 Challenger engines built by the American Locomotive Company (ALCO) in 1943–1944. All of this series were retired by 1959. (Goss Collection.)

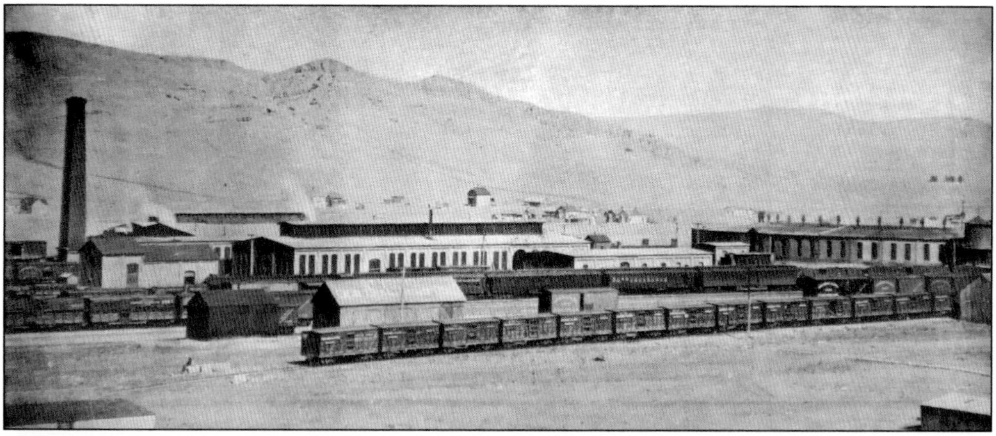

NPRR chose Livingston for repair facilities mainly because of its central location between terminal points. A half-million-dollar investment from 1883 to 1900 for construction of the shops produced the largest facilities between Minnesota and Puget Sound. Major shop expansion occurred in 1902, 1907, and in the 1940s, when the shops were enlarged to accommodate new diesel locomotives. (*Livingston Souvenir.*)

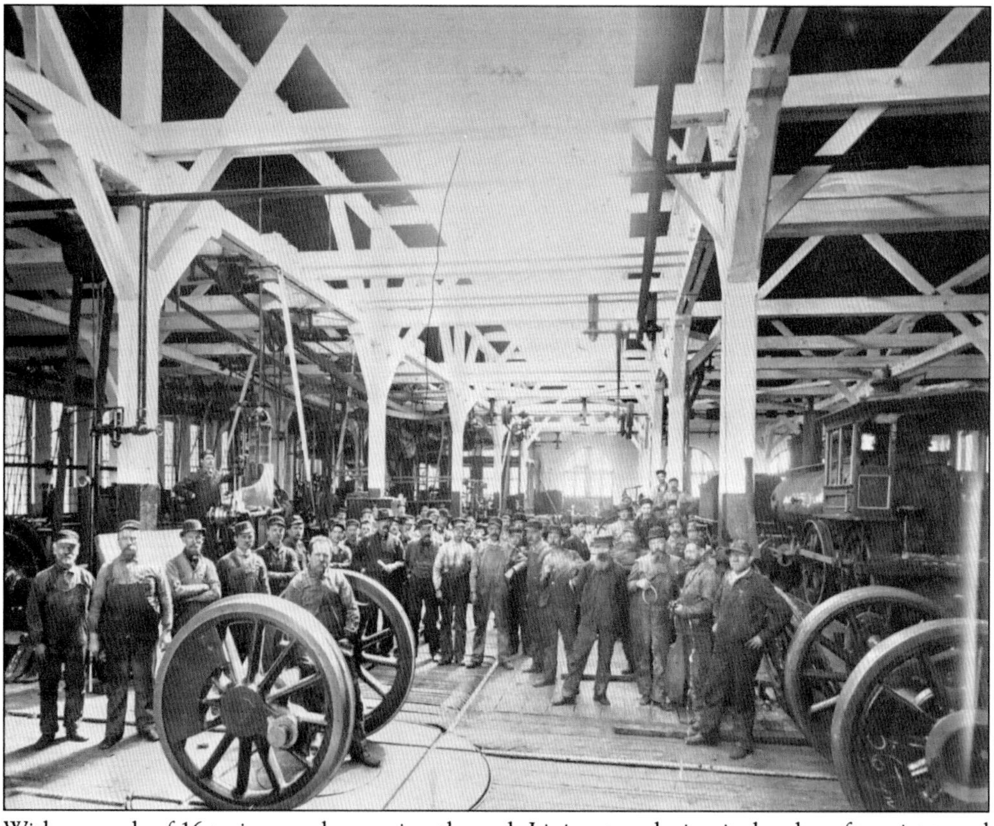

With upwards of 16 trains per day passing through Livingston during its heyday of tourist travel and freight transportation, the repair and manufacturing shops of the Northern Pacific Railroad became the center of activity as well as the base of Livingston's employment. By 1902, the payroll of the railroad averaged $45,000 per month. (Yellowstone Gateway Museum.)

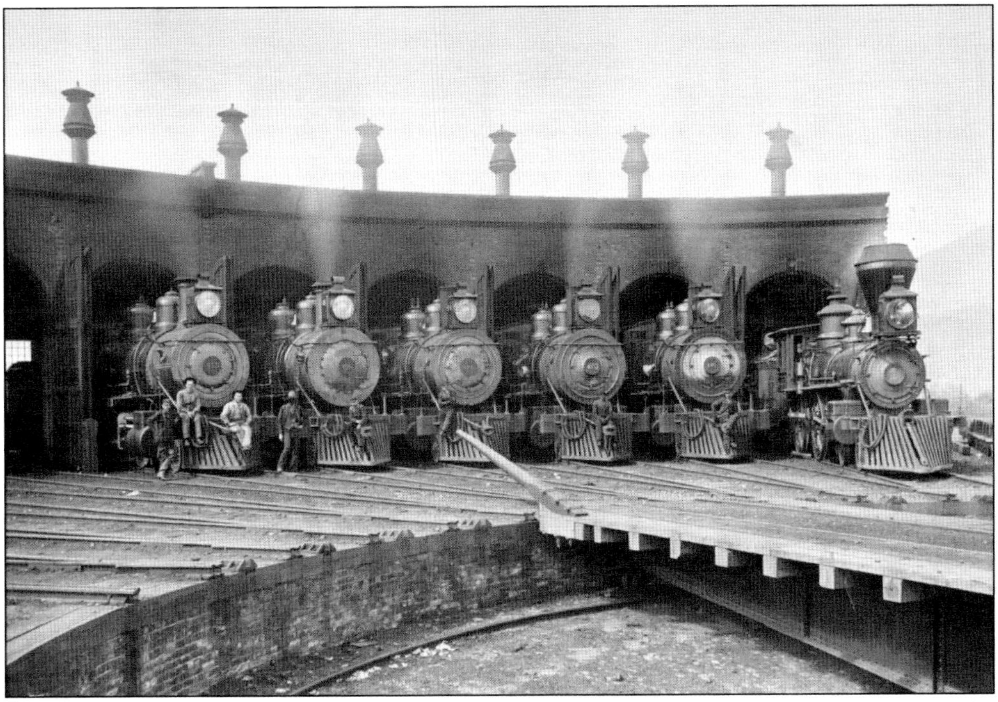

This brick roundhouse, built in 1883, encompassed 15 stalls and a 54-foot turntable. Accessed by turntables, roundhouses allowed locomotives to be turned around for the return trip since early steam locomotives could only travel forward. The introduction of diesel locomotives in 1944 diminished the need for Livingston's enlarged 44-stall roundhouse and 135-foot turntable. By 1983, the last three remaining stalls had been demolished. (Yellowstone Gateway Museum.)

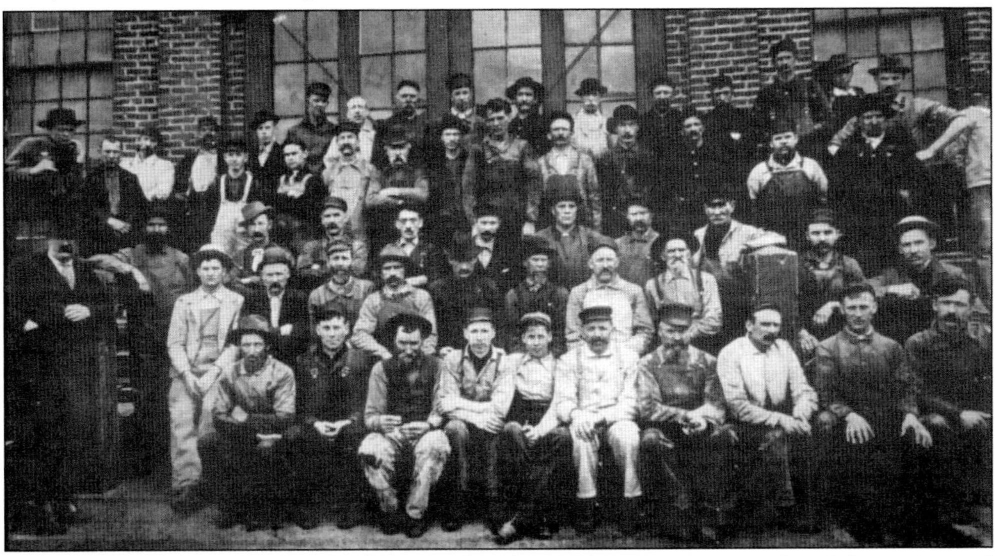

NPRR employed between 600 and 800 workers by 1900 in its various railroad shops. Around 1915, it was estimated that the employees of the railroad constituted one-sixth the population of Livingston. By 1935, employment in the Livingston shops division alone increased to more than 1,700. With the amplified use of private automobiles, rail service steadily declined after World War II and severely impacted employment in Livingston by the 1970s. (*Livingston Souvenir*.)

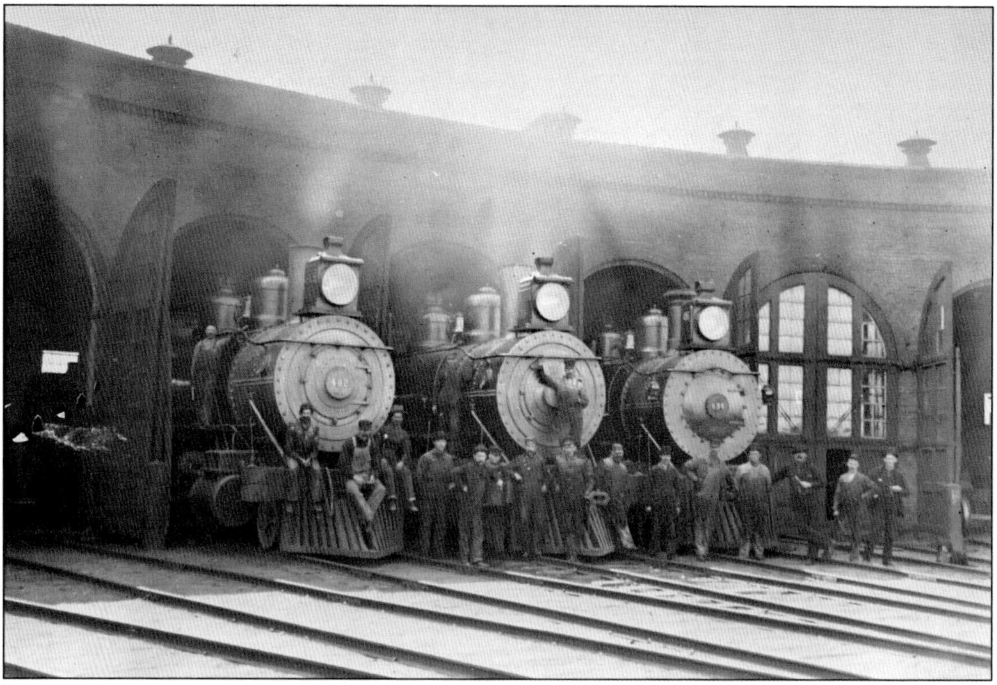

Livingston's roundhouse represented the principal maintenance facility at the midpoint of the Northern Pacific Railroad line. Enlarged in 1898 and again in 1907, this semicircular building served as repair facilities as well as temporary housing for engines between division runs. During the pinnacle of rail travel in America, Livingston's roundhouse, with its crew of 100, was the pride of the town as well as the NPRR. (Yellowstone Gateway Museum.)

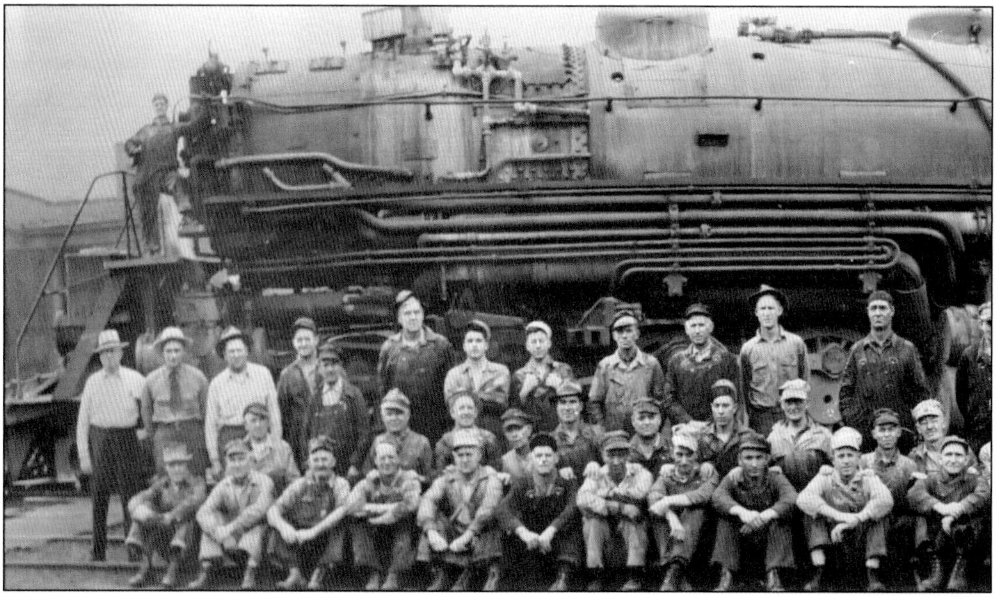

This railroad crew posed for a group photograph in front of NP 5000, a 2-8-8-4 Class Z-5 Yellowstone locomotive. Considered the largest in the world at the time, these locomotives eliminated the use of two engines on the head end of freight trains hauling heavy loads between eastern Montana and North Dakota. (Yellowstone Gateway Museum.)

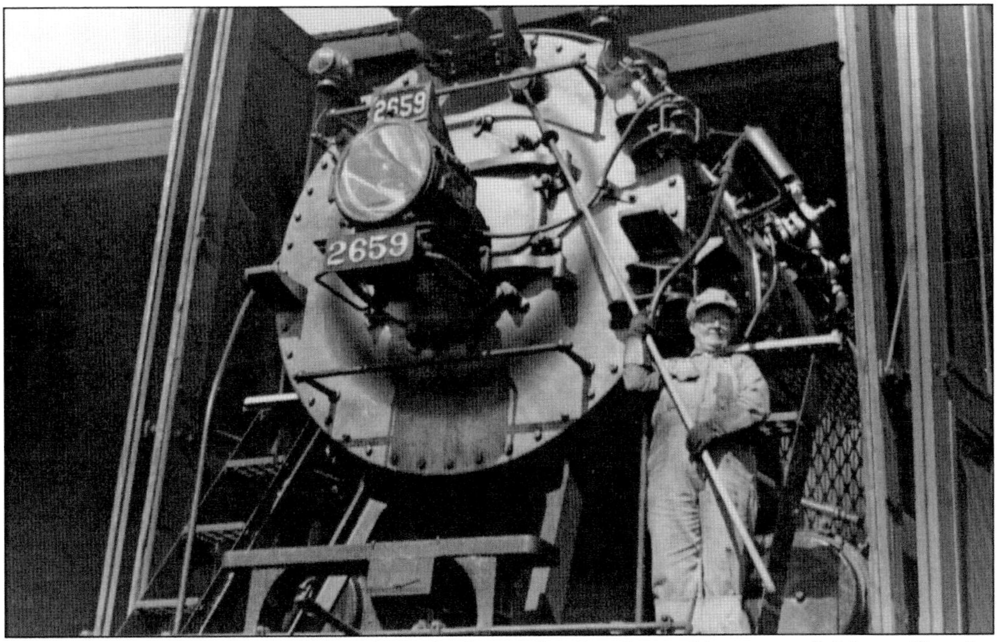

Following the death of her husband, Fredrick, Bertha Gonder and her nine children, all under the age of 12, came to Livingston in 1914. With most men serving in World War I, the NPRR employed Bertha and 22 other women in 1918. Armed with her 10-foot-plus scrub brush, Bertha, an engine wiper for 30 years, became a legendary figure when *Life Magazine* featured her unusual occupation in its November 21, 1938, issue. (Yellowstone Gateway Museum.)

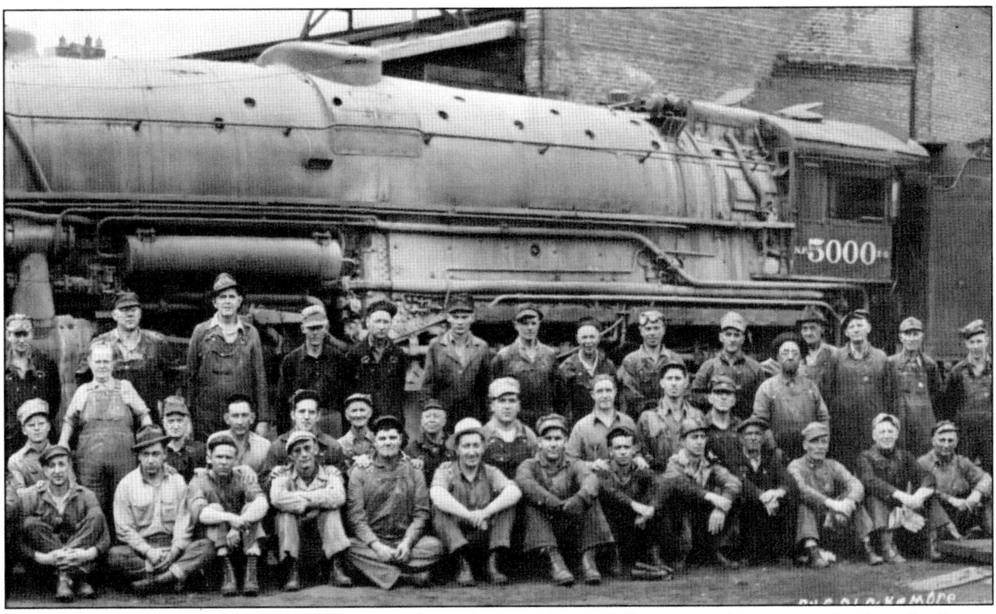

While many names of this predominantly male crew have fallen into obscurity, the female figure on the left side of this image represented an anomaly in the railroad business. Determined to "hold her own" after being widowed with nine children in 1914, Bertha Gonder dutifully served the NPRR eight hours a day, seven days a week, filling grease cups, operating the roundhouse turntable, and swabbing down smoky engines. (Yellowstone Gateway Museum.)

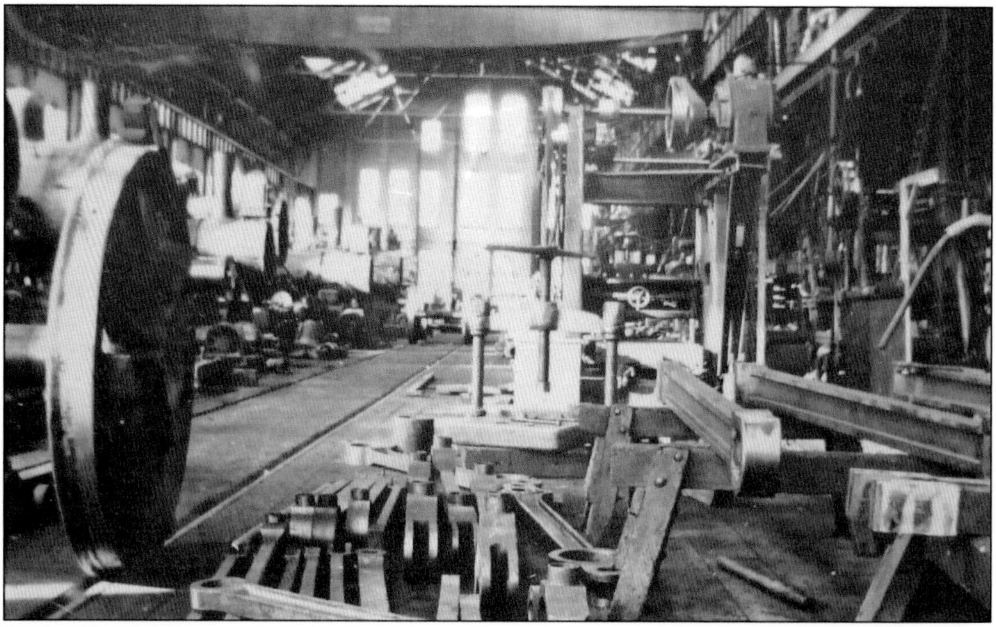

By far the most important industrial unit of the NPRR in Livingston was the machine shops. According to the *Livingston Enterprise* in 1900, the machine shop "is filled with machinery of the latest pattern and design for making and fitting parts necessary to repair disabled engines," and "its present equipment enables it to completely rebuild seven locomotives each month." (Private collection.)

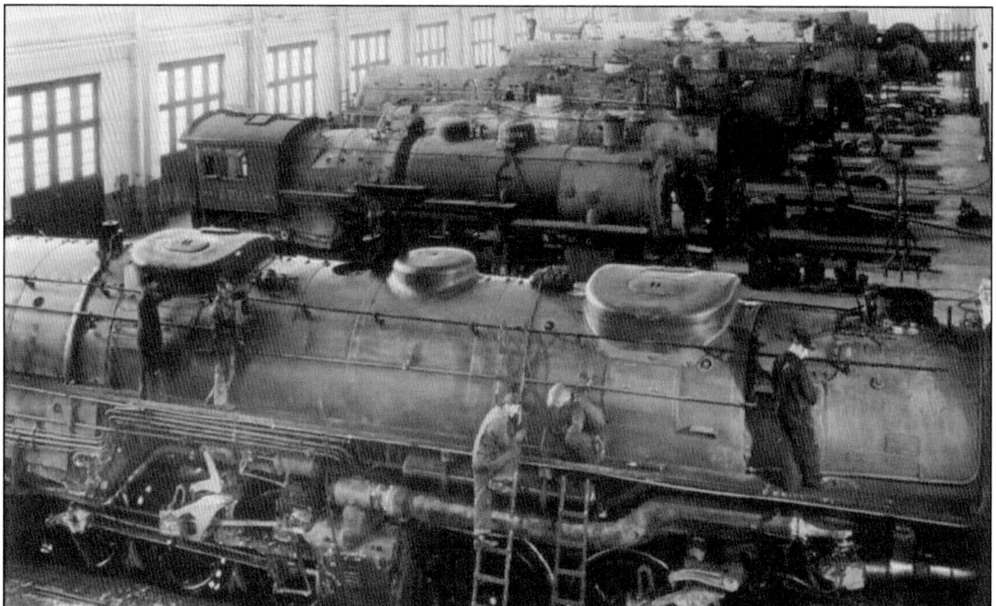

Crews worked on a wide variety of Northern Pacific locomotives in this engine shop. The boiler shop overhauled and repaired boilers of the locomotives, while the copper and tin shop facilitated covering and burnishing the engines. "Upon the tracks that traverse the building and connect it with the roundhouse may be seen engines in all stages of repair," claimed the *Livingston Enterprise* in 1900. (Goss Collection.)

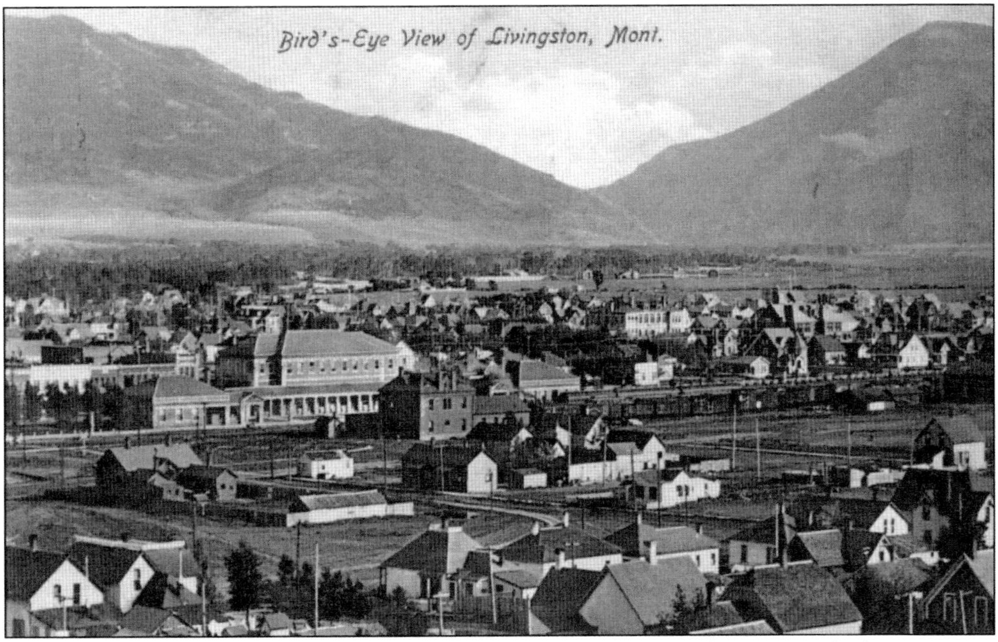

This 1909 Scheuber Drug postcard view, taken from a hillside north of town, reveals the expansion of residential housing on the northern side of the tracks. Primarily a residential area for railroad workers, the housing here reflects simpler construction. In the background (center), the monumental 1902 passenger depot looms large over the town's expanding footprint on the landscape. Visible on the right is the equally massive high school. (Goss Collection.)

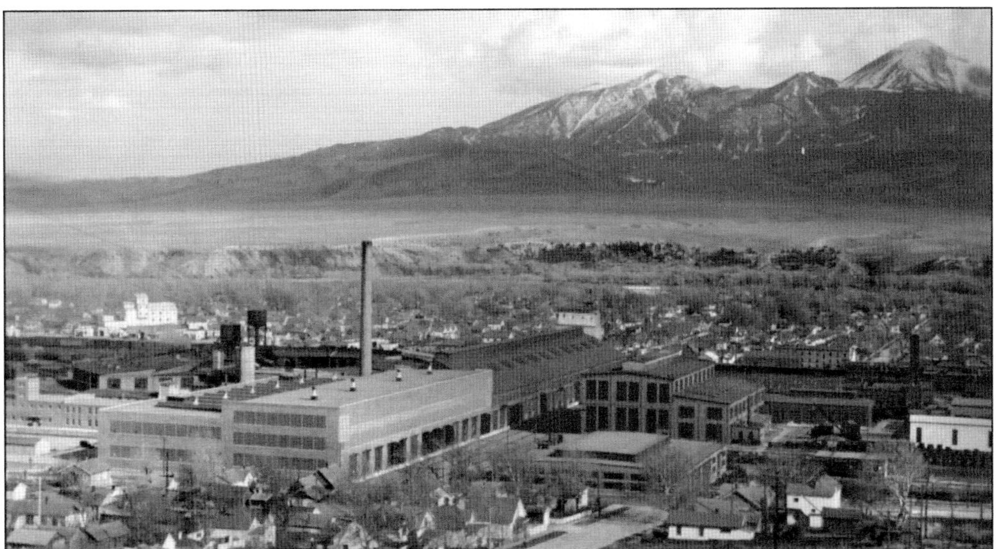

In 1970, Burlington Northern Railroad (BN) took over the Northern Pacific, and Livingston became a secondary line in the larger BN system, employing over 1,100 workers in the late 1970s. Employment gradually faded as passenger service ceased in 1979 and freight operations declined. BN closed the shops in May 1986. (Goss Collection.)

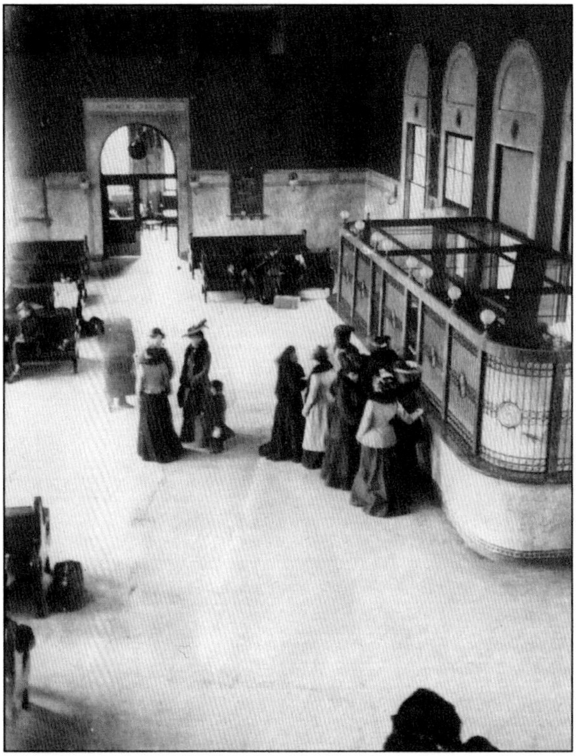

The ticket office, with its marble countertop, commanded center stage in the spacious waiting room of Livingston's third railroad depot. Constructed in 1902 with interior walls of chipped stone, the waiting room was illuminated with clusters of incandescent bulbs. The second story was accessed by two spiral staircases, one of which connected the ladies' parlor to a balcony that afforded an excellent view of the scenery. (Yellowstone Gateway Museum.)

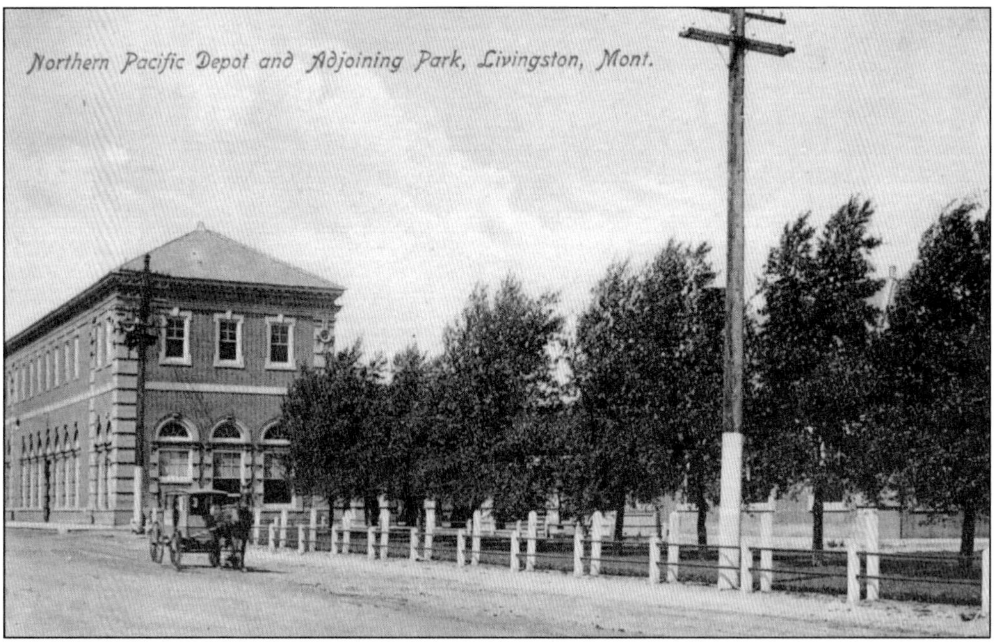

The majestic Livingston NPRR depot built in 1901–1902 was constructed of Menominee red brick and trimmed with St. Louis pressed yellow brick and terra cotta. In addition to laying the building's foundation in November 1901, workers were also excavating the grounds, setting fence posts, and fertilizing the soil for the park adjacent to the depot. The concrete walkway along Park Street furthered the depot's refined appearance. (Goss Collection.)

Three

METROPOLITAN AIRS

Launched in June 1883, the aptly named *Livingston Enterprise* newspaper reported weekly on the expansion of the budding town with an exuberance that drew the attention of many newspapers from afar who contributed enterprising stories of the town's progress. A June 24, 1883, *Butte Daily Miner* article echoed the extraordinary growth of Livingston, reporting, "The town is now all life and bustle" and "Livingston possesses elements of permanence and prosperity which few Montana towns enjoy."

Some of Livingston's earliest businesses included the Bank of Livingston, Thompson Brothers Department Store, A. L. Babcock and A. W. Miles Mercantile, Gordon Brothers Lumber, and John O. Saxe News and Fruits. Livingston's early progress and prosperity increased the possibility of courting new business enterprises to the thriving city by both railroad and city promoters. The Livingston Flouring Mill Company, Garnier Cigar Company, Nolan Brothers Hardware, Goughnour Lumber Company, Hruza's Cold Storage Market, Hefferlin Mercantile Company, and various A. W. Miles companies represented just a few of the business concerns that flourished in Livingston's booming economic climate.

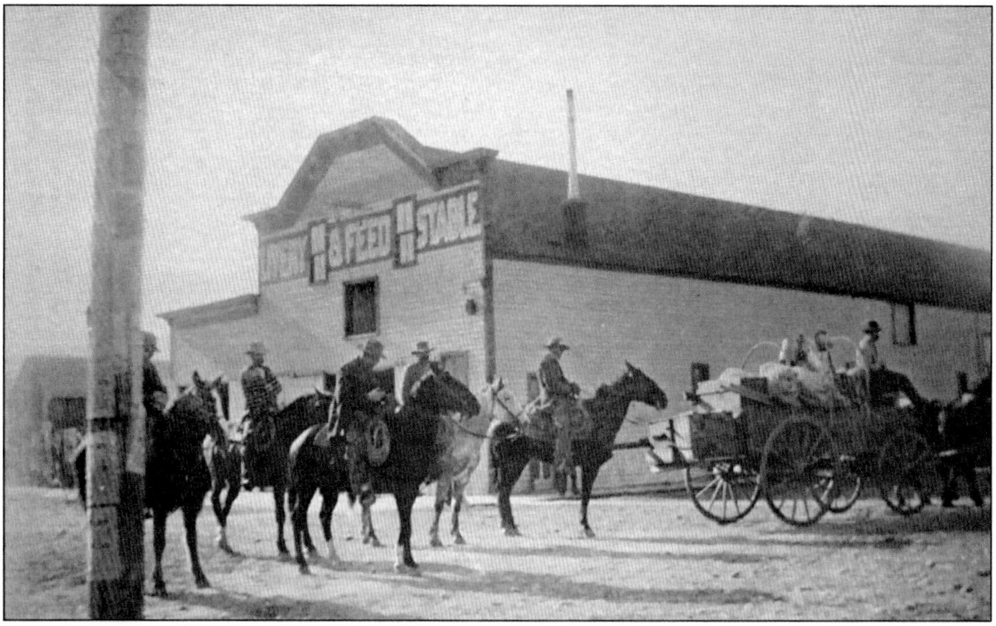

The Livery & Feed Stable depicted in this 1890s image was once owned by George Wakefield, who operated this concern on Callender and 2nd Streets from at least 1896. Operating passenger and mail stages in Yellowstone and surrounding areas since 1883, Wakefield began conducting camping parties into the park in 1896. Ennis & Robsons Livery previously occupied this location in 1891. (Private collection.)

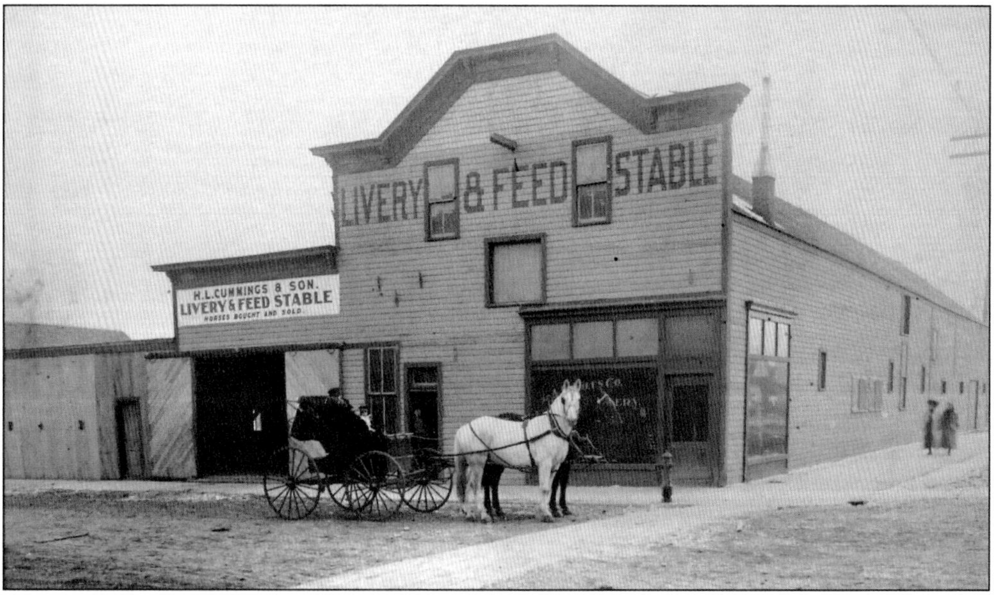

Arriving in Livingston around 1904, Herbert Cummings (Commings) and son Lyman took over Wakefield's old livery business in 1906. The Cummings business moved into a new brick building on Lewis and 3rd Streets in 1909. Businessmen Mertz and Blair took over the old livery location on Callender and 2nd Streets, establishing an automobile business. The advent of the horseless carriage steered the Cummings family into launching an automobile repair business and Chevrolet dealership. (Private collection.)

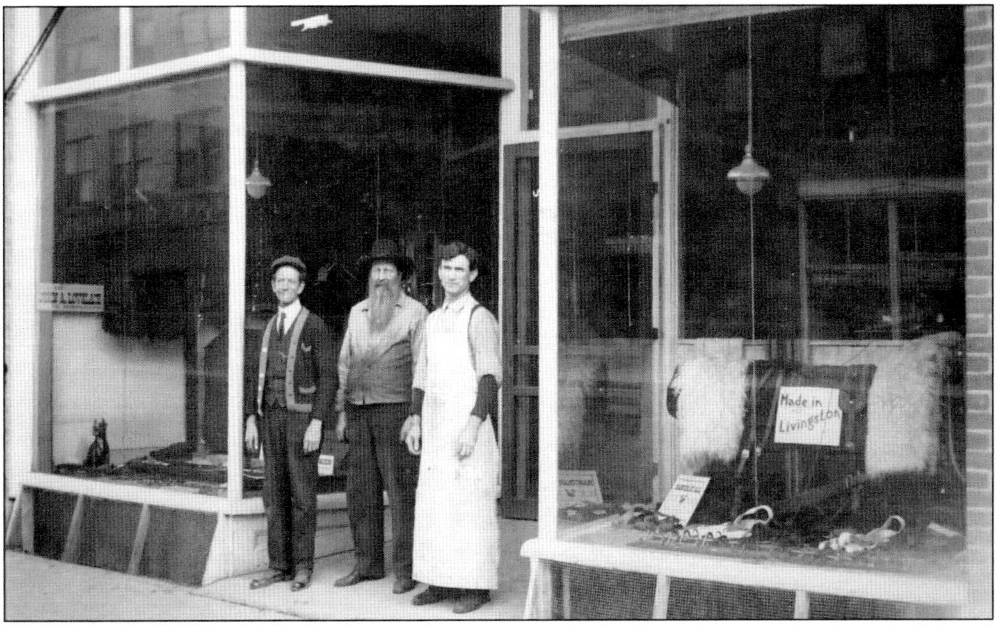

Learning the leather and harness craft at an early age in Indiana, Christian I. Alspaugh (center) moved to Livingston in 1907 and set up his saddle shop on the corner of Main and Lewis Streets at age 55. Together with son Joseph (right), they specialized in "Made in Montana" leather goods that accommodated horsemen and ranchers long after the automobile commandeered the highways and byways. (Private collection.)

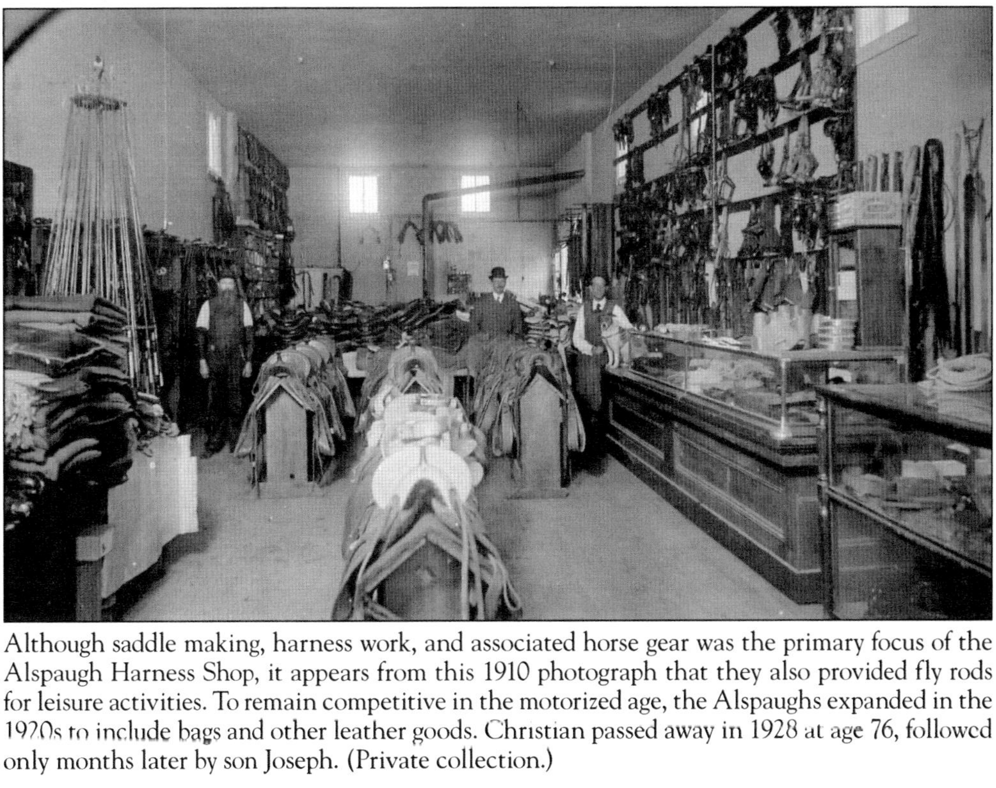

Although saddle making, harness work, and associated horse gear was the primary focus of the Alspaugh Harness Shop, it appears from this 1910 photograph that they also provided fly rods for leisure activities. To remain competitive in the motorized age, the Alspaughs expanded in the 1920s to include bags and other leather goods. Christian passed away in 1928 at age 76, followed only months later by son Joseph. (Private collection.)

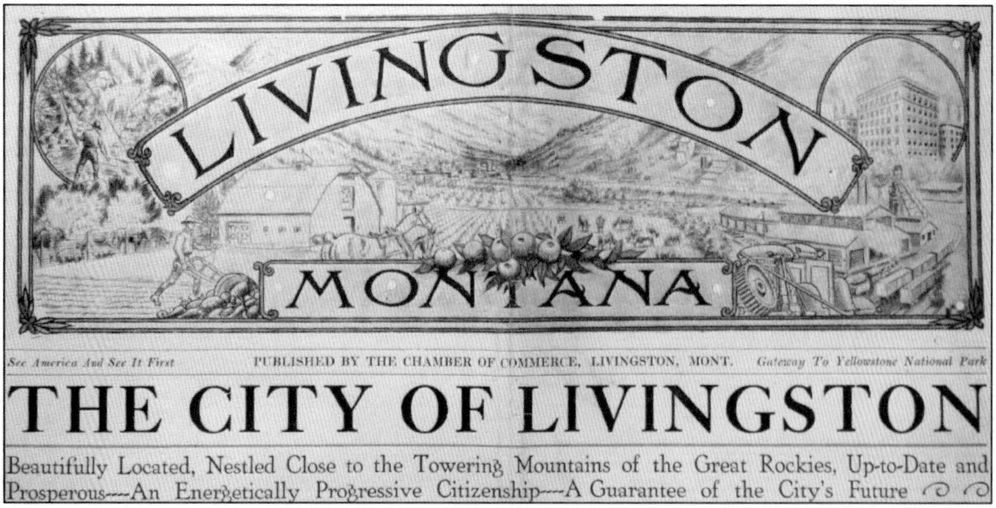

LIVINGSTON

MONTANA

See America And See It First PUBLISHED BY THE CHAMBER OF COMMERCE, LIVINGSTON, MONT. *Gateway To Yellowstone National Park*

THE CITY OF LIVINGSTON

Beautifully Located, Nestled Close to the Towering Mountains of the Great Rockies, Up-to-Date and Prosperous---An Energetically Progressive Citizenship---A Guarantee of the City's Future

This chamber of commerce newsletter headline proudly heralded Livingston's inviting locale as well as enthusiastic confidence in its citizenry and future prospects. Situated along the banks of the Yellowstone River in the heart of the Rocky Mountains, Livingston indeed commanded a premier location that offered the convenience of a forward-looking city, picturesque and productive agricultural valleys, and a plethora of outdoor recreational activities amid majestic mountain scenery. (Private collection.)

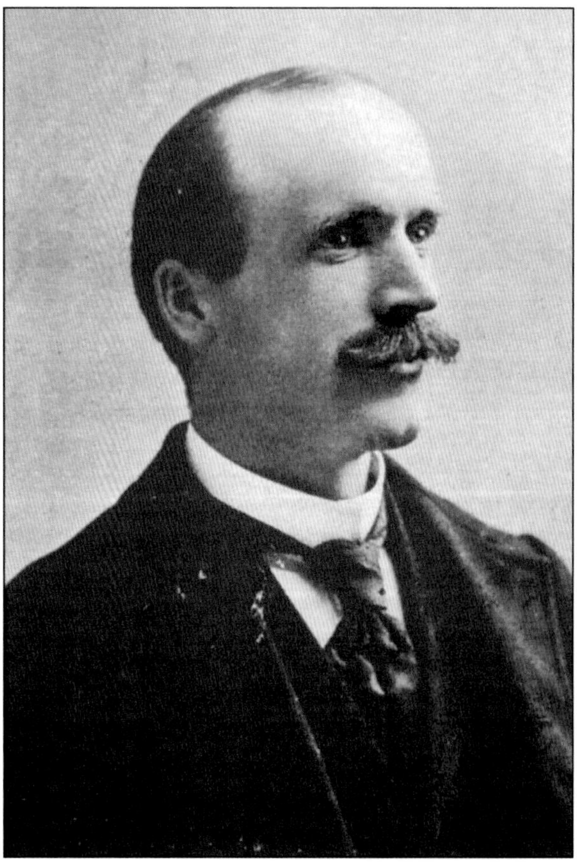

William N. Hefferlin was one of four brothers who immigrated from Kansas and Missouri to Livingston in the 1880s. Brothers John and Charles arrived in town in 1883 as employees of the NPRR. Five years later, convinced of a bright future, William and Orlando joined John and with $1,500 capital established Hefferlin Mercantile. By 1899, business was booming with $100,000 a year in sales. (*Livingston Souvenir.*)

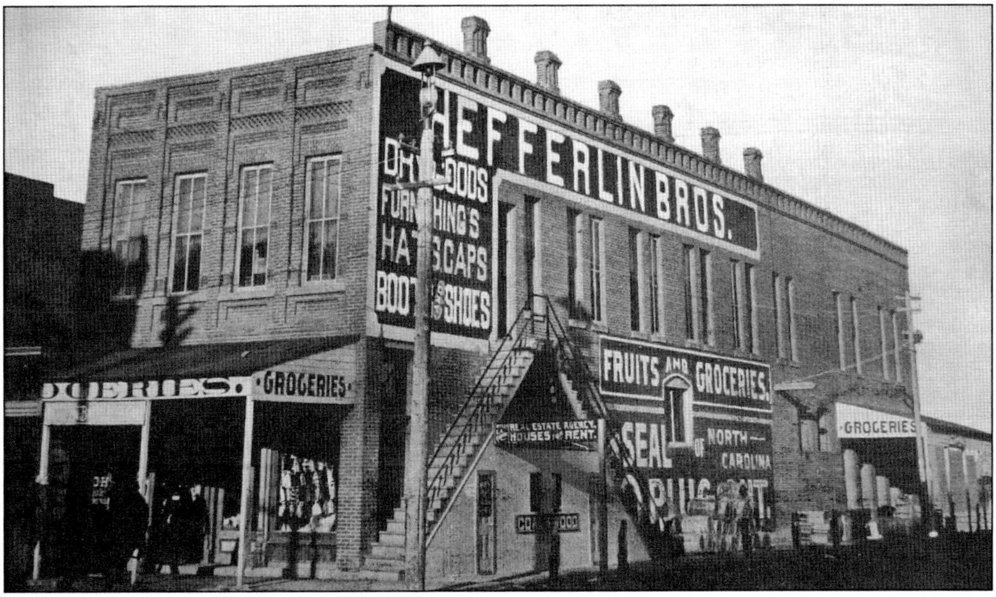

The three Hefferlin brothers built this handsome store on the corner of Main and Callender Streets in 1888 and the next year incorporated as the Hefferlin Mercantile Company. Around that time, they expanded and established branch stores at the neighboring communities of Fridley and Trail Creek. Meanwhile, Charles built the Merchants' Bank, Hefferlin Opera House, and a dozen other stores on Main Street. (*Livingston Souvenir.*)

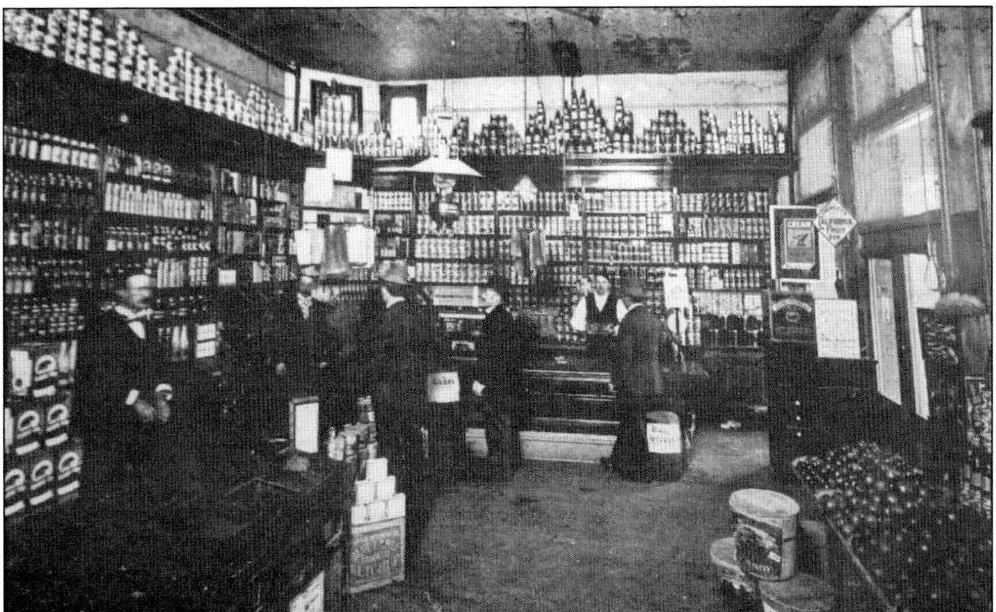

The Hefferlin Mercantile offered a wide array of goods that included groceries, clothing, hats, shoes, and assorted sundries. Specializing in mail-order goods, they issued yearly catalogs to bring big-city goods to local folk. A hotel, variously named Yellowstone Block and New York, operated on the second floor. By 1927, the store was vacant. The Mint Bar took residence after Prohibition and continues to operate to this day. (*Livingston Souvenir.*)

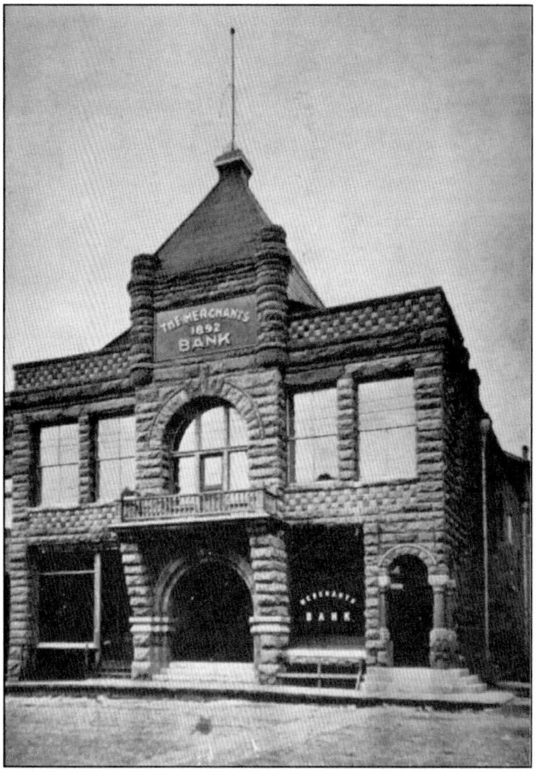

In 1889, Charles Hefferlin established the Merchants' Bank and in 1892 erected this imposing structure on North Main Street to accommodate his bank. This photograph, believed to date from 1892–1893, flaunts a cut-stone facade, plate-glass windows, and sandstone pillars. Toward the back, the Hefferlin Opera House was established and quickly became a hallmark for societal functions. The Chinese-run Opera House Restaurant also occupied part of the building. (*Livingston Souvenir.*)

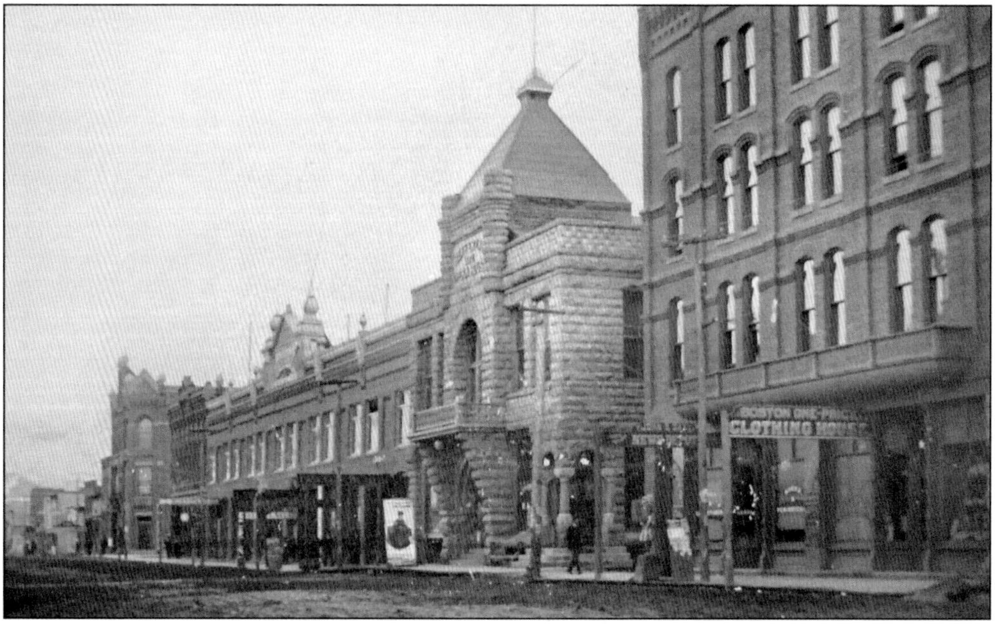

A nationwide economic collapse in 1893 also effected Livingston. The Merchants' Bank, along with other local banks, went bankrupt. Hefferlin later resurrected the bank but changed the name of the building from the Merchants' Bank to Hefferlin Opera House, as evidenced by this 1894 photograph. At this time, rudimentary electric light poles lined the streets and the Sax newsstand operated next door in the Albemarle Hotel Annex. (Private collection.)

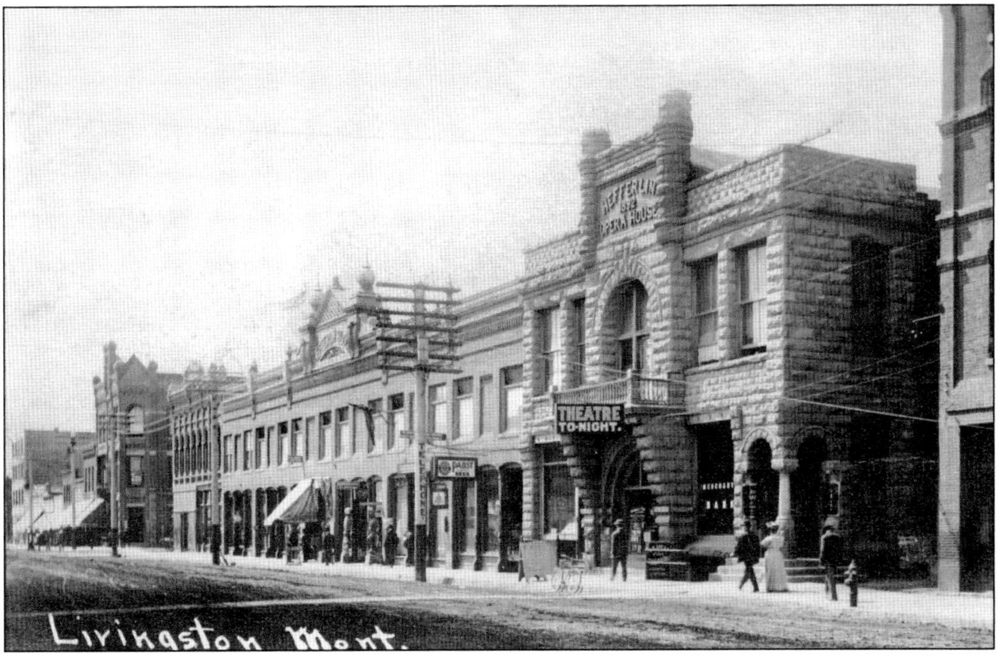

Fire struck the opera house January 31, 1896, and destroyed much of the interior and roof, inflicting $30,000 damage. Hefferlin soon rebuilt, but the steeple-roof feature no longer graced the edifice. Hefferlin reportedly "spared no labor or expense in making it a monument of beauty, convenience and comfort." Electric and telephone lines now cluttered the street view. In the 1920s, the Orpheum Theater assumed occupancy of the opera house. (Goss Collection.)

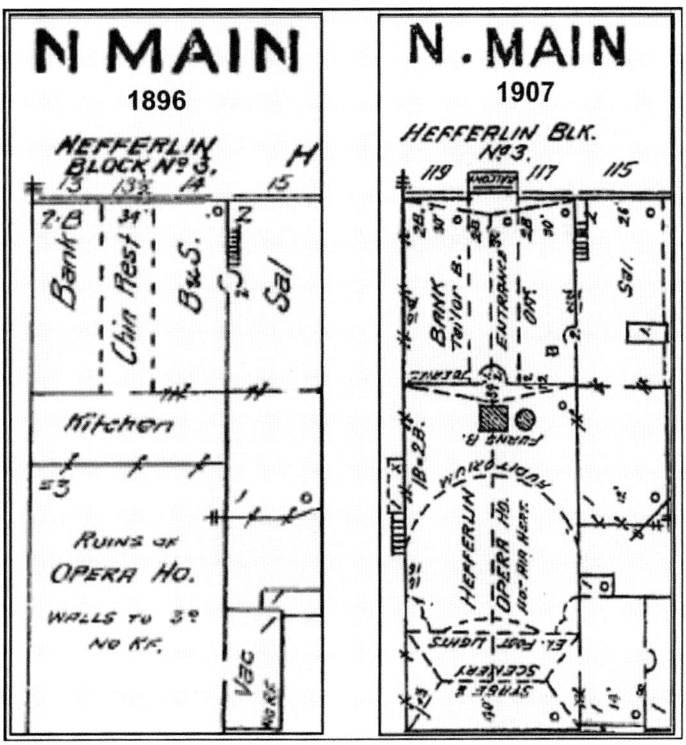

The 1896 map, produced less than a year after the fire, depicted the opera house building with a notation "Ruins of Opera Ho." The Merchants' Bank occupied the corner of the building with the Chinese restaurant in the center. The 1907 map revealed the new opera house design that seated 700. A moveable stage, combined with a stationary stage, offered an impressive 50-by-73-foot overall stage. (Goss Collection.)

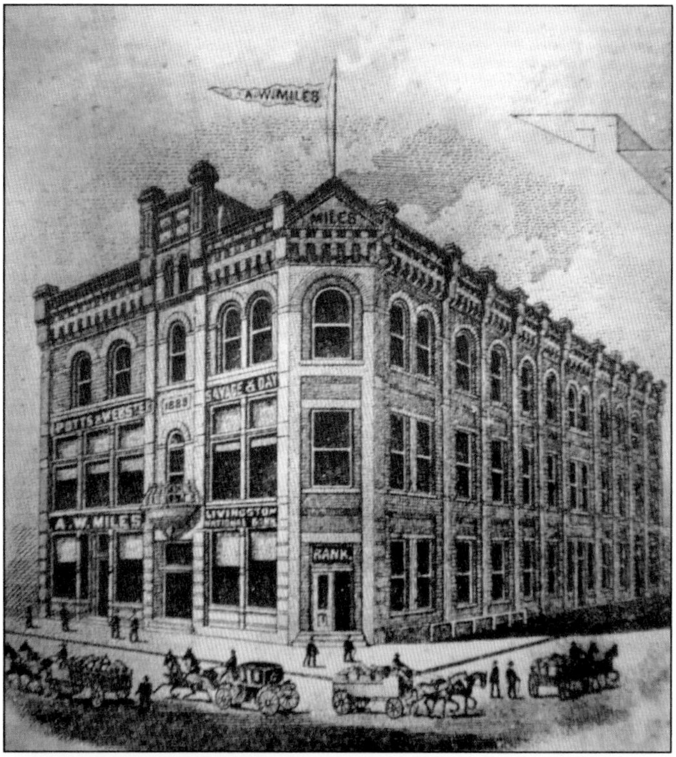

Arthur Wellington Miles, nephew to Gen. Nelson Miles, was among the earliest and foremost businessmen in Livingston. After constructing the first Billings business block in 1881, he removed to Livingston late in 1882 and with A. L. Babcock established Babcock & Miles Hardware. Capitalizing on his success, Miles erected this imposing edifice at Main and Callender Street that accommodated his hardware enterprise, the Livingston National Bank, and other entrepreneurs. (*Livingston Souvenir.*)

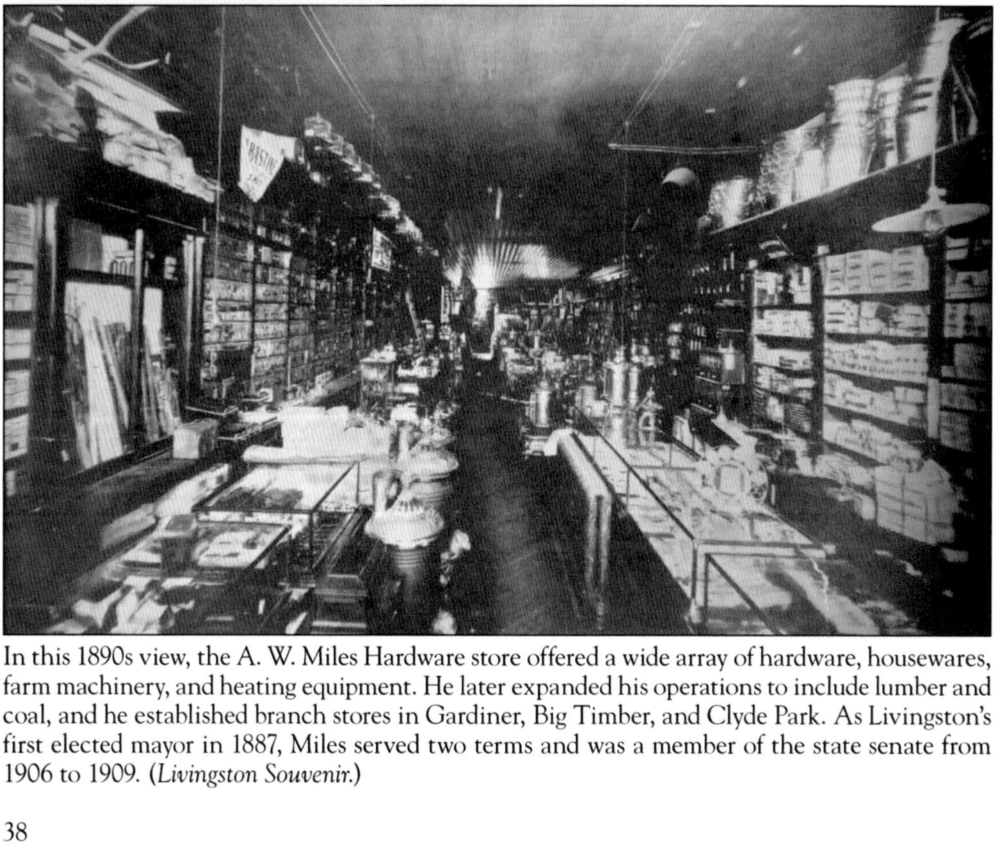

In this 1890s view, the A. W. Miles Hardware store offered a wide array of hardware, housewares, farm machinery, and heating equipment. He later expanded his operations to include lumber and coal, and he established branch stores in Gardiner, Big Timber, and Clyde Park. As Livingston's first elected mayor in 1887, Miles served two terms and was a member of the state senate from 1906 to 1909. (*Livingston Souvenir.*)

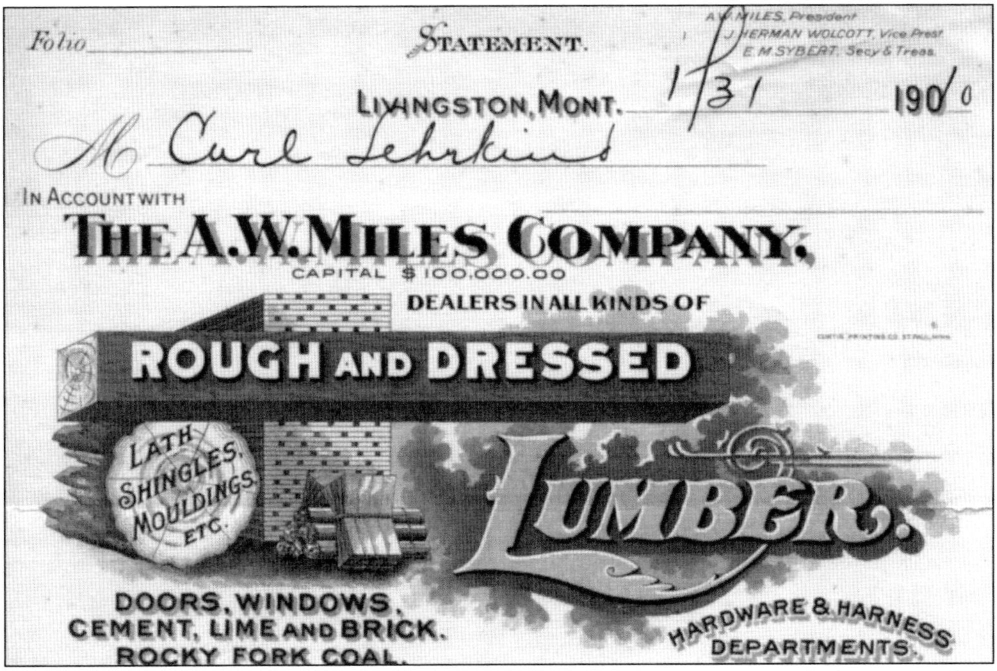
Folio

STATEMENT.

A. W. MILES, President
J. HERMAN WOLCOTT, Vice Prest.
E. M. SYBERT, Secy & Treas.

LIVINGSTON, MONT. 1/31 1910

M Carl Lehrkind

IN ACCOUNT WITH

THE A. W. MILES COMPANY.

CAPITAL $100,000.00

DEALERS IN ALL KINDS OF

ROUGH AND DRESSED LUMBER.

LATH, SHINGLES, MOULDINGS, ETC.

DOORS, WINDOWS, CEMENT, LIME AND BRICK. ROCKY FORK COAL.

HARDWARE & HARNESS DEPARTMENTS.

A. W. Miles Lumber Company was one of a myriad of business operations Miles invested in. The A. W. Miles Company, incorporated in 1901 with $100,000 capital, encompassed interests in lumber, coal, hardware, livery, saddlery, tin shop, and brick yard. Miles also established the A. W. Miles Land and Investment Company, operated a sheep ranch, and held majority interests in the Thompson Company, Gordon Brothers Lumber, and other businesses. (Goss Collection.)

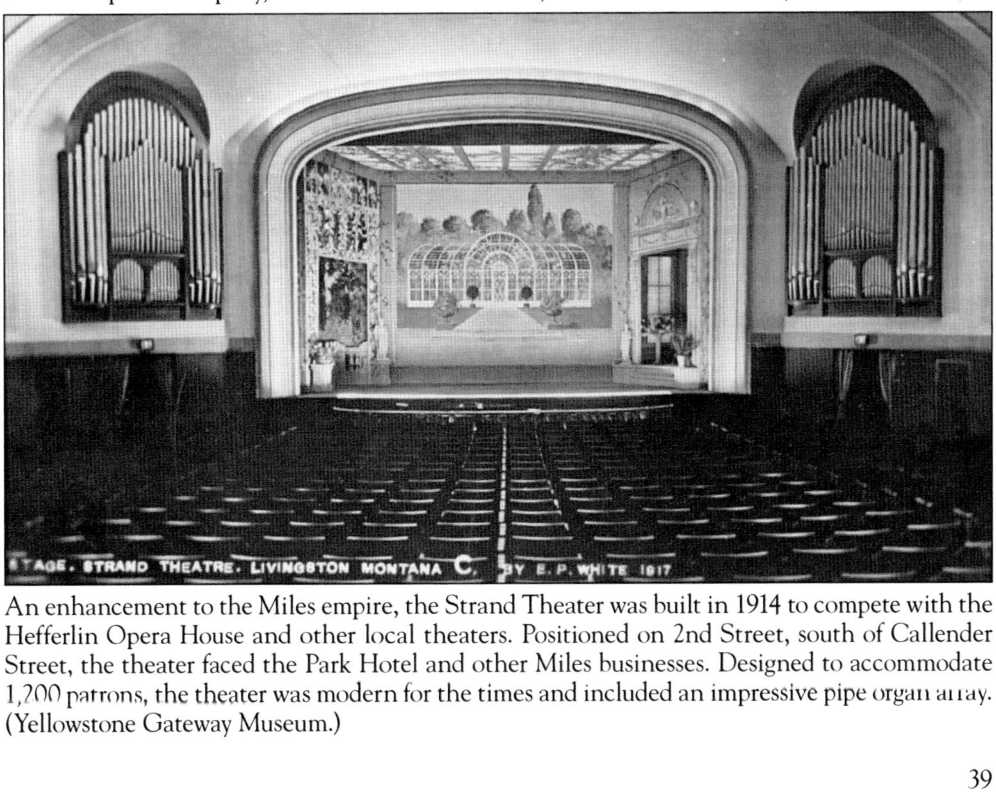

An enhancement to the Miles empire, the Strand Theater was built in 1914 to compete with the Hefferlin Opera House and other local theaters. Positioned on 2nd Street, south of Callender Street, the theater faced the Park Hotel and other Miles businesses. Designed to accommodate 1,200 patrons, the theater was modern for the times and included an impressive pipe organ array. (Yellowstone Gateway Museum.)

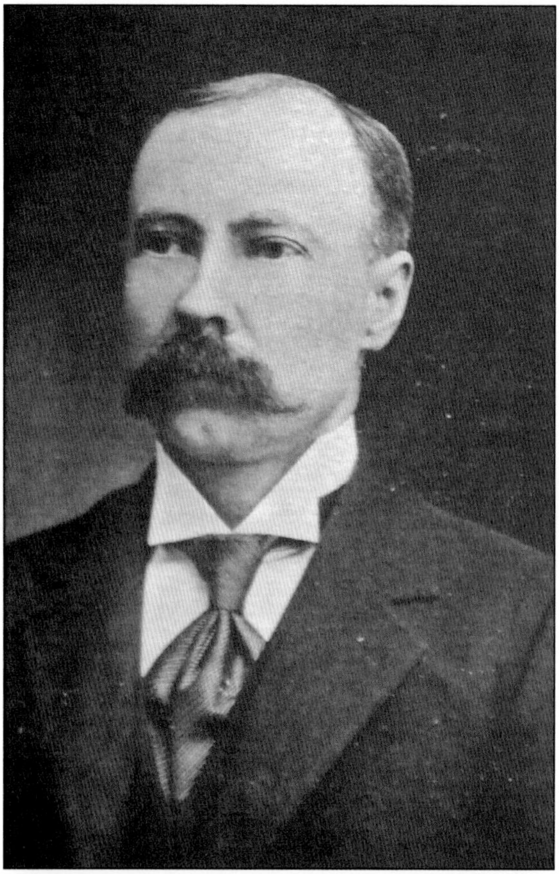

John O. Saxe and Alfred Croonquist followed the Northern Pacific to Livingston in 1883 as "news butchers." Saxe soon teamed up with F. W. Brown and set up a newsstand on Main Street known as Brown and Saxe. Apparently on his own by December 1883, Saxe advertised his enterprise as "John. O. Saxe—News and Fruit Dealers, and Confectioners" and offered the "latest eastern Dailies, Illustrated Journals, and Magazines." (*Livingston Souvenir.*)

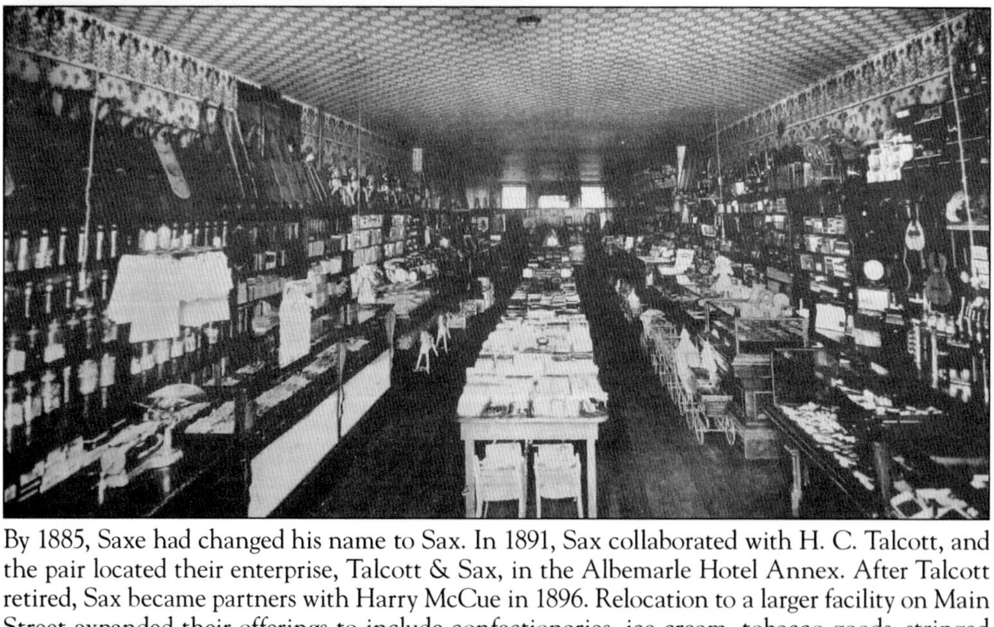

By 1885, Saxe had changed his name to Sax. In 1891, Sax collaborated with H. C. Talcott, and the pair located their enterprise, Talcott & Sax, in the Albemarle Hotel Annex. After Talcott retired, Sax became partners with Harry McCue in 1896. Relocation to a larger facility on Main Street expanded their offerings to include confectionaries, ice cream, tobacco goods, stringed instruments, school supplies, fishing gear, and Columbia bicycles. (*Livingston Souvenir.*)

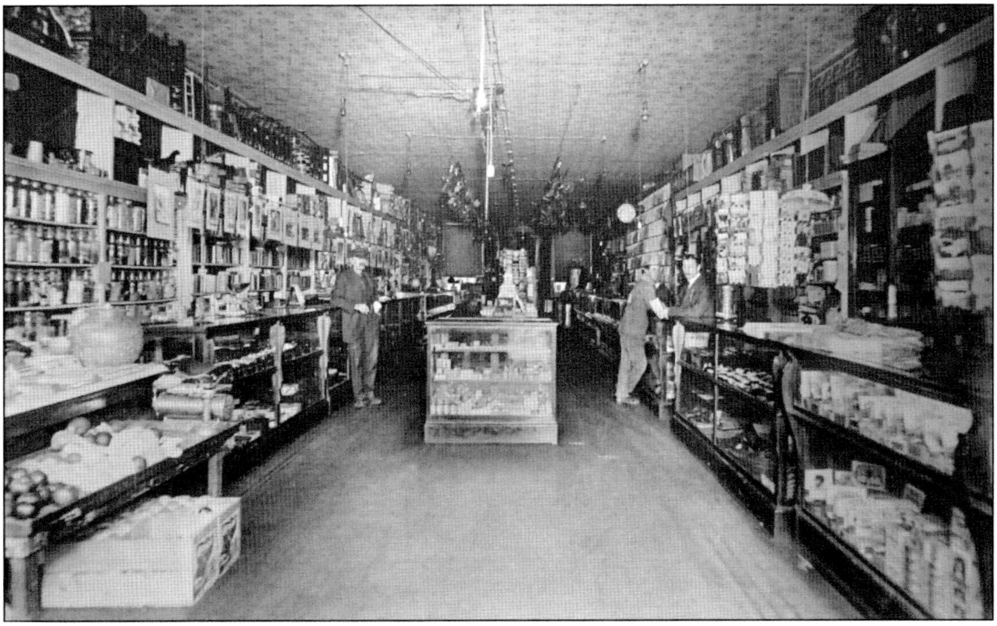

This 1911 photograph portrayed the recently renamed Sax & Fryer store operating at 109 North Main Street, the third store location. When colleague and recently elected Park County sheriff Harry McCue died in March 1911, John W. Fryer (standing behind the counter on the right) bought out McCue's interest in the store. Not long afterward, Sax & Fryer moved to its current location on 109 West Callender Street. (Fryer Collection.)

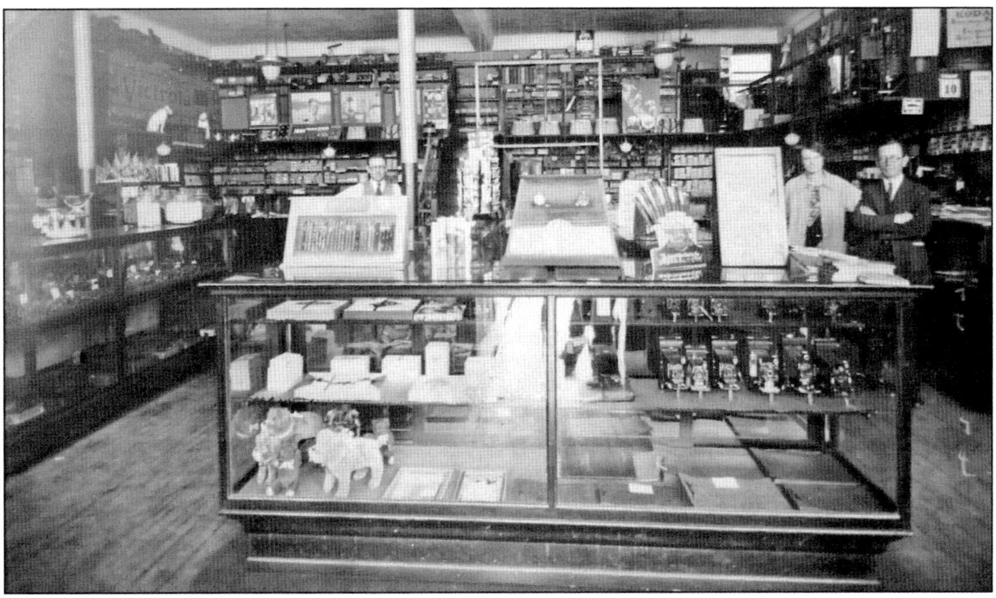

John's son Frank Fryer (at left) posed with associates in this 1920s photograph. The year 1925 proved noteworthy when Sax retired after 42 years and John W. Fryer was elected Livingston mayor and served two terms. John Haberstroh acquired Sax's share and remained with the company another 20 years. Following Haberstroh's retirement, this steadfast endeavor has remained in the Fryer family these past 64 years with John W. Fryer's grandson John Fryer directing the 125-year-old firm. (Fryer Collection.)

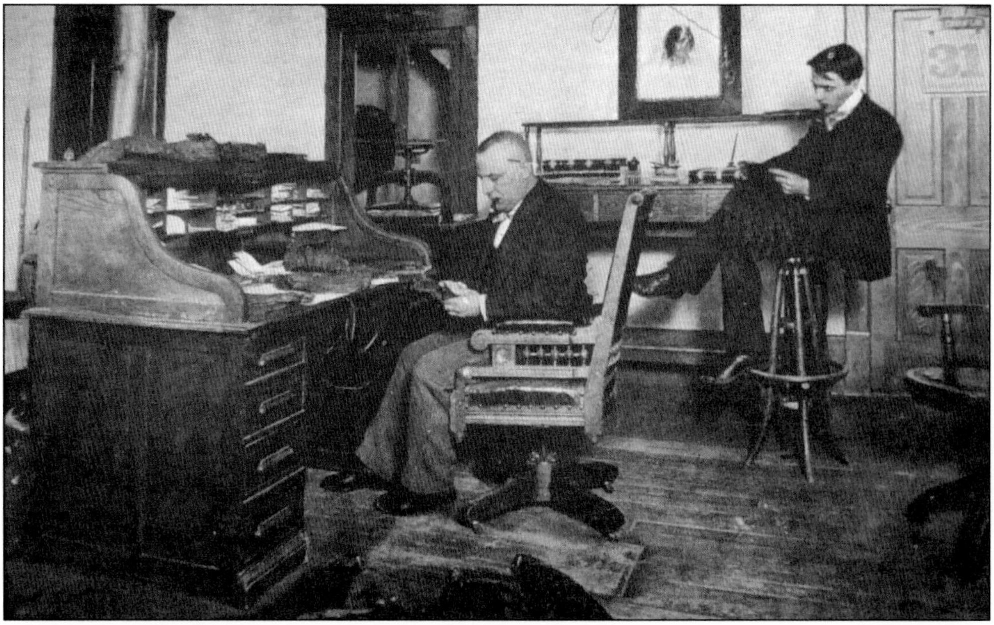

It seems no early Western town was complete without a local cigar factory that catered to the gentlemanly pleasure enjoyed by kings and commoners alike. Livingston was no exception, and for almost 50 years, the Garnier Cigar Company provided the smoke enjoyed by railroad workers, tourists, businessmen, and probably Calamity Jane! Charles Garnier and son Charles Jr. for a time supported a payroll surpassed only by the Northern Pacific. (*Livingston Souvenir.*)

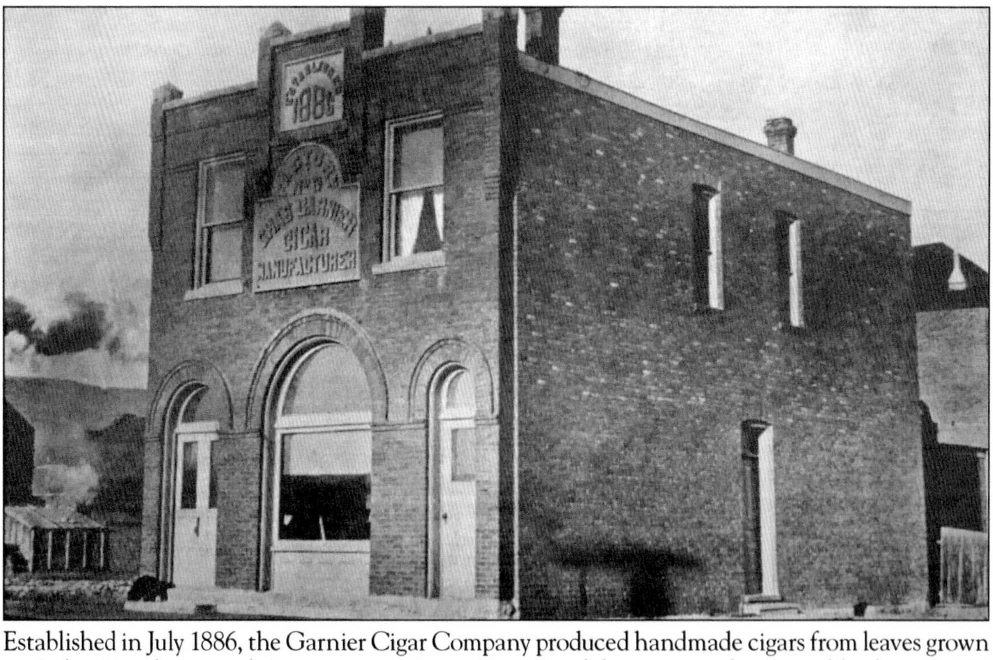

Established in July 1886, the Garnier Cigar Company produced handmade cigars from leaves grown in Cuba, Honduras, and Connecticut. Garnier's original factory was devastated by fire in 1897 but was soon replaced by this brick edifice on North 2nd Street. One of several manufacturers in town, Garnier competed with Charles Manley and James Shipton's cigar brands, J. S. and Livinston Favorite. Garnier also served as mayor and city treasurer. (*Livingston Souvenir.*)

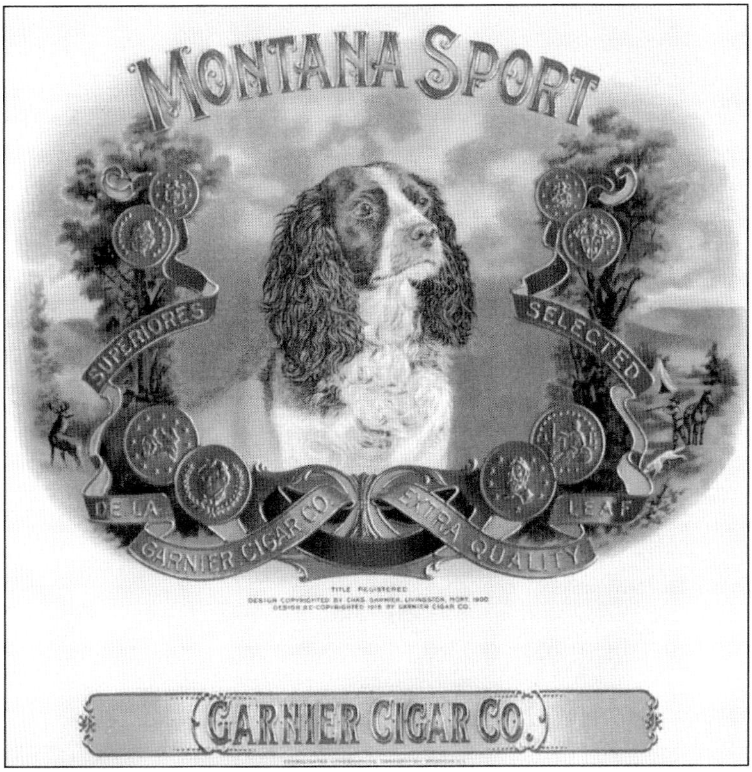

Crafted in different shapes and sizes, the Montana Sport was Garnier's only cigar. However, upward of 40,000 cigars per month were produced to supply local and regional demand. Featuring a droopy-eared black and white Springer spaniel, Garnier's trademark logo graced cigar boxes, bands, and advertising materials for many years. Charles Sr. died in 1939 and Charles Jr. followed in 1944, bringing an end to this historic enterprise. (Watry Collection.)

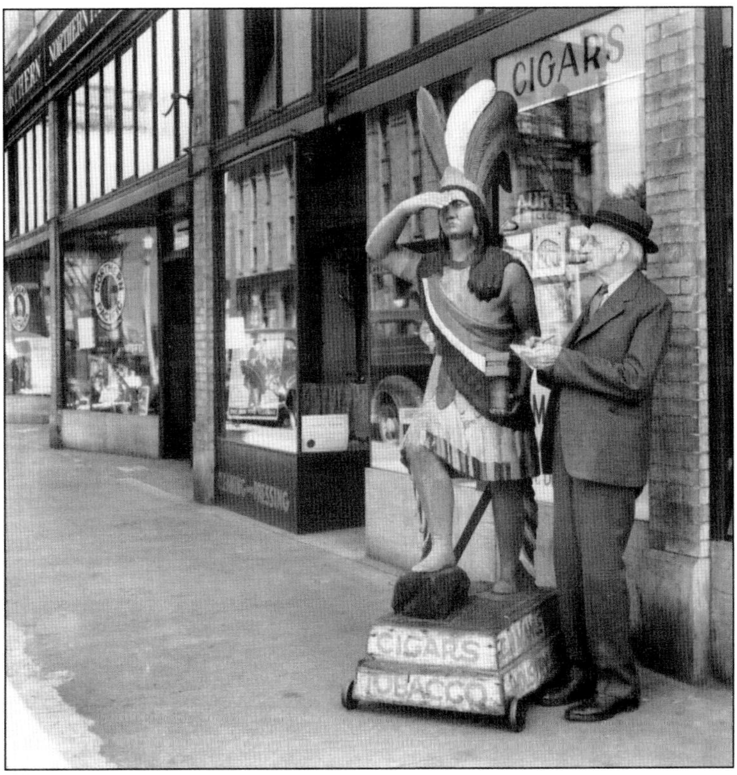

Carved by a Chicago firm in 1883, this gaily painted cigar-store Indian was shipped by rail to Charles Manley's cigar factory in Livingston. "Chief Skookum" guarded Manley's factory on North Main Street until fire destroyed the operation July 4, 1887. Manley and his wooden friend moved to Tacoma, Washington, where they managed a cigar store for 50 years. Charles confers with "The Chief" in this 1938 Tacoma photograph. (Tacoma Public Library.)

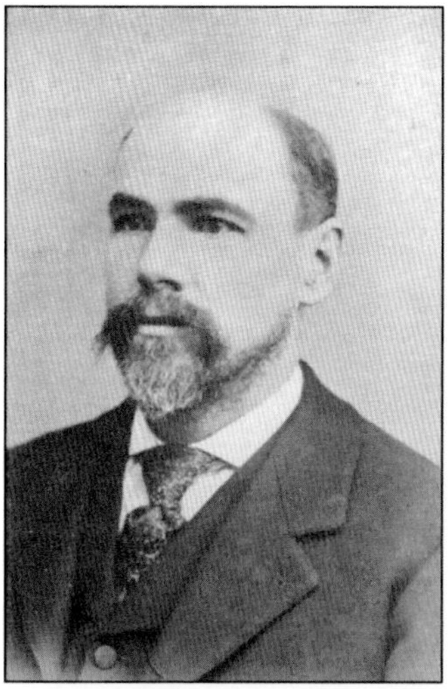 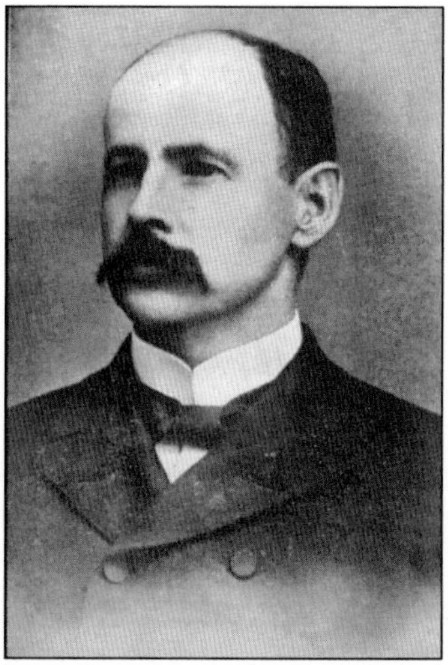 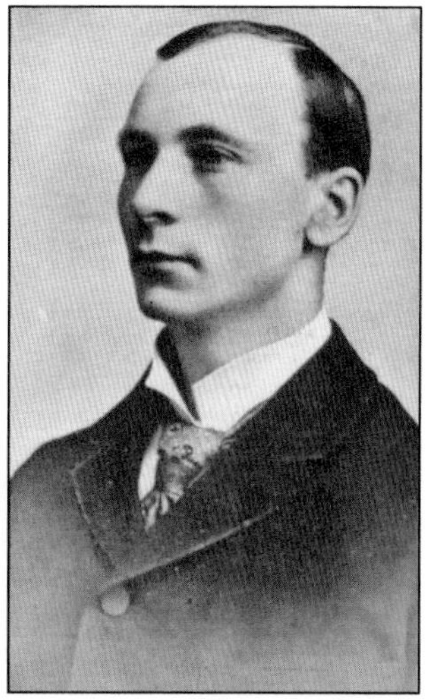

Natives of New York, brothers James, William, and Floyd Thompson were pioneer merchants in the fledgling town of Livingston. James journeyed west in 1880, settled in the Black Hills, and engaged in merchandizing. William joined him in 1881 and taught school in Lead City. Moving to Coulson, Montana, James soon realized the business potential of Livingston and relocated. William followed, and together they inaugurated the Thompson Brothers Mercantile. (*Livingston Souvenir.*)

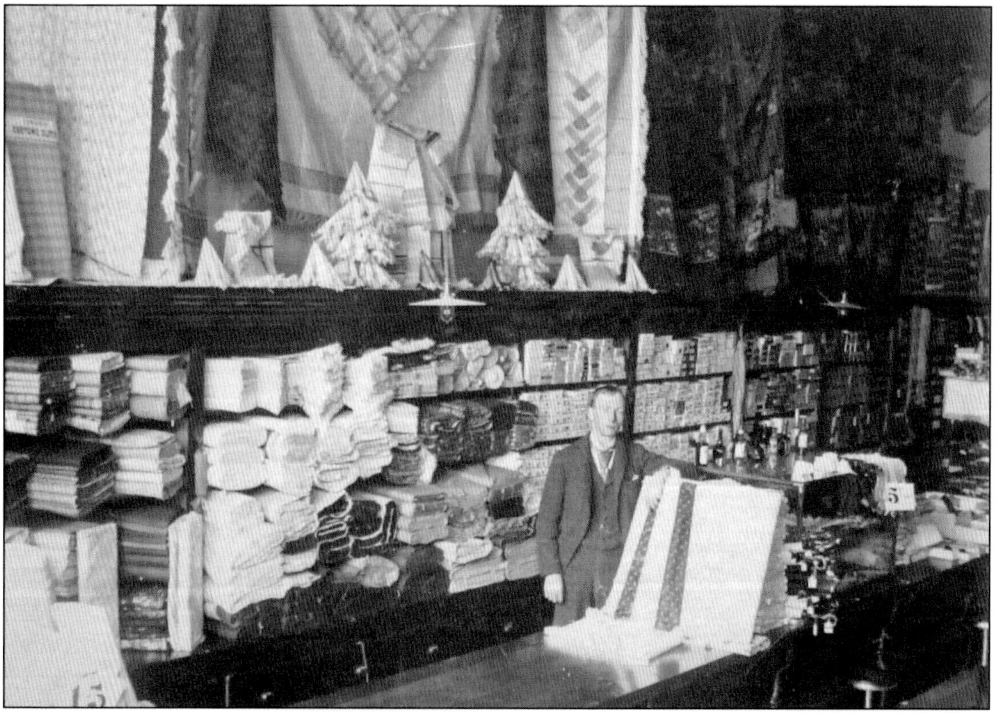

In 1886, Floyd Thompson made the trek west to Livingston and joined the Thompson Brothers partnership. The enterprise boomed, and the brothers built a new complex on the corner of Main and Callender Streets. This 1890s view depicts Floyd tending the counter in the dry goods department of the mercantile store at Main and Callender. Floyd, still in his thirties, passed away before 1906. (Private collection.)

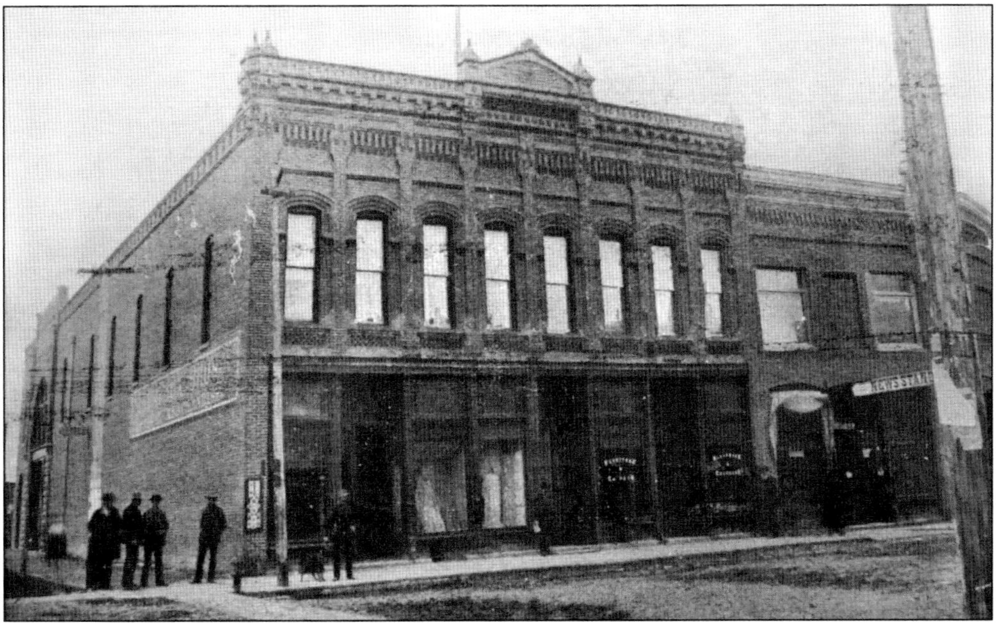

The Thompsons erected this handsome brick edifice around the early 1890s and shared the right portion of the building with Krieger Brothers Furniture. Early advertisements trumpeted "fancy groceries," dry goods, clothing, gents' furnishings, cashmeres, woolens, and ladies' underwear. In 1900, William purchased Carver Mercantile on the corner of Park and Main Streets and a year later sold his share of the family business to brother James. (*Livingston Souvenir*.)

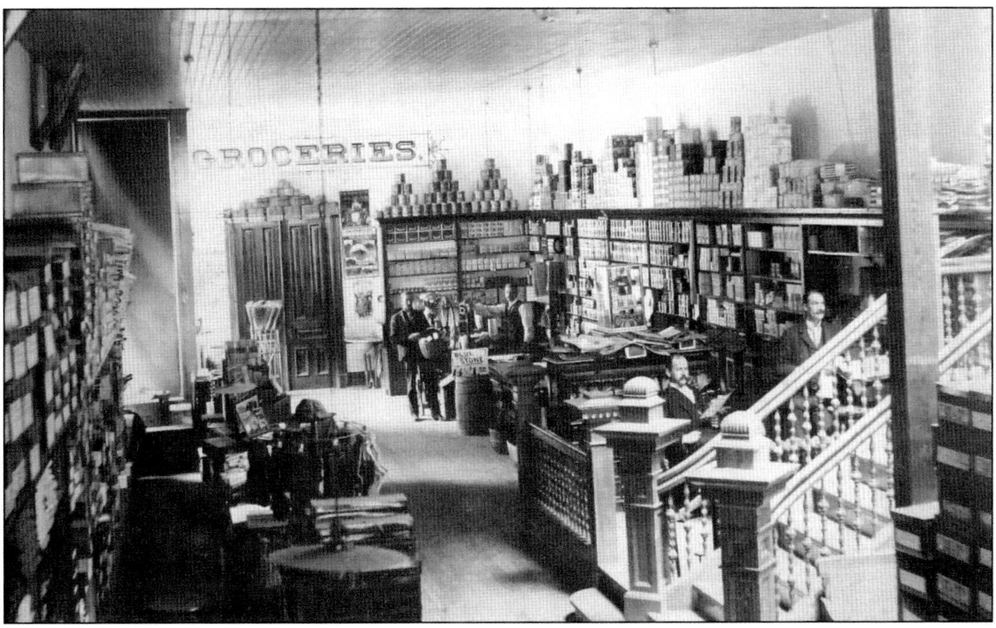

William Thompson, seated in the foreground, shares the office with Lew Shannon while grocer C. A. Talbot and Ed Wright stand to the rear in this early-1890s view of the Thompson Brothers grocery department. With William's departure from the business in 1901 and Floyd's passing soon after, James moved to San Diego and the Thompson Brothers became the Thompson Company in 1902 under the ownership of A. W. Miles. (Private collection.)

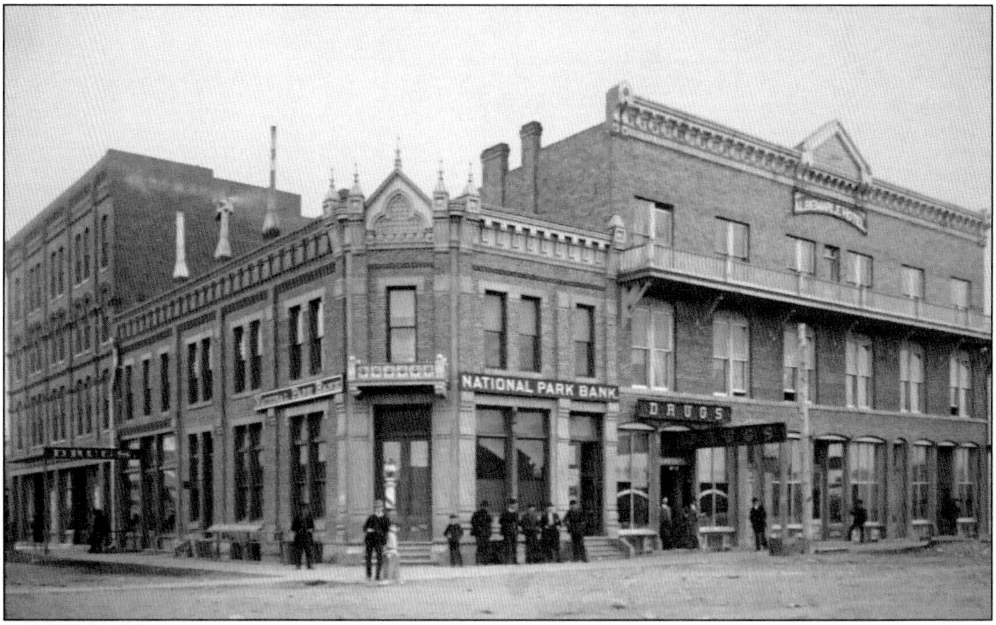

Livingston's first financial institution was created early in 1883 when Stebbins, Mund & Company established the Bank of Livingston. Competition rapidly followed as the First National Bank opened in mid-July. Late in 1886, the Bank of Livingston reorganized as the National Park Bank and moved into this impressive new edifice on the corner of Park and Main Streets, bordered by the Albemarle Hotel. (Private collection.)

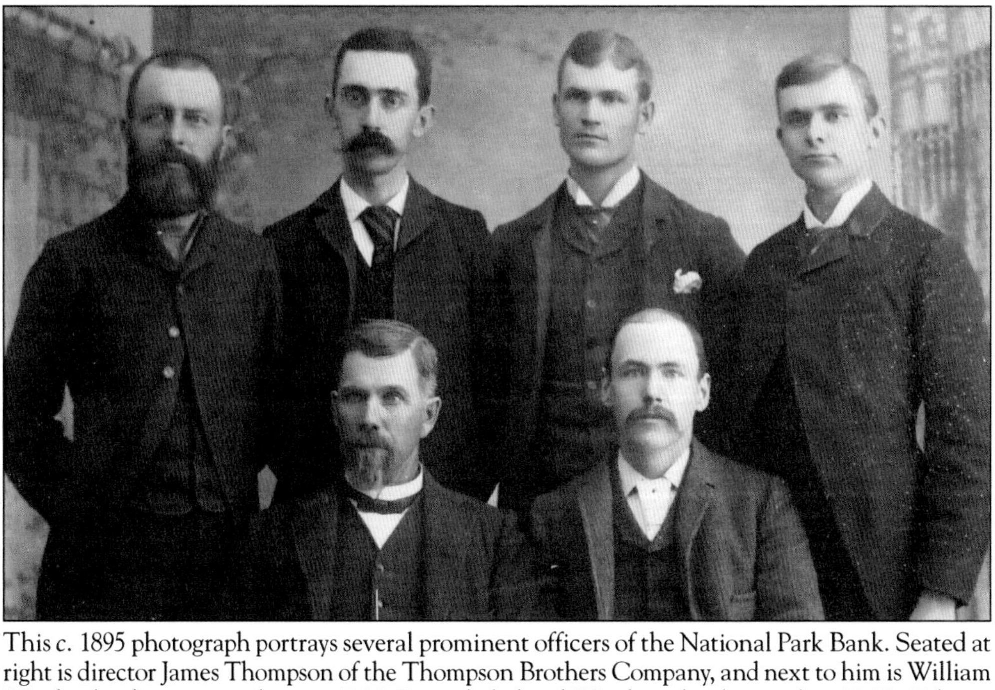

This *c.* 1895 photograph portrays several prominent officers of the National Park Bank. Seated at right is director James Thompson of the Thompson Brothers Company, and next to him is William Wright, bank vice president in 1886. Directly behind Wright is bank president E. H. Talcott, and the gentleman at left may be bank founder W. R. Stebbins. Other early directors included E. Goughnour, J. T. Smith, J. C. Vilas, and F. A. Krieger. (Private collection.)

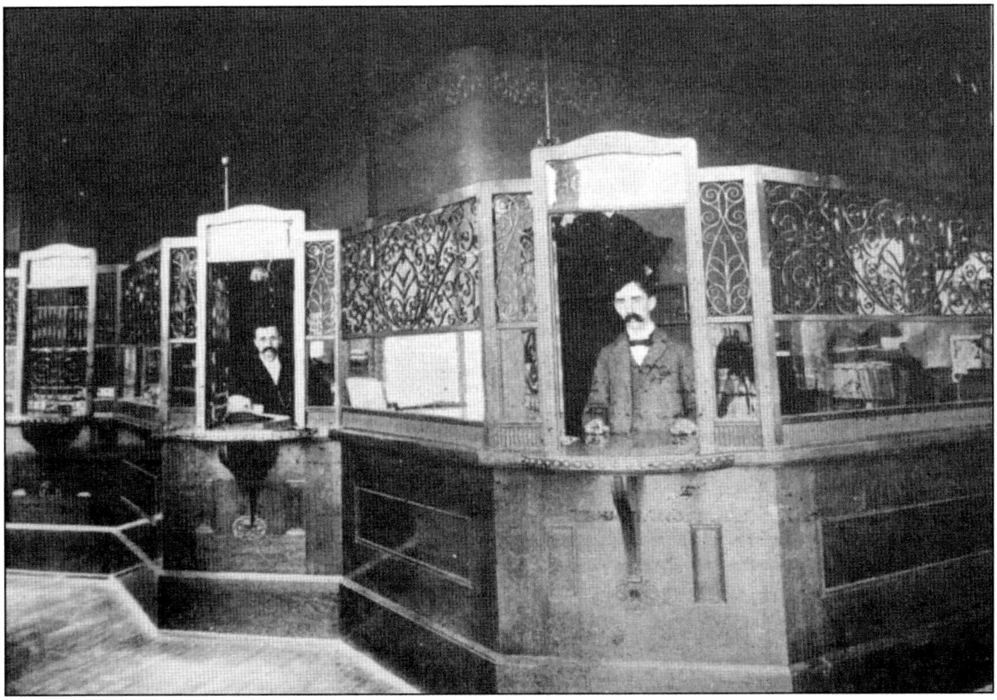

Although a successful enterprise, the National Park Bank suffered the throes of the 1893 financial panic and like other banks in Livingston was forced close its doors. The NP Bank recovered in two months, several years ahead of Livingston's other financial institutions. The 1905 advertisements boasted the NP Bank as the "oldest and leading bank in Park County." E. H Talcott may be the lead cashier in this 1890s photograph. (*Livingston Souvenir.*)

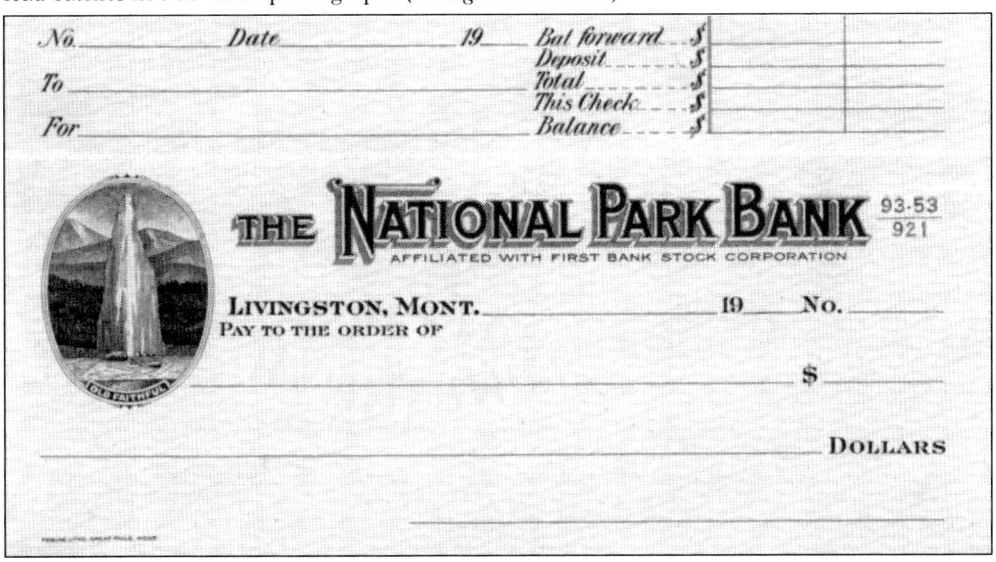

No. Date 19 Bal forward $
Deposit $
To Total $
This Check $
For Balance $

THE NATIONAL PARK BANK 93-53/921
AFFILIATED WITH FIRST BANK STOCK CORPORATION
OLD FAITHFUL
LIVINGSTON, MONT. 19 No.
PAY TO THE ORDER OF
$
DOLLARS

In 1930, the National Park Bank decided additional space was necessary and a new two-story building was erected on the corner of Callender and 2nd Streets at a cost of $100,000. The name was changed to First National Park Bank in 1957, and it continues as a successful business. With Sax & Fryer, it ranks among the oldest businesses in town. This 1930s check features Old Faithful Geyser. (Goss Collection.)

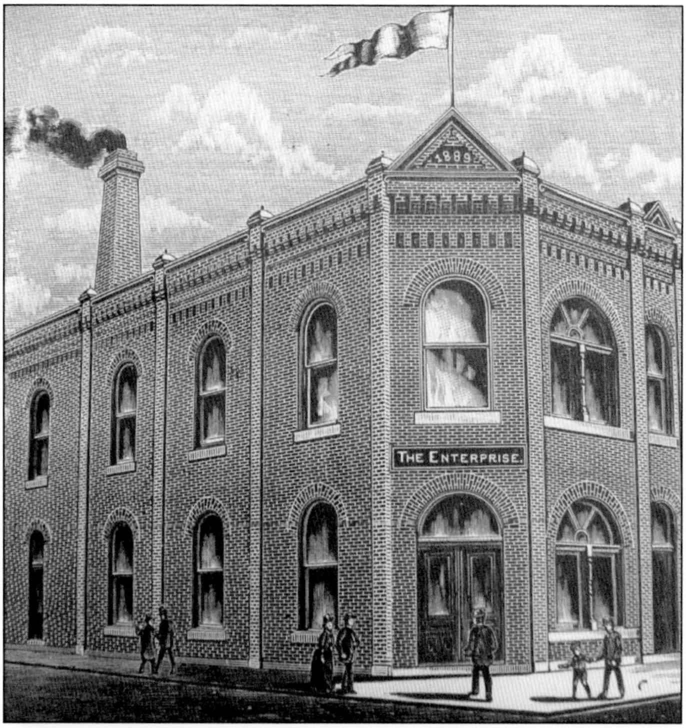

Newspapers have traditionally been the mainstay of small communities. The *Livingston Gazette* published Livingston's first newspaper on December 4, 1882. The *Livingston Enterprise* followed on June 4, 1883, and has remained in publication since, making it among the oldest continuously operated businesses in Livingston. Erected in 1889, this impressive edifice on the corner of Park and 2nd Streets hosted the *Enterprise* until 1919. (*Livingston Souvenir.*)

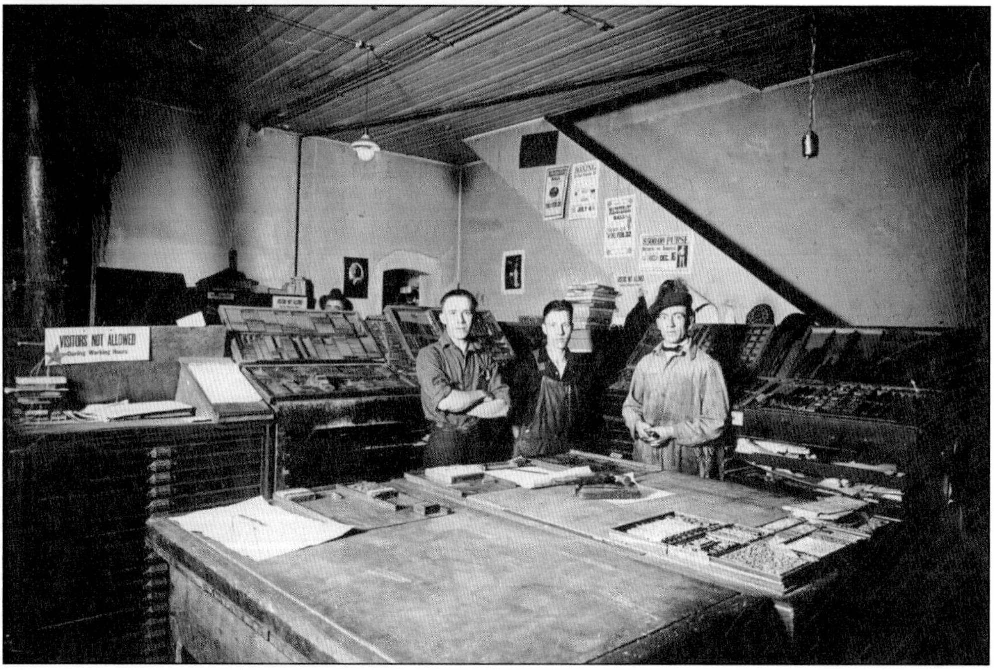

This undated photograph portrayed the typeset room, the heart of the newspaper, where ink-stained hands deftly positioned the type that spelled out the days' news. Founded by Wright and Hendry and originally located upstairs in the Orschel Building on Park Street, the *Livingston Enterprise* changed hands and locations several times over the years and included ownership by the Anaconda Copper Company from 1918 to 1959. (Yellowstone Gateway Museum.)

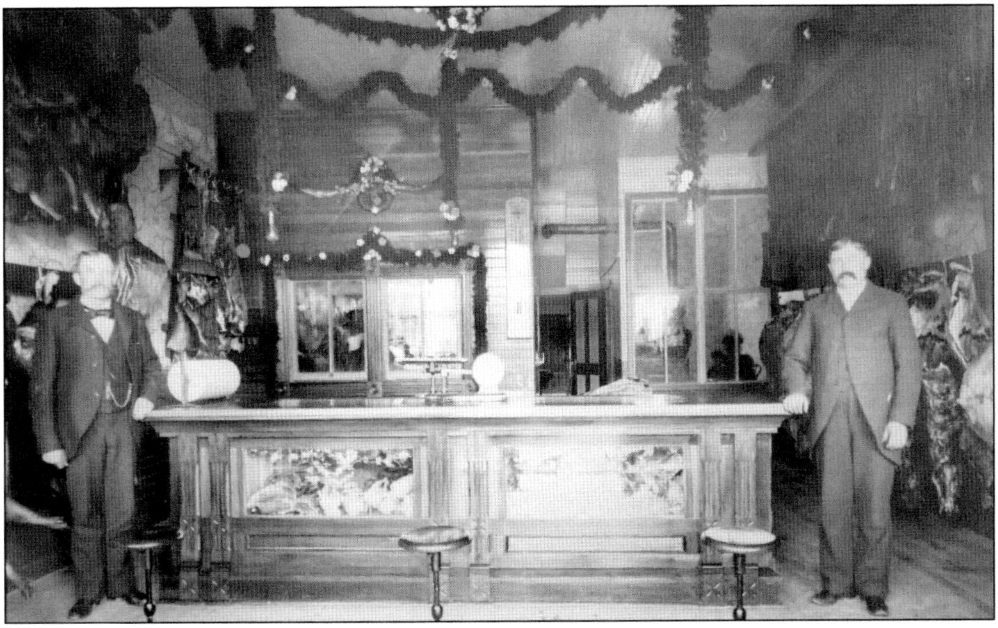

Arriving at Livingston in 1884 with his wife, Mary, William Hruza worked for nine years as a butcher for S. L. Holliday and Harvey & Company before establishing the Cold Storage Market. With business expanding, he moved to larger quarters at 106 South Main Street. Pictured at left, Hruza proudly presents his wares in the front counter area of his gaily decorated emporium. (Private collection.)

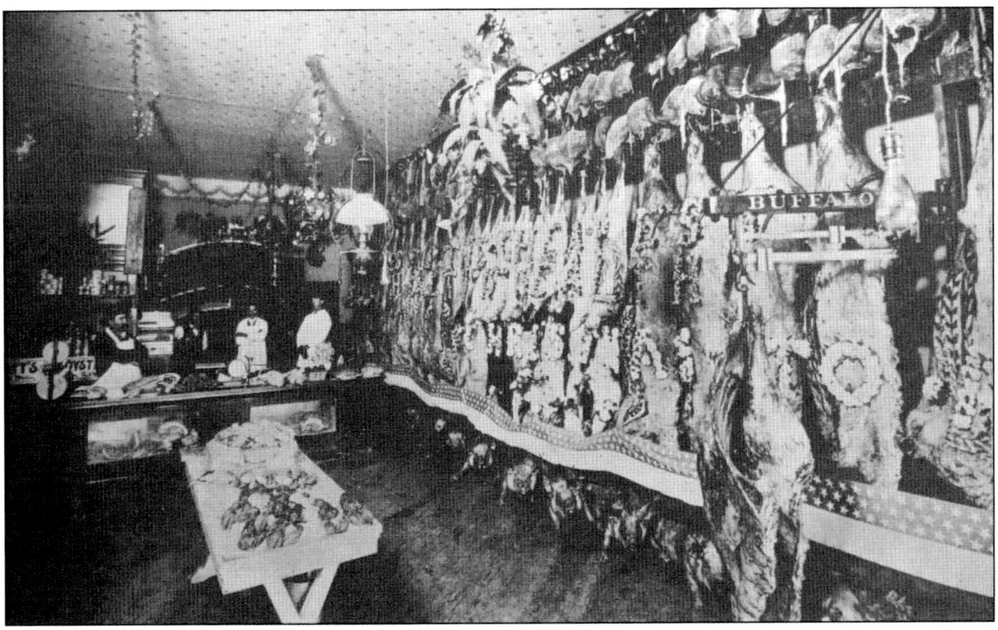

Festive Christmas decorations enliven this photograph of the Cold Storage Market. Hruza offered an array of meats that included beef, buffalo, poultry, pork, lobsters, and oysters. Newspaper advertisements proclaimed it the "Best Sausage Factory West of Chicago." By 1900, upwards of 20,000 pounds of locally raised meat was processed in his ranch slaughterhouse south of town. He retired from the enterprise in 1915. (*Livingston Souvenir.*)

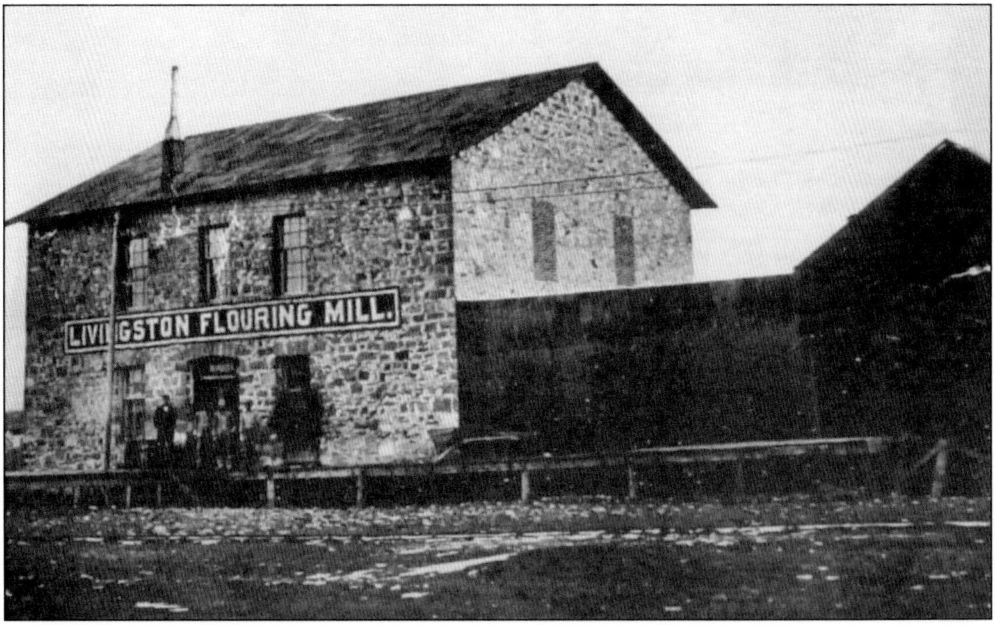

A. W. Miles and William Grabow opened this flouring mill in November 1898 that was capable of producing 75 barrels of high-grade flour a day. Frank Huot, who had previously operated mills in Minnesota, Nebraska, and Big Timber, Montana, managed the operation. Shortages of wheat caused inconsistencies in production the first few years, and in October 1902, a catastrophic fire gutted the native-stone building. (*Livingston Souvenir.*)

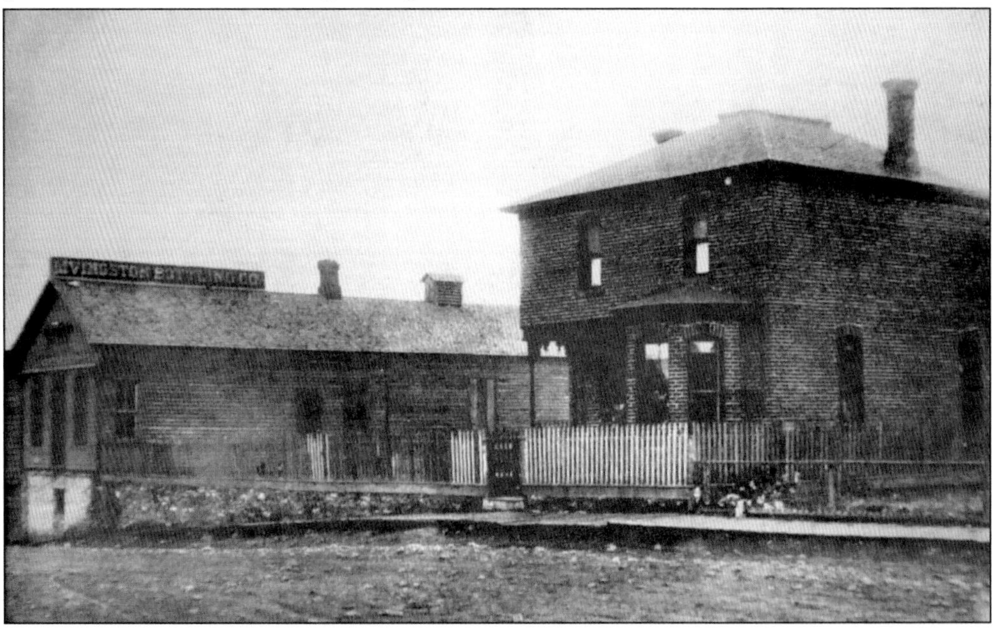

The Livingston Bottling Company was established around 1888 following Frank Beley's move to Livingston from a Butte brewery. The company bottled all manner of drinks with the exception of beer. Success followed as Beley became a city alderman and was elected mayor in 1893. He later served as Park County sheriff, county commissioner, concrete contractor, and drugstore owner. He departed life in 1944 at age 83. (*Livingston Souvenir.*)

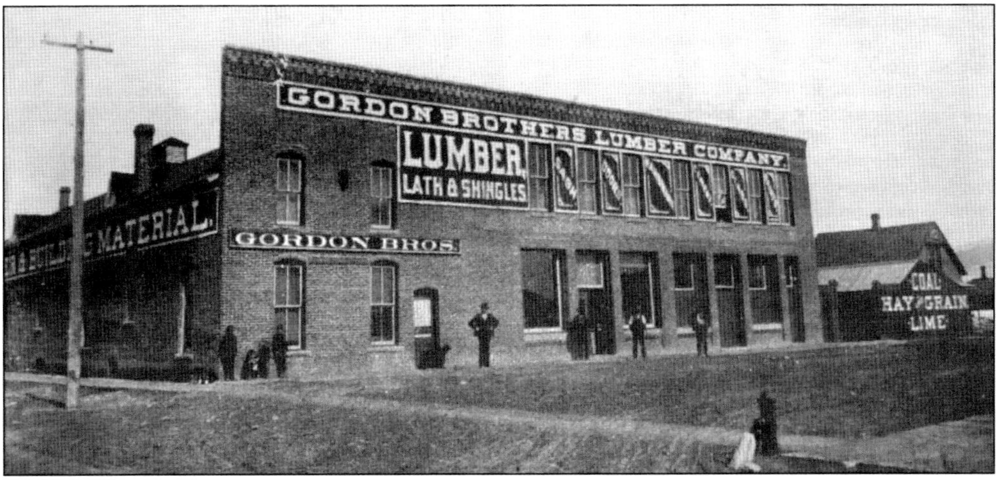

George and William Gordon started their lumber business in 1883 and erected this substantial operation on Park Street after an 1889 fire destroyed their original premises on B Street. Spreading over the entire block between D and E Streets, their yard was directly accessed by a railroad spur to facilitate shipping operations. Businessman Arthur Miles purchased the concern in 1900, and it became A. W. Miles Lumber Yard. (*Livingston Souvenir.*)

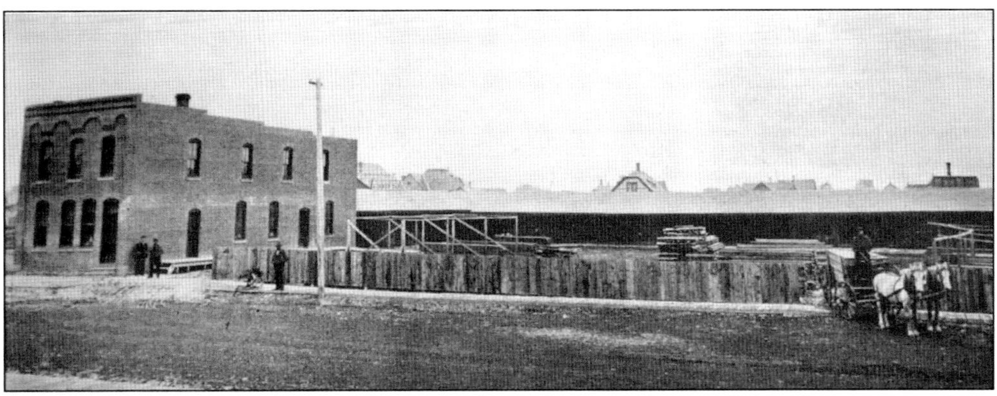

Prior to relocating to Billings, Montana, in the early 1880s, Emanuel Goughnour spent three years in Placerville during the 1849 California Gold Rush. Finding better prospects in Livingston, Goughnour opened a lumberyard on the corner of Lewis and 2nd Streets. Goughnour sold the business, which the new owners incorporated as Livingston Lumber Company in 1903. (*Livingston Souvenir.*)

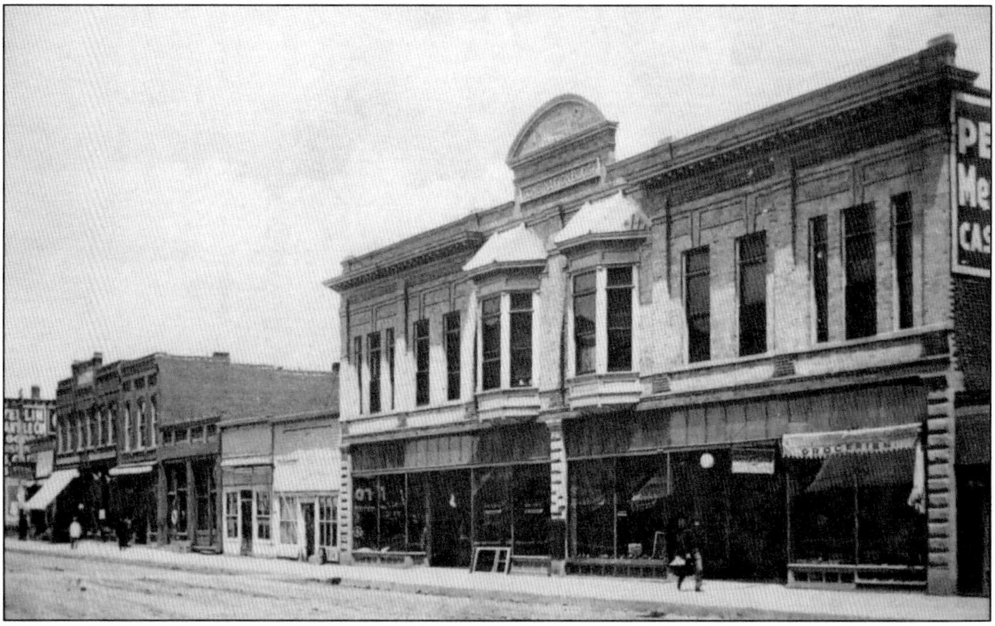

Still standing proudly on South Main Street between Callender and Lewis Streets, the Combination Block was erected in 1904 and hosted Scheuber Drug among the first tenants. Moving from his original 1893 store, Scheuber remained at this location until the mid-1930s. Other tenants included Peoples Mercantile, formerly Yellowstone Grocery, a butcher shop, and Davenport's Furniture. The Livingston Club and boarders occupied the second floor. (Private collection.)

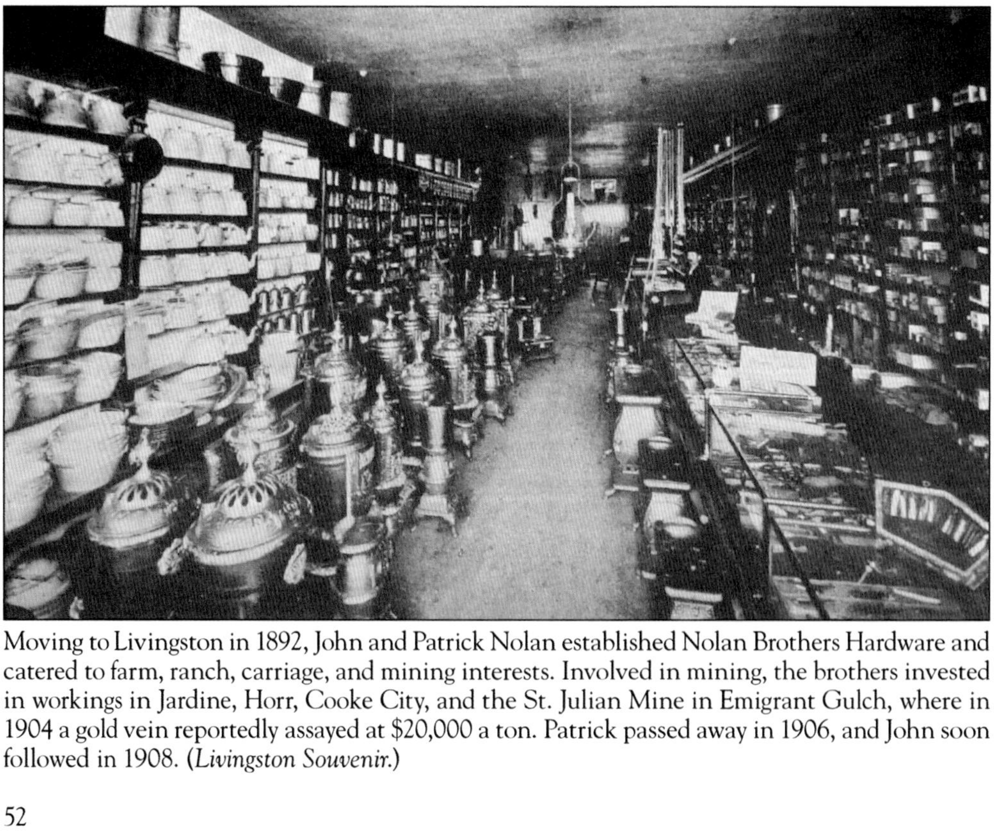

Moving to Livingston in 1892, John and Patrick Nolan established Nolan Brothers Hardware and catered to farm, ranch, carriage, and mining interests. Involved in mining, the brothers invested in workings in Jardine, Horr, Cooke City, and the St. Julian Mine in Emigrant Gulch, where in 1904 a gold vein reportedly assayed at $20,000 a ton. Patrick passed away in 1906, and John soon followed in 1908. (*Livingston Souvenir.*)

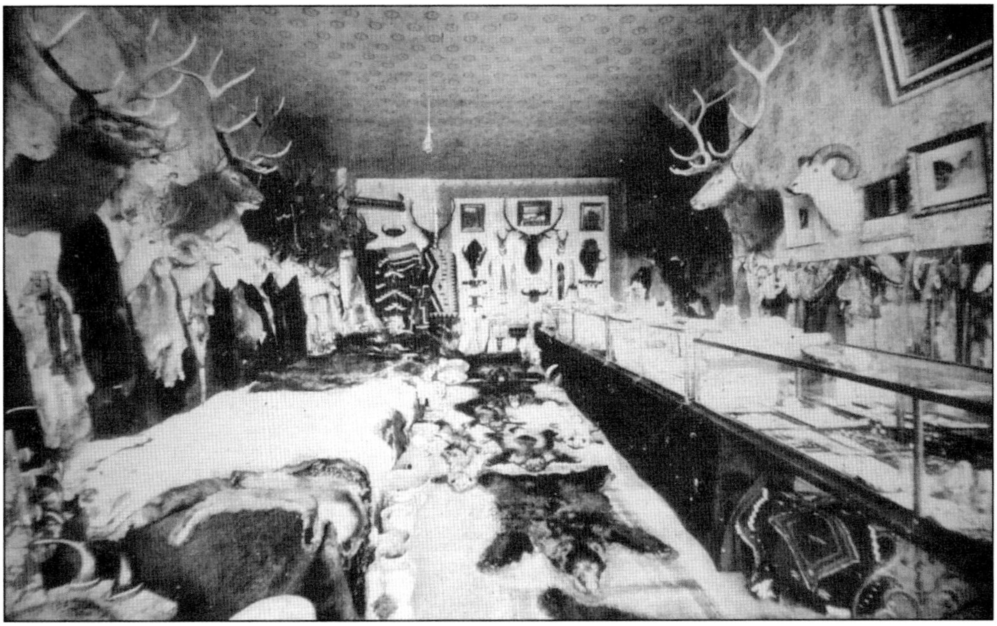

Establishing this taxidermy business on 2nd Street prior to 1900, famed hunter Frank B. Tolhurst traded furs and sold elk horn furniture, robes, and specimens. He advertised a "Choice selection of Rocky Mountain game heads, including Bison, Moose, Elk, Caribou, Mountain Sheep, Mountain Goat, Deer, Antelope, and Musk Ox." Tolhurst's business suffered a fire in 1913 that devastated much of his work, and by 1920, he relocated to Gardiner, Montana. (*Livingston Souvenir.*)

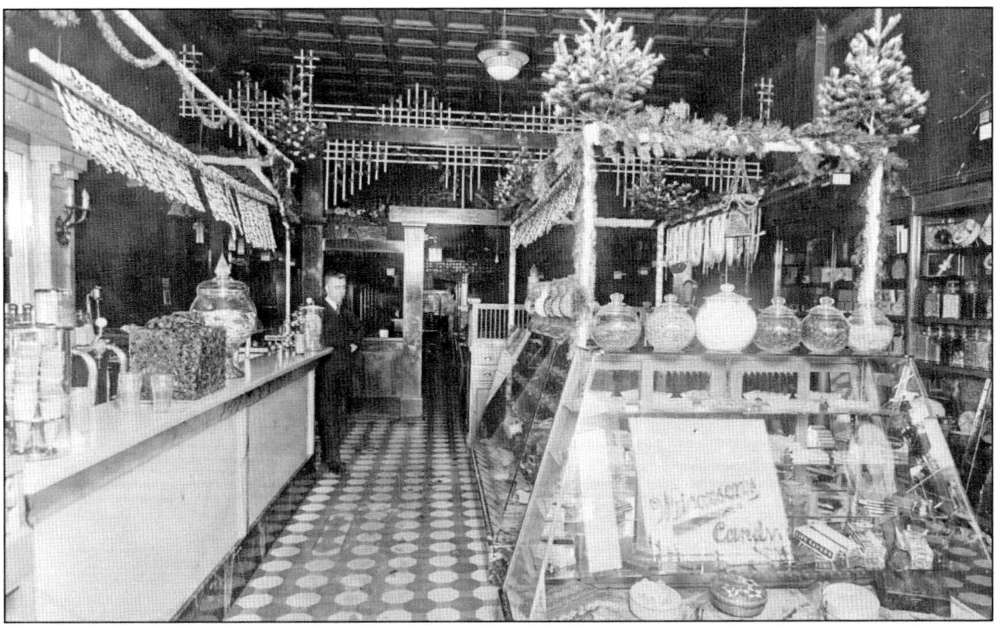

Carl Wilcoxson and Harry Swingley founded Wilcoxson's Kandy Kitchen in 1912 on Main Street. Early advertisements claimed, "Klean Kandy, Karefully Koncocted Konfections, Kream Karamels." The company began manufacturing its now famous ice cream in 1917, and over the years, this emporium served as candy store, manufacturing plant, ice cream parlor, soda fountain, and restaurant. (Yellowstone Gateway Museum.)

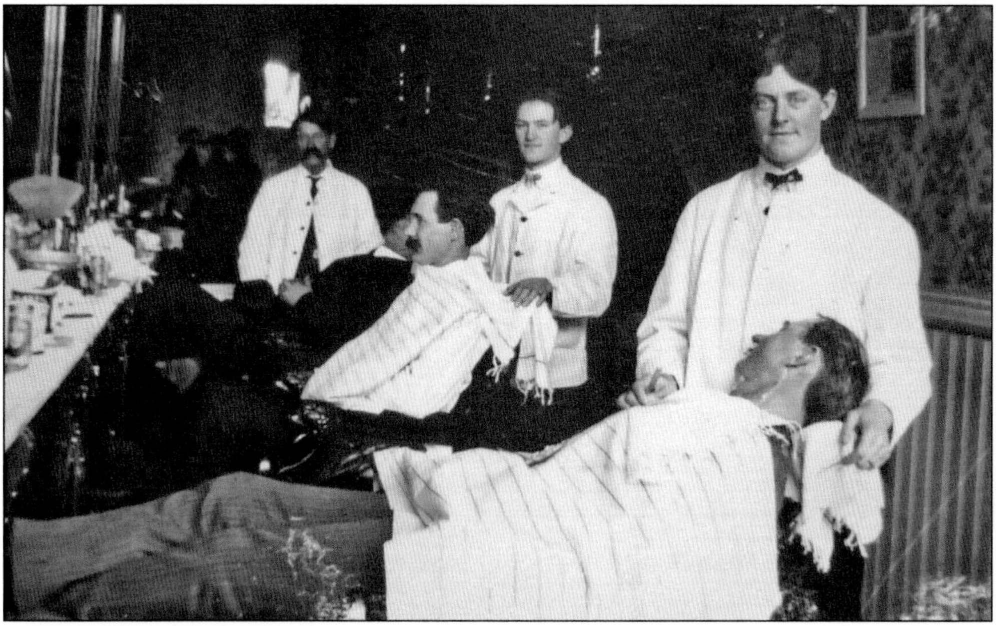

After pursuing his trade for seven years in South Dakota, Alexander VanBrocklin introduced Livingston to his tonsorial parlor on Thanksgiving Day in 1889. From the basement of the National Park Bank, he soon moved to new quarters on Main Street, where son George later joined the endeavor. The parlor reportedly provided all that was "necessary to cleanse the body and promote the moral and physical health." (Private collection.)

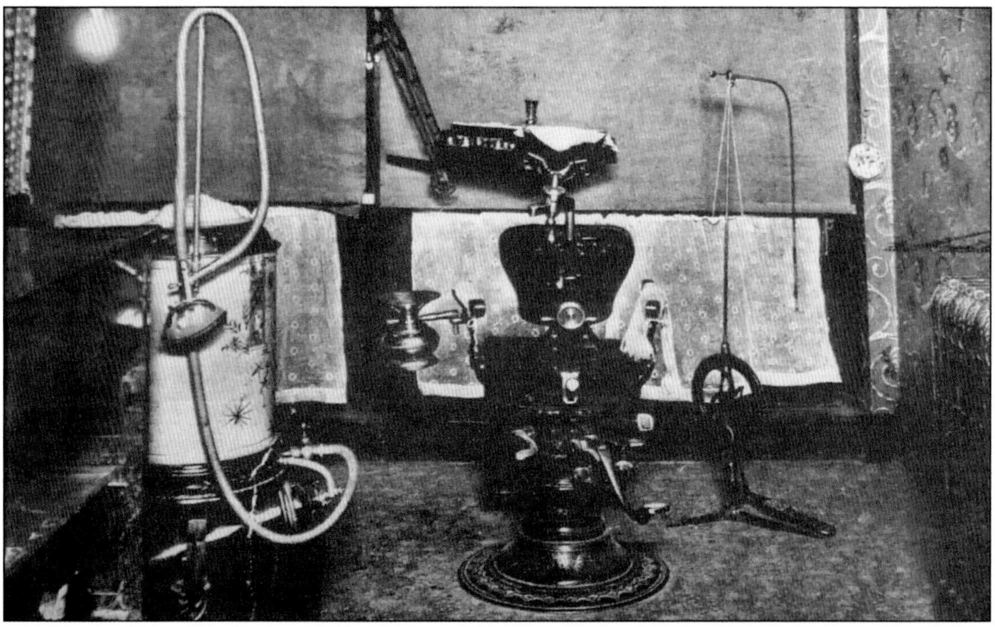

Graduating from the Chicago College of Dental Surgery in March 1891, Steven C. Pierce relocated forthwith to Montana, following the footsteps of uncles who participated in Montana's early gold rush. He established his Livingston practice in "elegantly equipped parlors" on the second floor of the Miles Block. In 1902, *Progressive Men of Montana* named him "one of most successful and popular dentists in the state." (*Livingston Souvenir.*)

Four

Civil Matters

According to the New York *Sun* in September 1883, "the social and business development of the [railroad] town generally follows this order: Saloons, stores in which the necessities of life are sold, gambling establishments, daily newspapers, school houses, a bank, a church." Livingston seemed to follow this casual convention of the day, with a tally of 39 saloons before the 1884 erection of a schoolhouse.

The first school built in Livingston was the East Side School in 1884. By 1918, Livingston had added the North Side School, West Side School (later renamed Lincoln School), Central School, and Park County High School to its educational facilities. Livingston's construction of a courthouse, city hall, post office, and library by 1914 provided the essential structures for conducting the city's civil matters.

While some buildings in Livingston were being erected, others were burning down. A series of fires occurring in May, August, and November 1885 nearly destroyed the business area of the fledgling town. In 1894, a one-horse hose and ladder wagon was finally purchased and one paid firefighter was hired. Fires in 1896, 1897, 1903, 1904, and 1913 continued to devastate structures of the city but not the spirit of the stalwart citizens who continually rallied to rebuild their enterprising community.

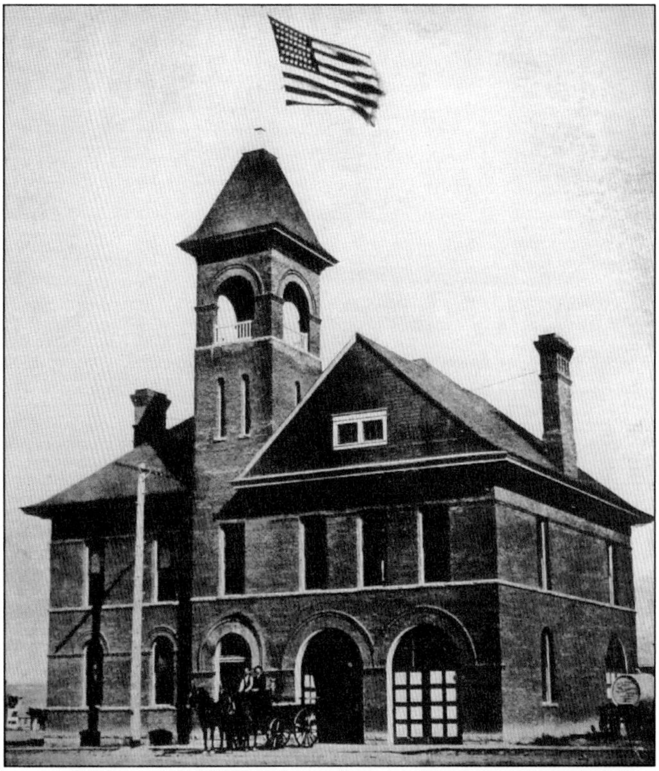

Late in 1888, local voters elected to incorporate the town and obtained city status by December 3. Eight years later, a $10,000 bond facilitated the erection of this impressive brick city hall in 1896 at Callender and B Streets. The signature bell tower was removed in 1953 because of earthquake concerns. When city–county government moved into new offices, the building was sold in 1975 to a private enterprise. (*Livingston Souvenir.*)

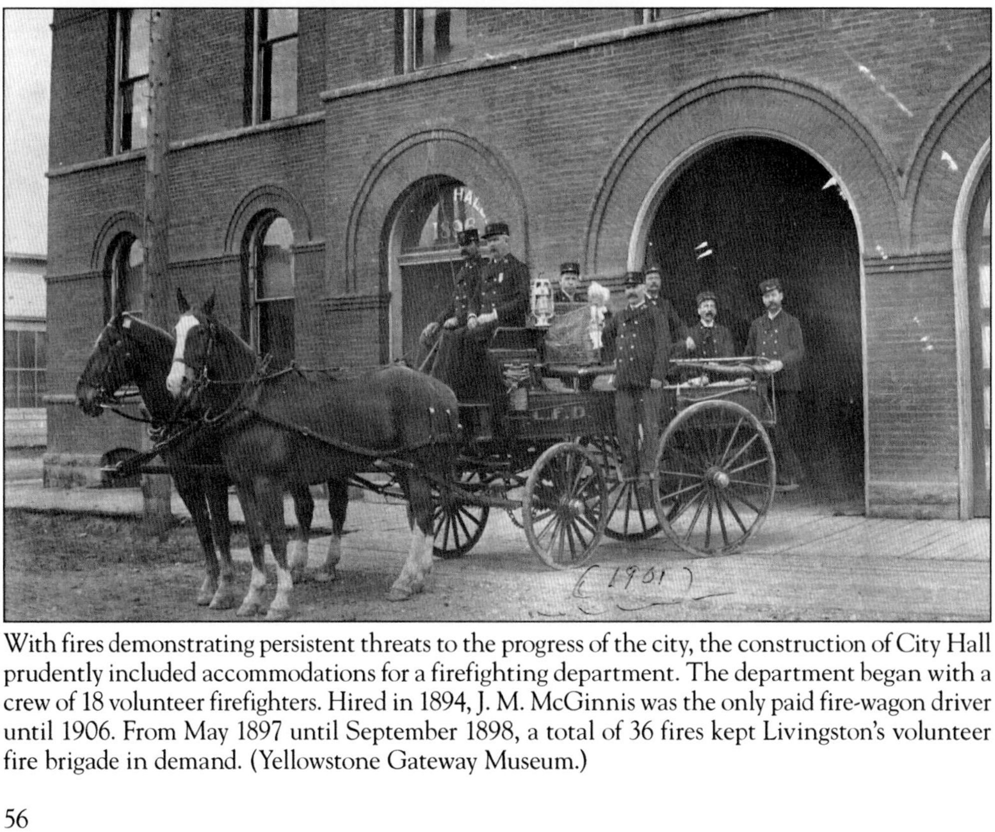

With fires demonstrating persistent threats to the progress of the city, the construction of City Hall prudently included accommodations for a firefighting department. The department began with a crew of 18 volunteer firefighters. Hired in 1894, J. M. McGinnis was the only paid fire-wagon driver until 1906. From May 1897 until September 1898, a total of 36 fires kept Livingston's volunteer fire brigade in demand. (Yellowstone Gateway Museum.)

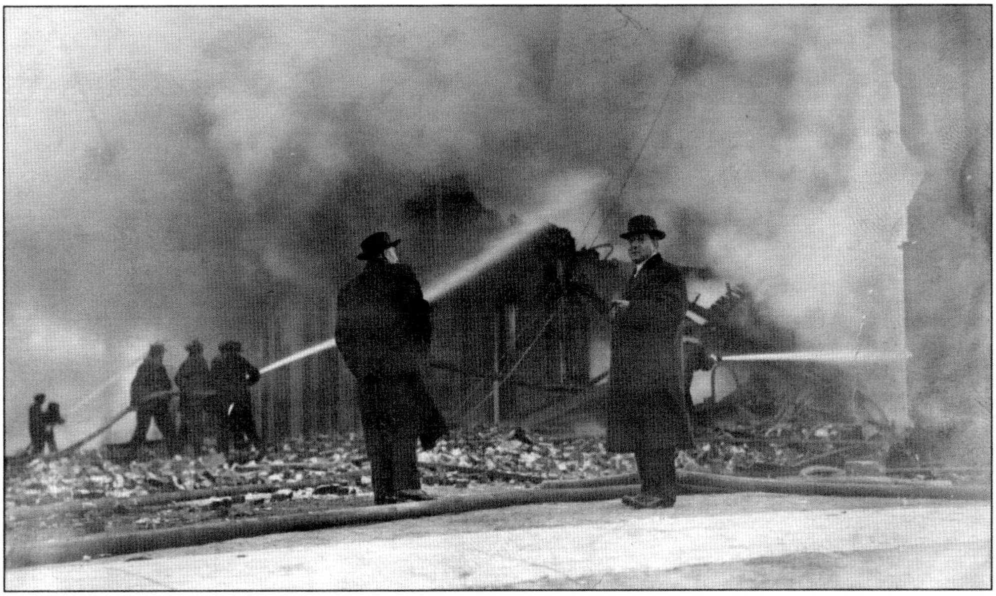

The scorching devastation of fire became a relentless occurrence in Livingston throughout its history. This blaze captured on December 16, 1913, began in the A. W. Miles Hardware store, ravaging six buildings, including the First State Bank. While the bank's vault with its contents survived this major inferno, the financial sacrifice of buildings and businesses was estimated to be upwards of $150,000 to $200,000. (Goss Collection.)

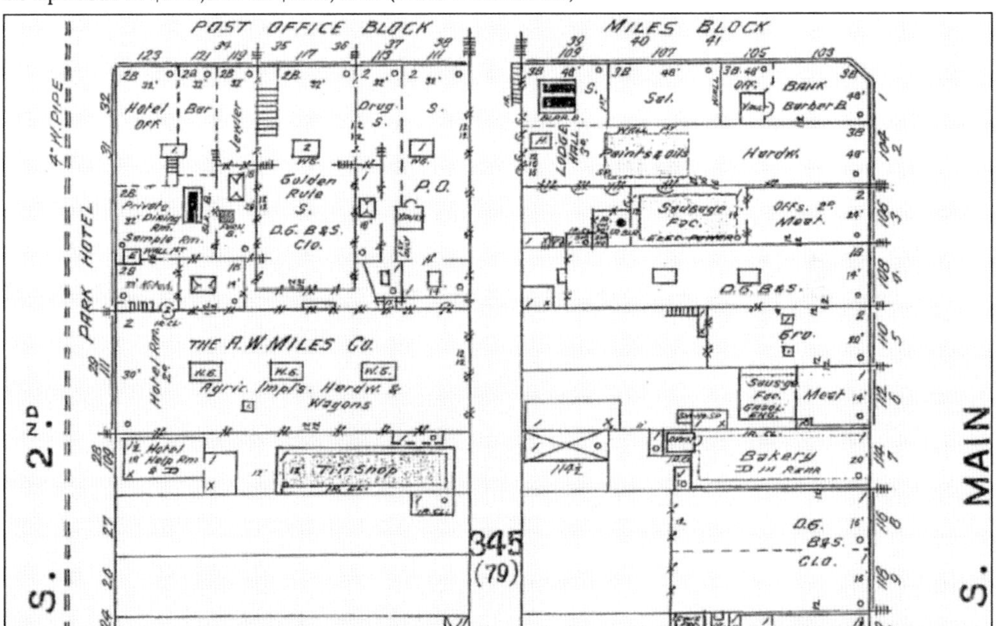

This 1907 map of the Miles block gives a visual perspective of the location of the 1913 fire that consumed the A. W. Miles Hardware store, the First State Bank, Dr. S. C. Pierce's dental office, O. M. Harvey's law office, Smith's Saloon, and the Modern Rooming House operated by Hattie Murphy. The 4:00 a.m. fire sent 40 roomers into the streets in nothing but underwear and coats. (University of Montana.)

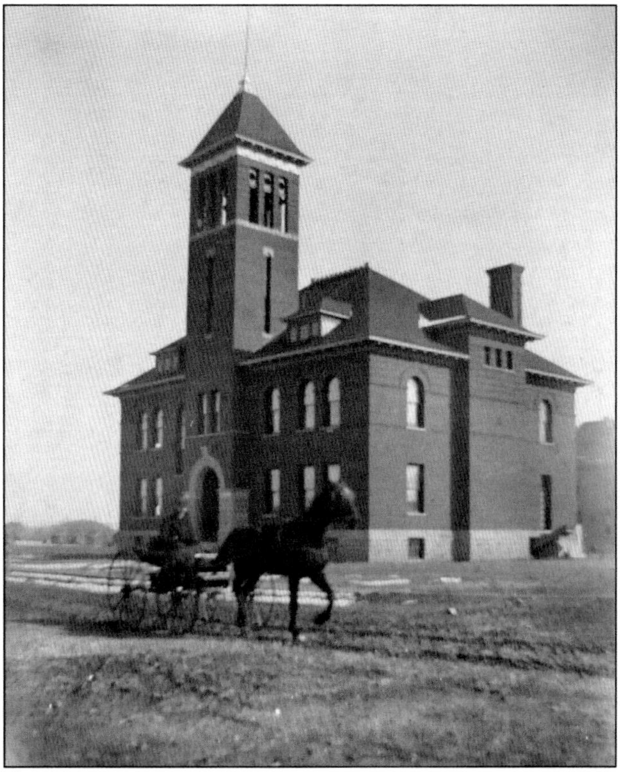

This impressive brick courthouse, shown shortly after construction, opened August 1, 1896, amid much fanfare. Initially part of Gallatin County, one of nine original Montana territorial counties, Park County had been created nine years earlier in February 1887, with Livingston as county seat. Despite some opposition, this venerable landmark was razed in 1974 to make way for the new city–county government complex. (Private collection.)

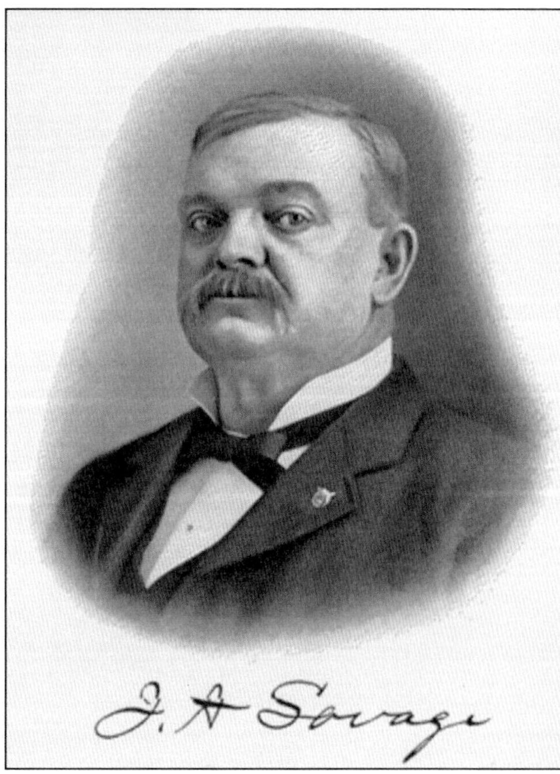

New York native Judge John A. Savage contracted gold fever in 1867 and traveled to Fort Benton, Montana, arriving after a 54-day steamboat voyage on the Missouri River. He mined in Last Chance Gulch and spent time in Nevada and Utah before removing to Livingston in 1882 to practice law. Eminently popular with a kindly disposition, Savage adjourned from life in March 1904 at age 64. (*Livingston Souvenir.*)

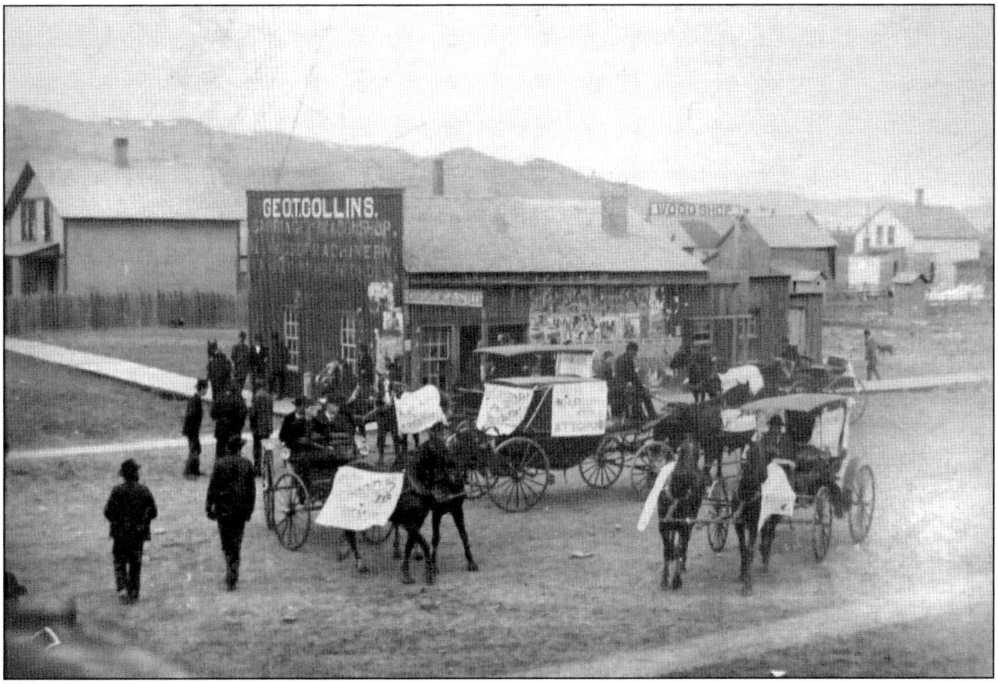

This image captures the unique style of campaigning during horse-and-buggy days near George T. Collins's blacksmith shop at Clark and South Main Streets. The only legible name on a banner is most likely William H. Poorman, who practiced law in Livingston from 1889 to 1901. This is probably a city election in 1891–1895, as the county did not have "Police" positions as one of the banners advocates. (Private collection.)

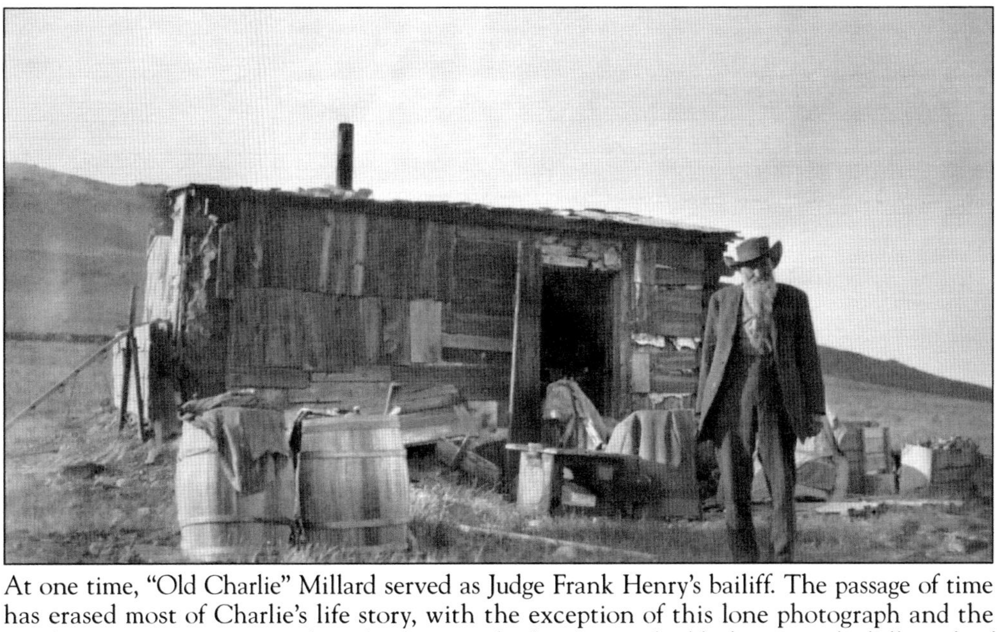

At one time, "Old Charlie" Millard served as Judge Frank Henry's bailiff. The passage of time has erased most of Charlie's life story, with the exception of this lone photograph and the handwritten caption stating that Charlie was "the first man to build a home on the hill north of Livingston." His name last appeared in the R. L. Polk Livingston City Directory in 1908–1909. (Private collection.)

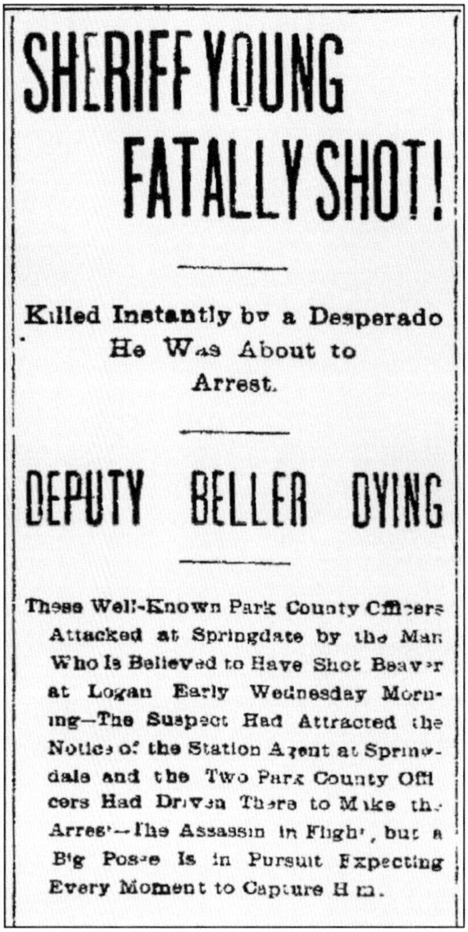

SHERIFF YOUNG FATALLY SHOT!

Killed Instantly by a Desperado He Was About to Arrest.

DEPUTY BELLER DYING

These Well-Known Park County Officers Attacked at Springdale by the Man Who Is Believed to Have Shot Beaver at Logan Early Wednesday Morning—The Suspect Had Attracted the Notice of the Station Agent at Springdale and the Two Park County Officers Had Driven There to Make the Arrest—The Assassin in Flight, but a Big Posse Is in Pursuit Expecting Every Moment to Capture Him.

Waking up Saturday, November 10, 1900, Montana residents were shocked to read this *Anaconda Standard* headline. Rated as Park County's "most efficient and popular sheriff," George Young was gunned down in cold blood at the Springdale railroad depot while attempting to apprehend a man suspected of murdering a rancher in a nearby town. The 44-year-old father of four served twice as Livingston city marshal and three terms as sheriff. (*Anaconda Standard*.)

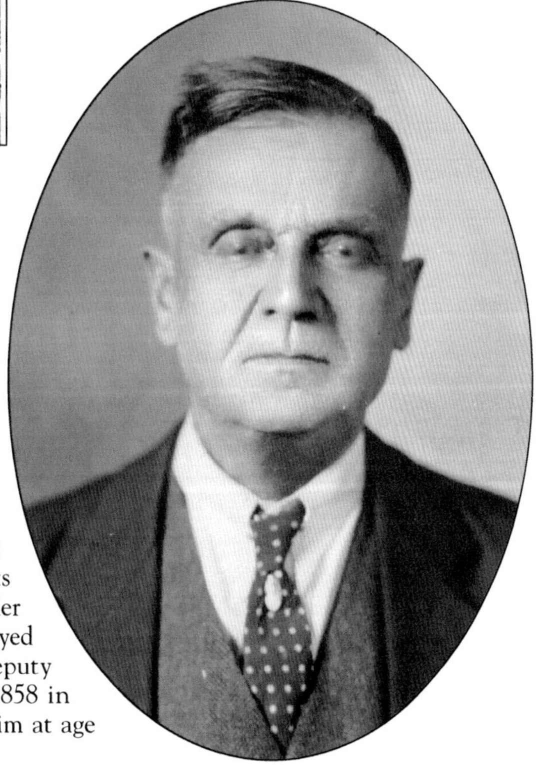

Also shot that fateful day in Springdale was Under-sheriff Frank Beller. The newspapers initially reported him "fatally wounded," but as Mark Twain once commented, "Reports of my death were greatly exaggerated." Beller survived the life-threatening wound and enjoyed a long life in Park County, serving as deputy game warden well into his 70s. Born in 1858 in Pennsylvania, this photograph captures him at age 79. (Private collection.)

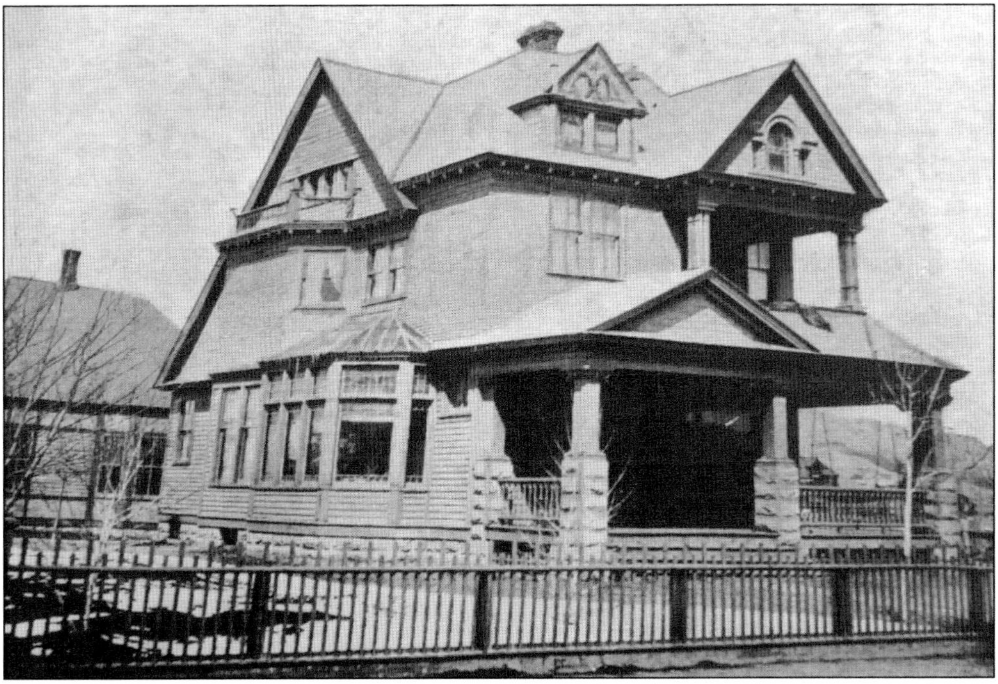

Edith Lott, who began her lifelong nursing vocation with Park Hospital proprietor Dr. George Windsor, founded Livingston's second major hospital in this former residence of Judge Frank Henry in 1928. While she sold the hospital in 1947, it remained in operation until 1955. Lott continued to care for the ill until she retired in 1958. Remembered as a most benevolent soul, Lott died at age 93. (*Livingston Souvenir.*)

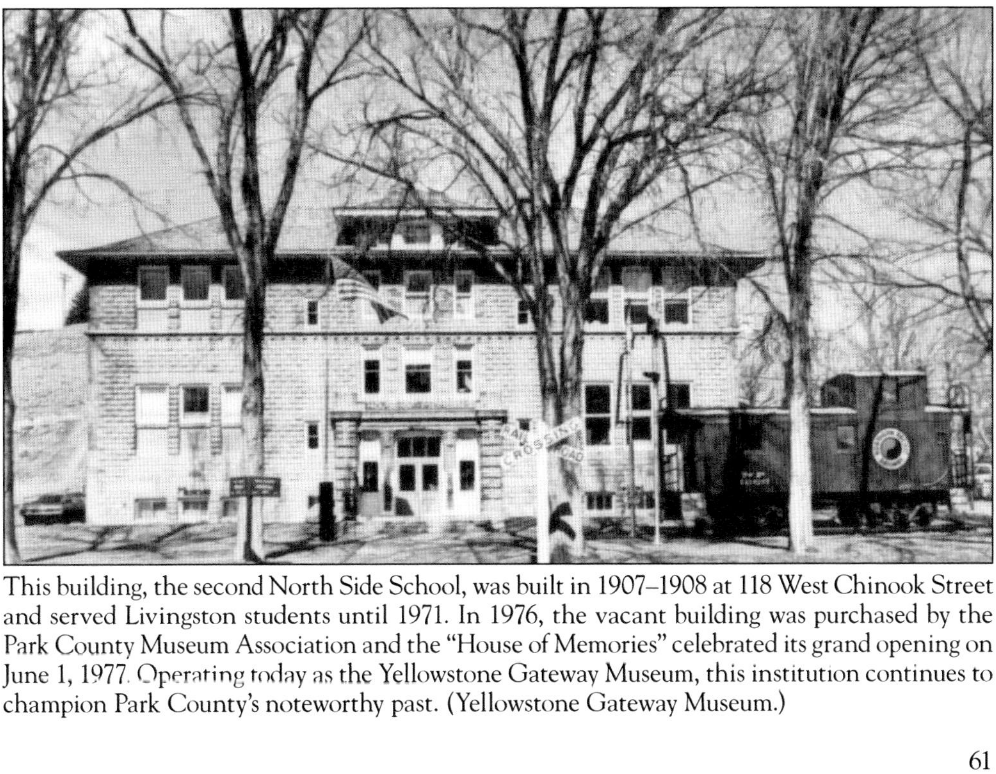

This building, the second North Side School, was built in 1907–1908 at 118 West Chinook Street and served Livingston students until 1971. In 1976, the vacant building was purchased by the Park County Museum Association and the "House of Memories" celebrated its grand opening on June 1, 1977. Operating today as the Yellowstone Gateway Museum, this institution continues to champion Park County's noteworthy past. (Yellowstone Gateway Museum.)

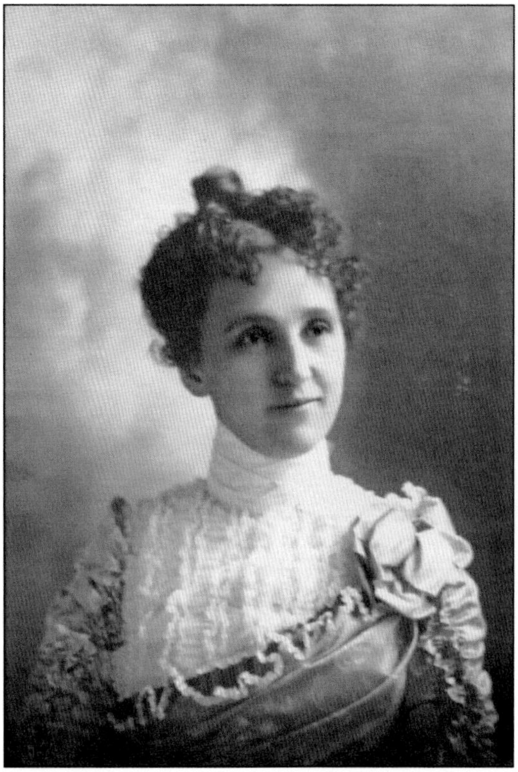

Brunette "Nettie" Ballinger served as the first county school superintendent from May 1887 to January 1888. It was an appointed position until elections could be held in the newly formed county. Subsequently she worked as stenographer in the court of brother-in-law District Judge Frank Henry. After 1900, Nettie spent time working in Santa Barbara, California, as a stenographer. Never married, she died in 1938 in Bozeman at age 86. (Private collection.)

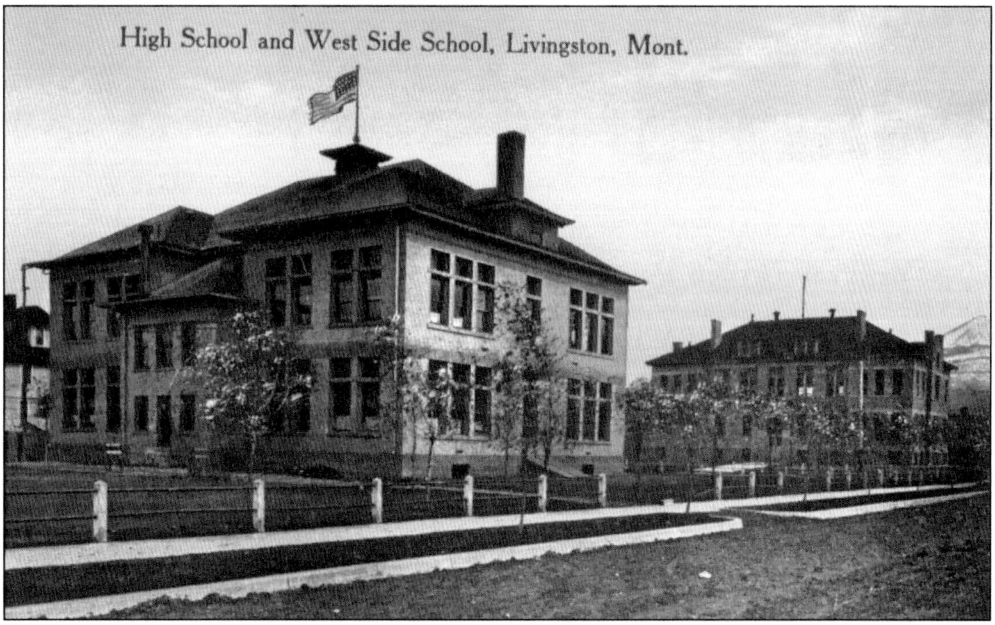

Due to overcrowding at the 1885 East Side School, the North Side School on C and Gallatin Streets and the West Side School on Callender and 5th Streets (foreground) were both constructed in 1892. West Side suffered fire damage in 1907 to the roof and upper floor. Reconstructed, the education process continued until 1967. Shown on the right side is the high school, built in 1905. (Goss Collection.)

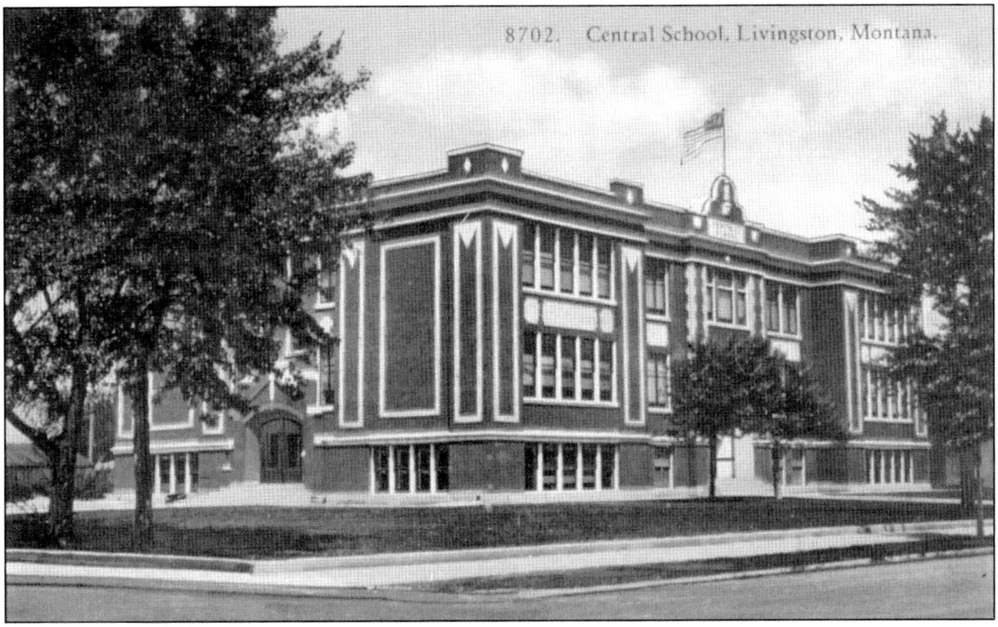

Increased enrollment probably prompted the building of the Central School in 1914 at Lewis and B Streets. During the Spanish influenza epidemic of 1918, Central was used as a temporary hospital. It was renamed Lincoln School in 1926, closed in 1974, and reopened at a later date. (Goss Collection.)

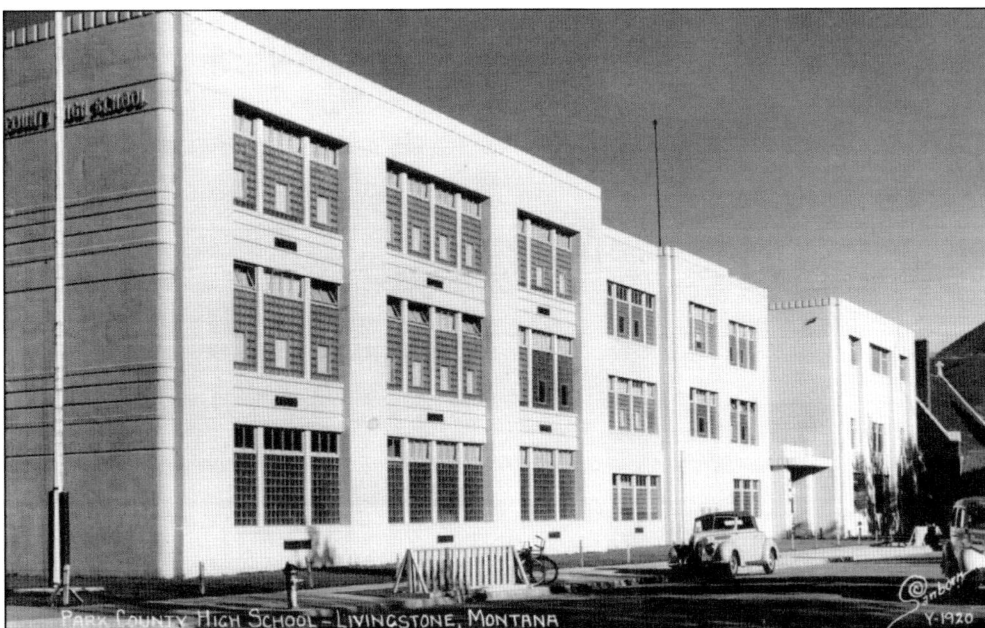

The first high school classes were conducted in 1894 on the top floor of West Side School. In 1905, Park County High School, bordering 5th Street, was constructed. This original building was replaced in 1939, but an addition from 1918 was retained. Thirty years later, a new school was built on McLeod's Island at a cost of over $1.5 million. The old school was converted to Middle School. (Goss Collection.)

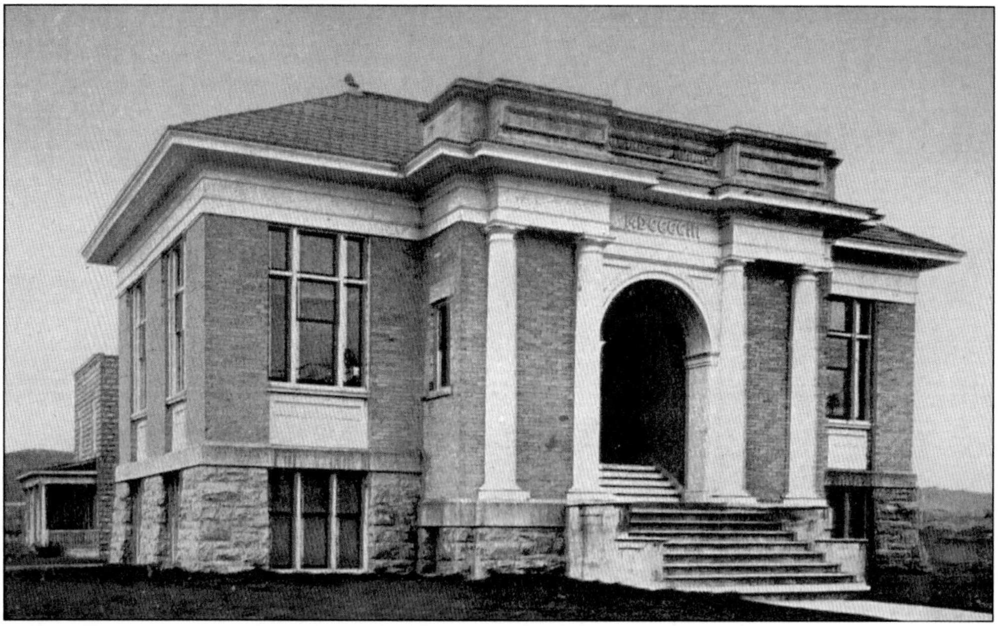

Philanthropist Andrew Carnegie offered Livingston a $10,000 gift for the creation of a library provided that the town secured a suitable location. In May 1903, five lots on the corner of Callender and 3rd Streets were purchased and Carnegie was notified that Livingston had fulfilled the requirements. By July 4, 1903, the promised library funds arrived and thus provided the foundations for Livingston's stone monument of self-education. (Goss Collection.)

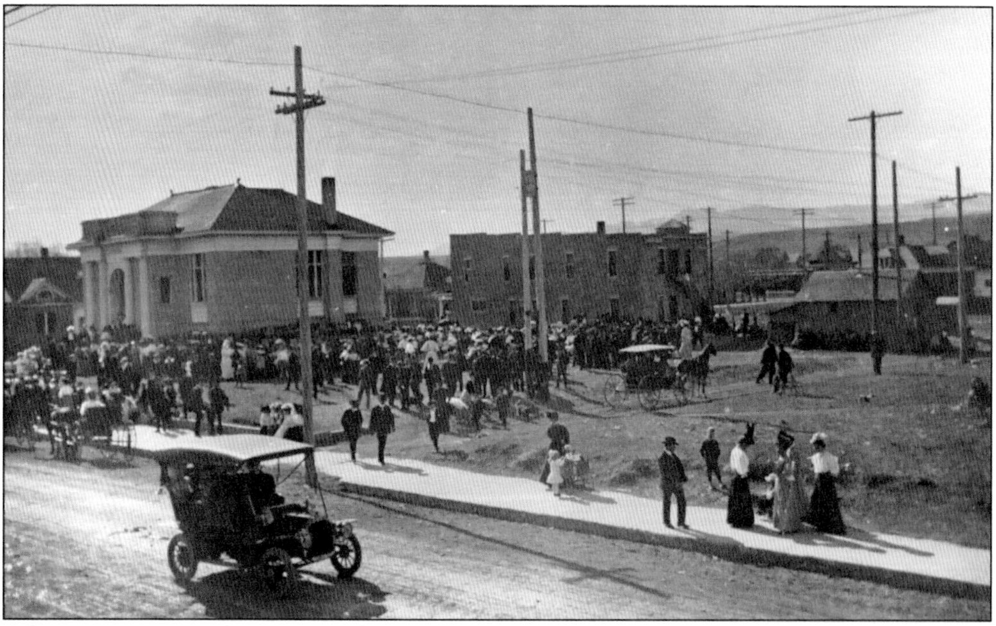

After petitioning residents to vote for a tax to create a public library, the ladies of the Yellowstone Club victoriously announced its passage in June 1902. Approval of plans presented by C. E. Bell of Helena for a Colonial Revival–style building in August 1903 initiated the commencement of construction by October. This jubilant dedication of the Livingston Free Library was held in the spring of 1905. (Yellowstone Gateway Museum.)

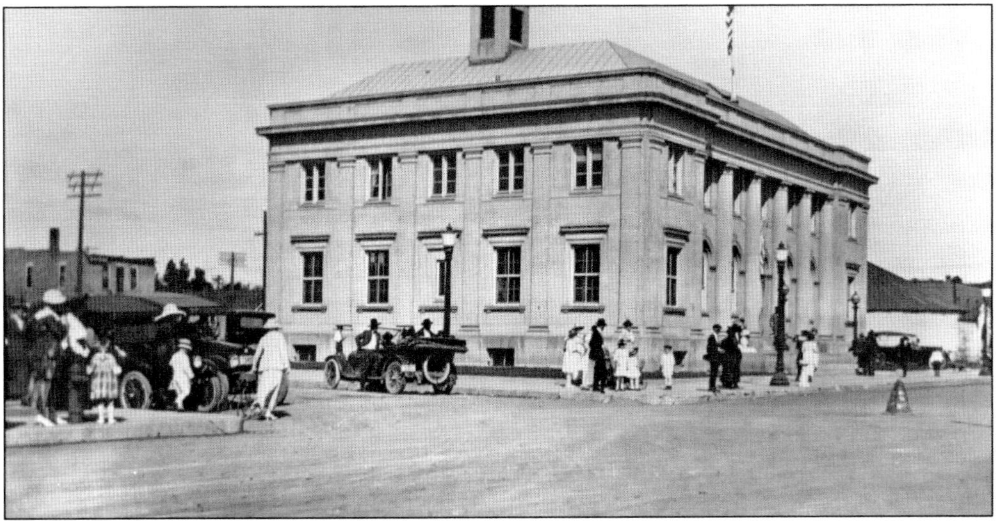

Architect Oscar Wenderoth designed this stately Classical Revival–style post office on the corner of 2nd and Callender Streets, with projected costs of $100,000. Construction commenced in spring 1913 with well-attended cornerstone ceremonies on May 20. Opening April 1914, it replaced the facility built by A. W. Miles on Callender Street in 1900. Livingston's first post office opened November 13, 1882, on Main Street between Callender and Lewis Streets. (Yellowstone Gateway Museum.)

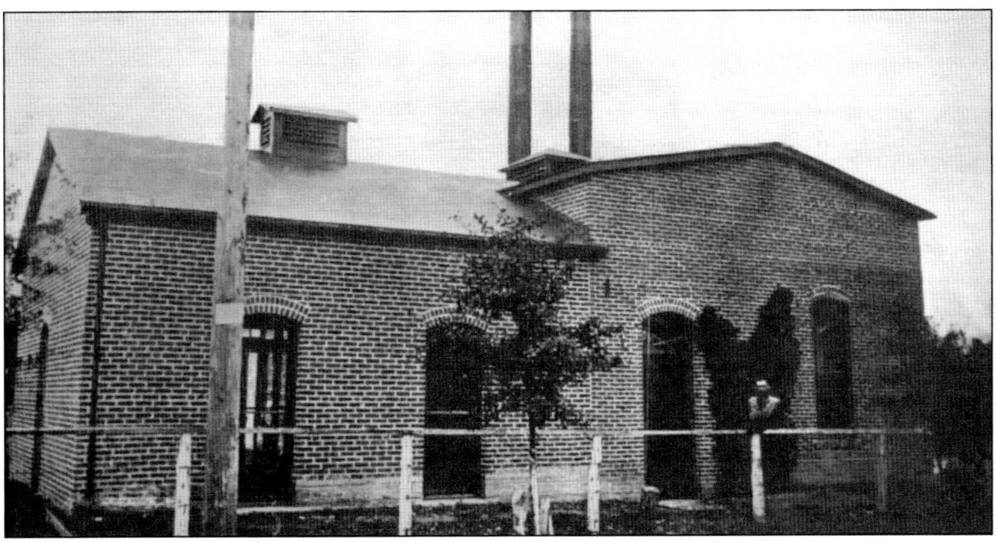

Businessmen Orschel, Stebbins, and Bundock obtained a 20-year franchise in 1889 to supply city water and built the Livingston Water Works in 1890 at the foot of 3rd Street, near the Yellowstone River. Supplied by a 14-by-60-foot well, three steam pumps were capable of producing over 2.5 million gallons per 24 hours. (*Livingston Souvenir.*)

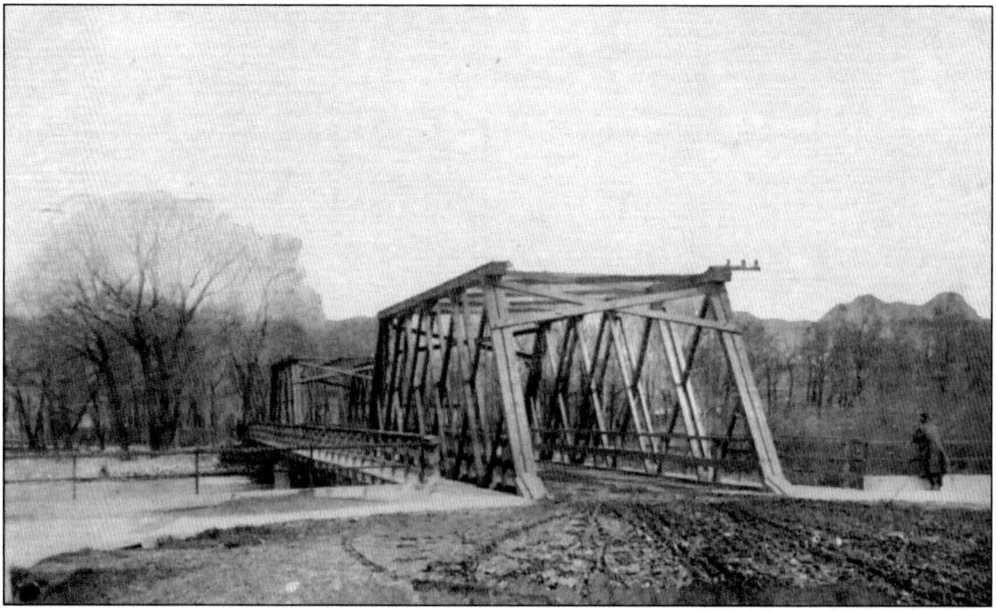

Crossing the West Branch of the Yellowstone River in the late 1800s, Main Street Bridge provided access to McLeod's Island and traffic from the east. After it was rechanneled in later years, only a relative trickle of the West Branch flows today. In 1915, Frederick Todd, a former Livingston photographer, located the Yellow Nugget placer gold claim on a minor island adjacent to the bridge. After test drilling, Todd reported the island gravel was "lousy with gold." (Goss Collection.)

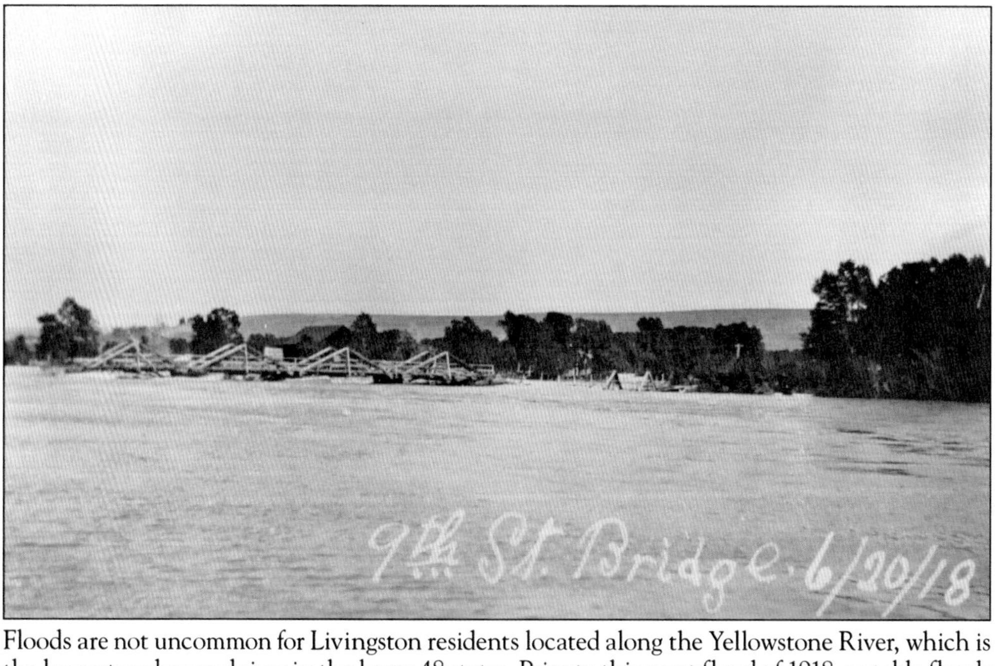

Floods are not uncommon for Livingston residents located along the Yellowstone River, which is the longest undammed river in the lower 48 states. Prior to this great flood of 1918, notable floods occurred in 1894 and 1905. The river peaked on June 16, flooding vast areas of the Livingston valley. This 9th Street Bridge washed out, along with Harvat and Carter's bridges, and isolated huge portions of the county. (Yellowstone Gateway Museum.)

In 1918, W. M. Finck & Company of Detroit established an overall factory in Livingston, one of five nationwide facilities. Fifty employees and 75 electric machines produced durable overalls for railroad workers and other regional markets. This 1918 advertisement from *The Railroad Trainmen Magazine* proclaimed that union-made overalls wore "like a pig's nose." In March 1920, a devastating fire with over $100,000 in losses silenced Finck's once industriously whirring machines. (Goss Collection.)

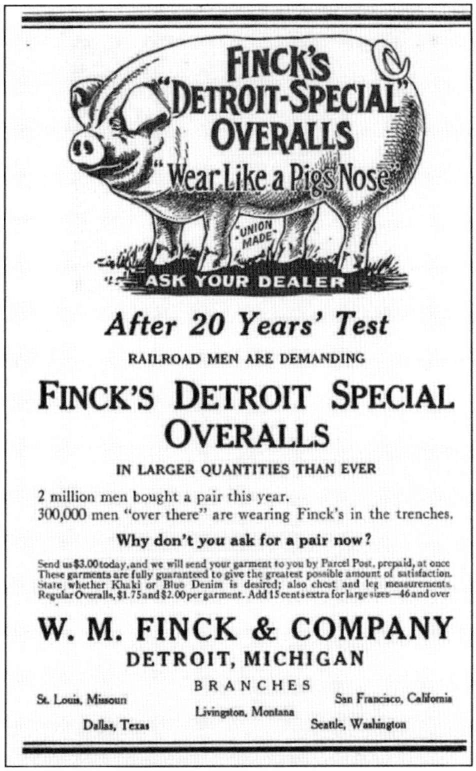

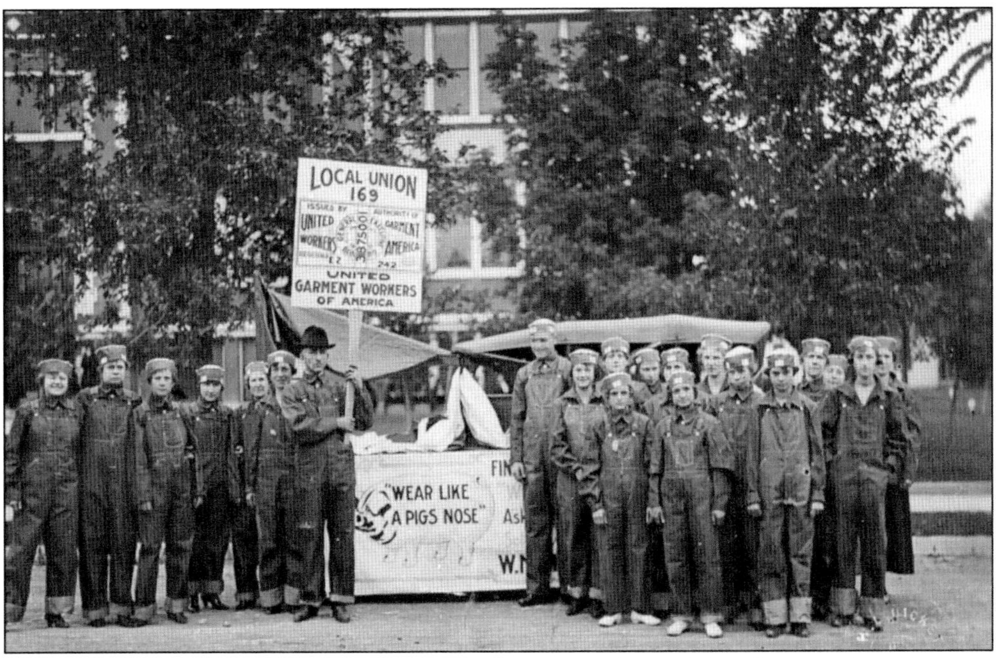

William Muir Finck believed in Montana and in a union workforce. The W. M. Finck & Company overall factories employed over 600 union workers nationwide. Finck's label proudly displayed "Union Made" on its tickets, and according to a 1908 compendium of Detroit history, the business stood second to none in the union. (Yellowstone Gateway Museum.)

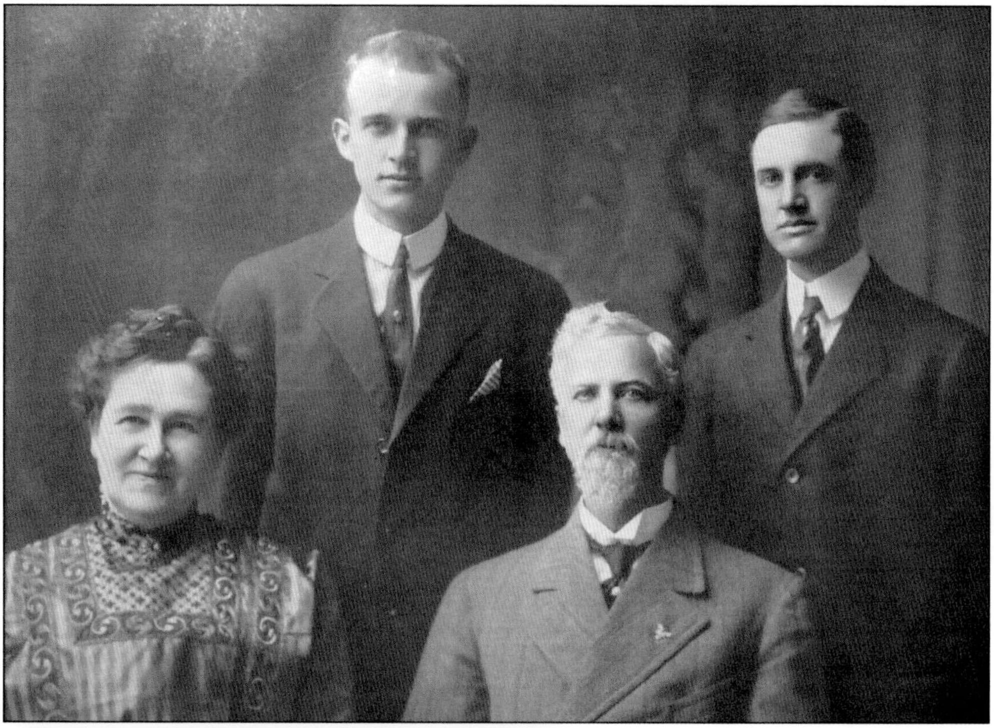

Pictured are John T. Smith, his wife, Ida, and sons Kirk and Vard. Arriving in Livingston from Missouri in 1890, Smith began practicing law. He served as city attorney, city mayor, and school director, and he held numerous other political and community posts. Kirk, a graduate of Bozeman Agricultural College, superintended the Smith's 3,800-acre ranch. Elected county attorney in 1912, Vard also practiced law with his father. (Private collection.)

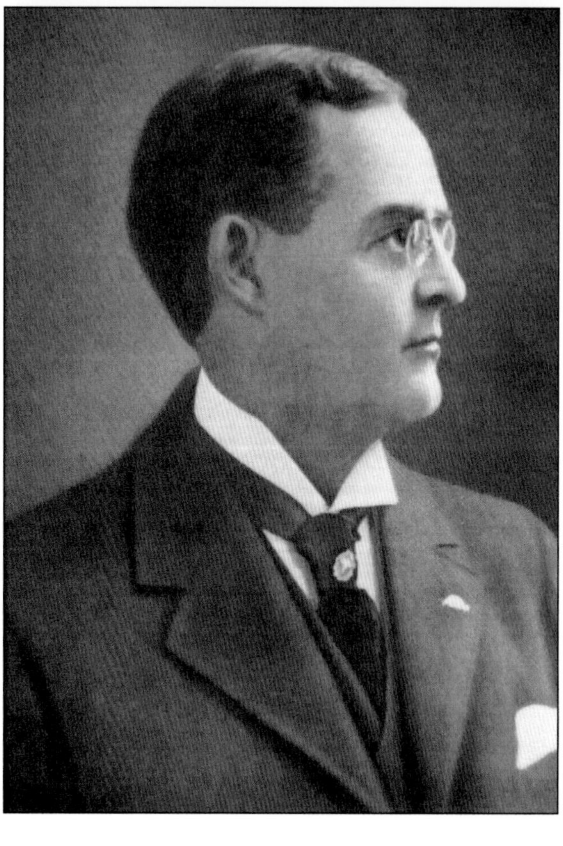

Arthur Wellington Miles, a prominent businessman and Republican, was elected Livingston's first mayor in 1889. Only 30 years of age at the time of his election, Miles became the youngest mayor in the United States. According to Heringshaw's *National Library of American Biography*, Miles served two terms as mayor, performed duties as Montana's state senator from 1905 to 1909, and became lieutenant governor of Montana in 1909. (Stout.)

Five

Bird's-Eyes and Boulevards

The townscape of Livingston in 1883, with its layout oriented to the tracks, mirrored many of the railroad towns sprouting up across the Great Plains. With the railroad as the center of its economic base, Livingston's commercial district developed south of and perpendicular to the tracks. This "T-town" design, typical of many railroad planned communities, reserved the north side of the tracks for future railroad shops and the roundhouse. Park Street, which paralleled the Northern Pacific right-of-way on the south side, advanced nearly overnight, with hotels, restaurants, and general merchandise stores that ran the length of the town site.

With each railroad facility expansion, the town extended its boundaries, which also prompted the residential area to spread out to the north side of the tracks. In 1908, construction of a Main Street underpass provided railroad workers and residents alike safe access between the north side of town and the main business district.

"Livingston has to her credit more miles of sidewalks, parking, and boulevards, when population is considered, than any city in the West. These sidewalks and boulevards extend to practically every part of the city and give to the town an attractive and permanent appearance," observed the *Anaconda Standard* in 1909. The 1916 paving of Livingston's streets finally gave the flourishing city a more polished appearance, not to mention a respite from muddy boulevards.

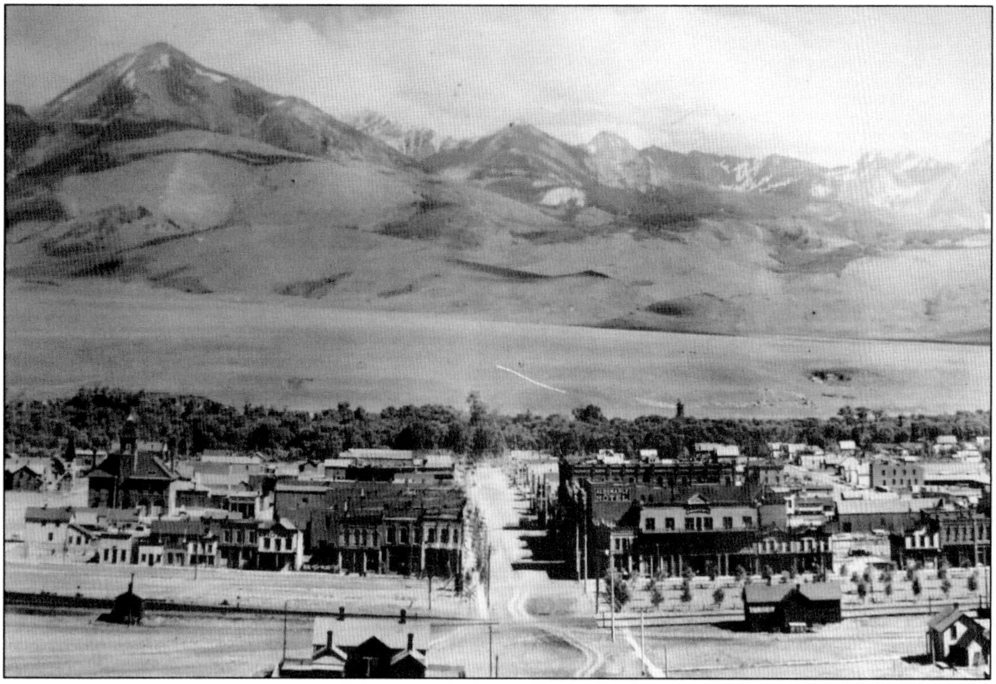

Wagon tracks wind across the railroad crossing in this *c.* 1900 view of Main Street. A park with a young growth of trees shows future promise and awaits construction of the new depot. The Albemarle Hotel stands across from the park, while the huge edifice behind the hotel is the Miles Block. Across from the Albemarle, the NPRR lunchroom awaits incoming passengers. City Hall dominates the view to the left. (Private collection.)

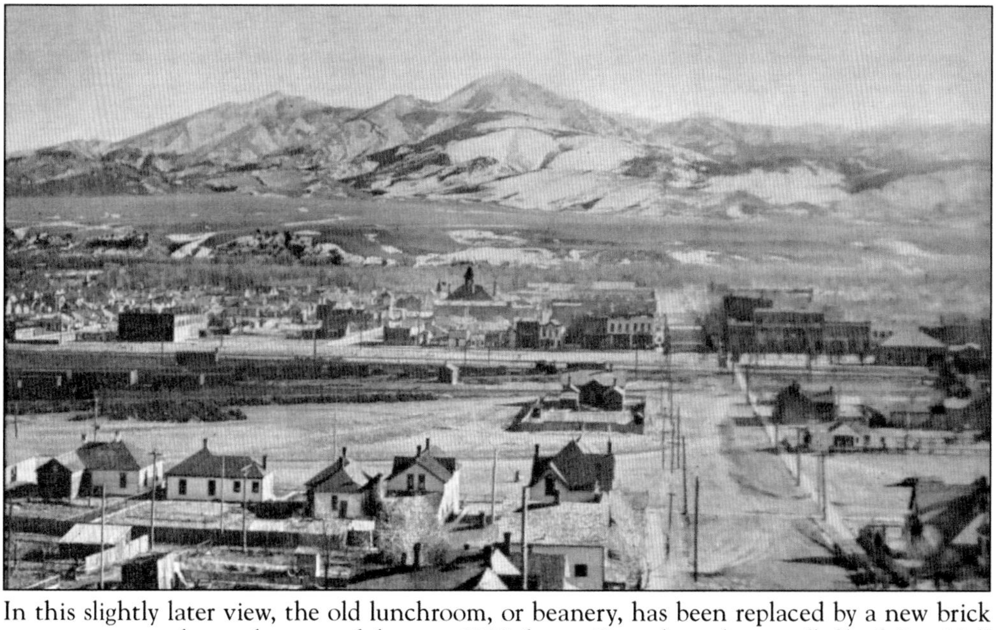

In this slightly later view, the old lunchroom, or beanery, has been replaced by a new brick structure across the tracks, part of the new 1902 depot. Growth to the east (left) of City Hall shows the residential area filled with simple bungalows that housed the increasing number of railroad workers. (Goss Collection.)

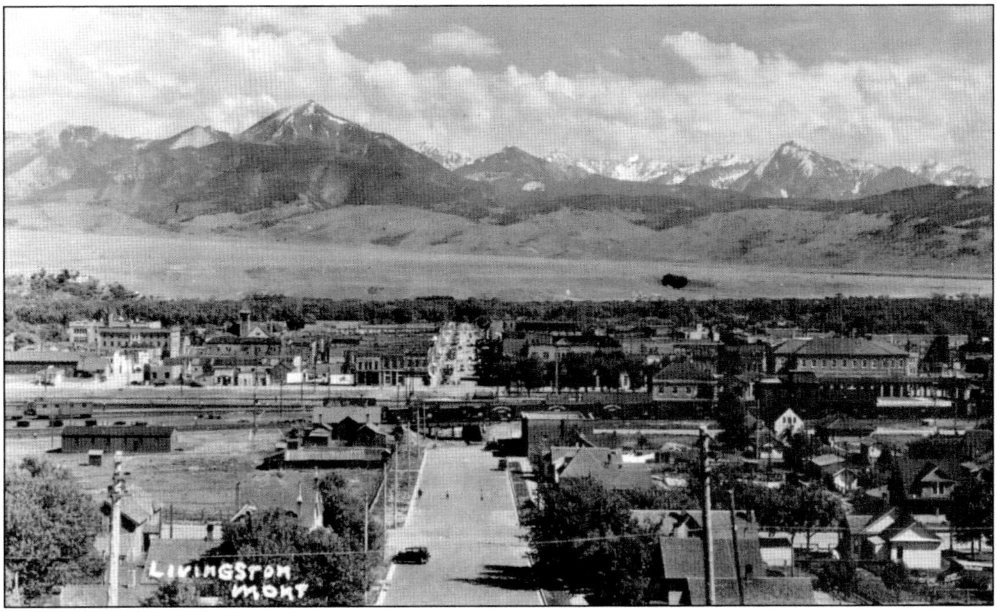

In this 1930s view, the railroad crossing of Main Street has become safer and more modern. An underpass, built in 1908, provided an easy access for workers and residents commuting between the north and south sides of town. In 1949, Main Street, just south of the underpass, was curved east to exit onto B Street. (Goss Collection.)

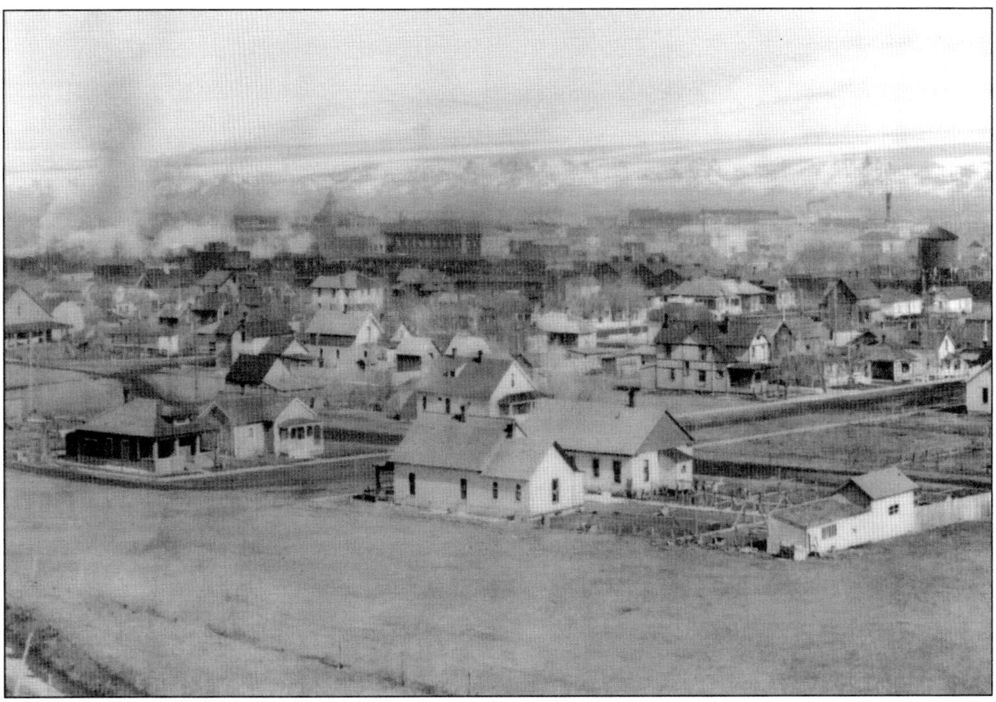
Looking eastward across Livingston from the hill north of town, smoke belched from the belly of the Northern Pacific railroad shops as workers went about the daily grind of building and rebuilding railroad cars and engines. Many of these homes in the foreground were relatively simple abodes, owned by those who earned an honest living by the sweat of their brow. (Goss Collection.)

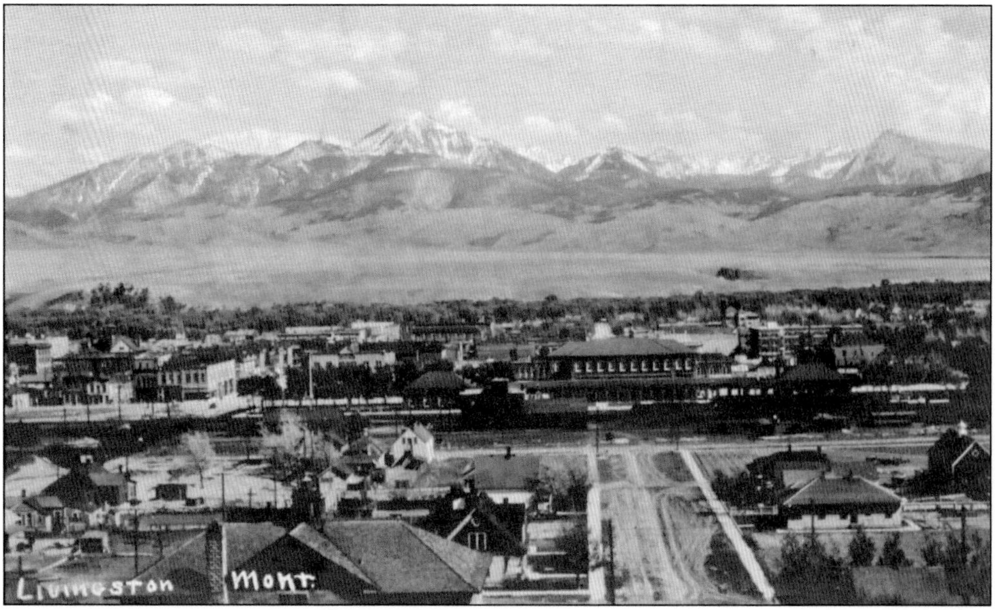

In this *c.* 1910 postcard view, published by Sax & Fryer, a broad, dirt-covered 2nd Street leads to the NPRR tracks and depot, but its primitiveness is belied by the presence of concrete sidewalks that portend progress. In the left foreground is the North Side School, currently occupied by the Yellowstone Gateway Museum. (Goss Collection.)

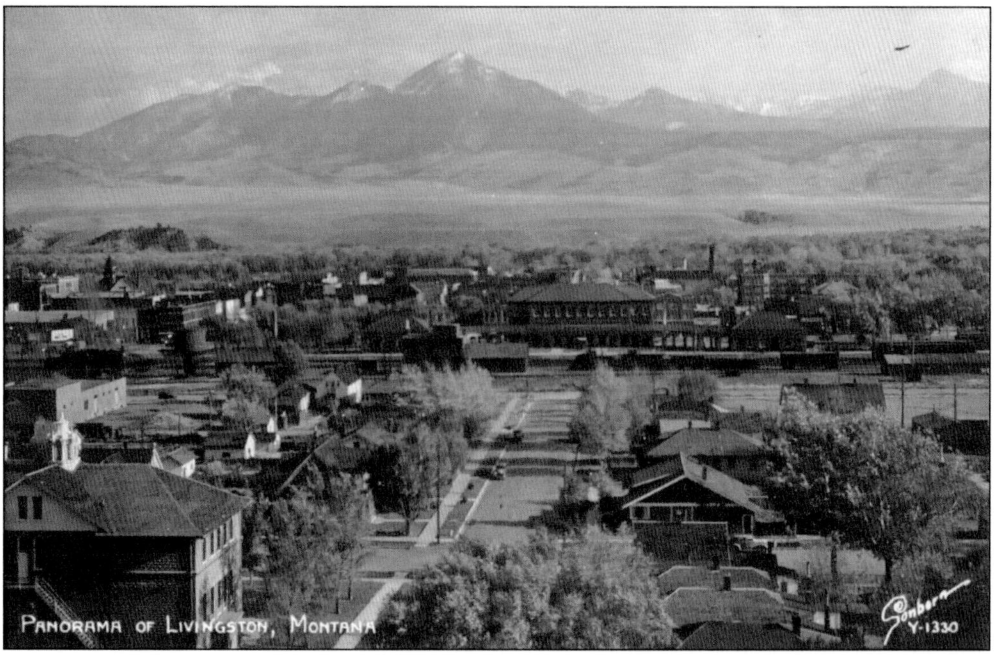

The 1902 NPRR depot dominated the still-extant 1889 depot across the tracks in this *c.* 1940 Sanborn real-photo postcard view. Gone are the alternatively dusty and muddy streets from days of yore. Paved avenues lined with mature trees and neatly manicured lawns portrayed an air of modernism and prosperity. (Goss Collection.)

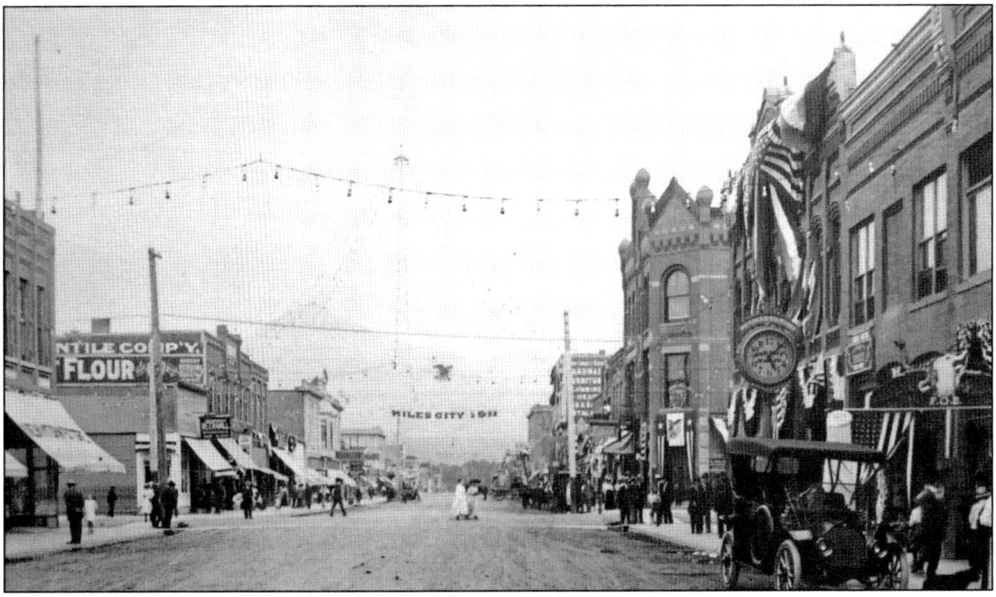

Celebrating the 1910 Montana Eagles Convention in Livingston, Main Street was festooned with decorations. The Thompson Brothers store, shown behind J. L. Murphy's clock, was heavy with flag bunting, while across Callender Street, the classic 1889 Miles Block displayed banners at the entrance. Opposite the Miles building, the German Beer Hall appeared to be among the few remaining wooden structures on Main Street. The Miles City banner advertised next year's convention. (Private collection.)

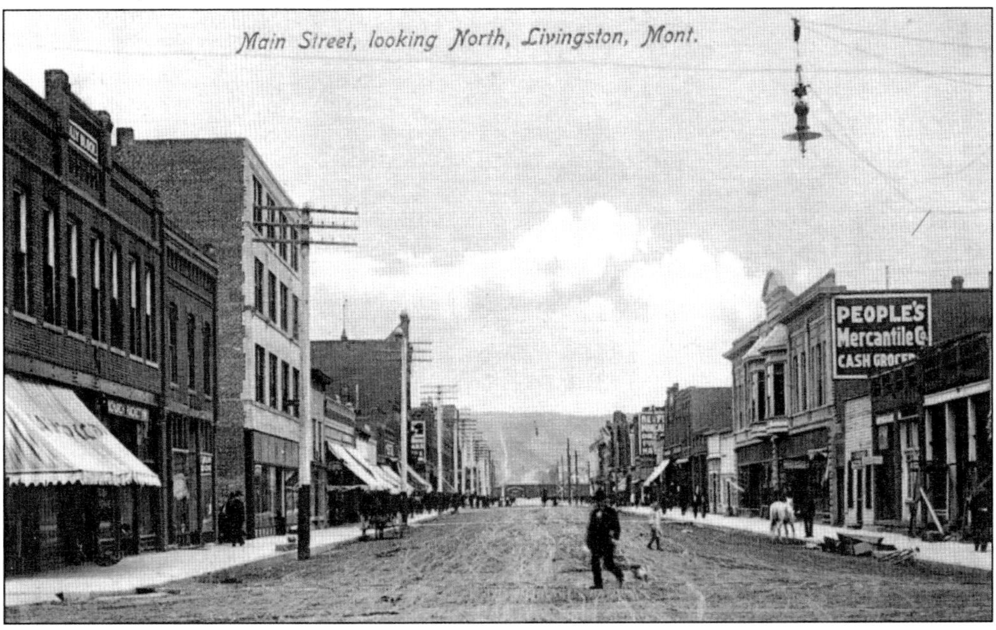

Looking north on Main Street from Lewis Street, one of the predominant features shown is the Combination Block. Home of People's Mercantile, the building also housed Frank Scheuber's drugstore. This *c.* 1908 postcard view was produced by Scheuber Drug (No. 516), who published numerous postcard views of Livingston, Park County, and more than 100 postcards of Yellowstone Park between the years 1905 and 1910. (Goss Collection.)

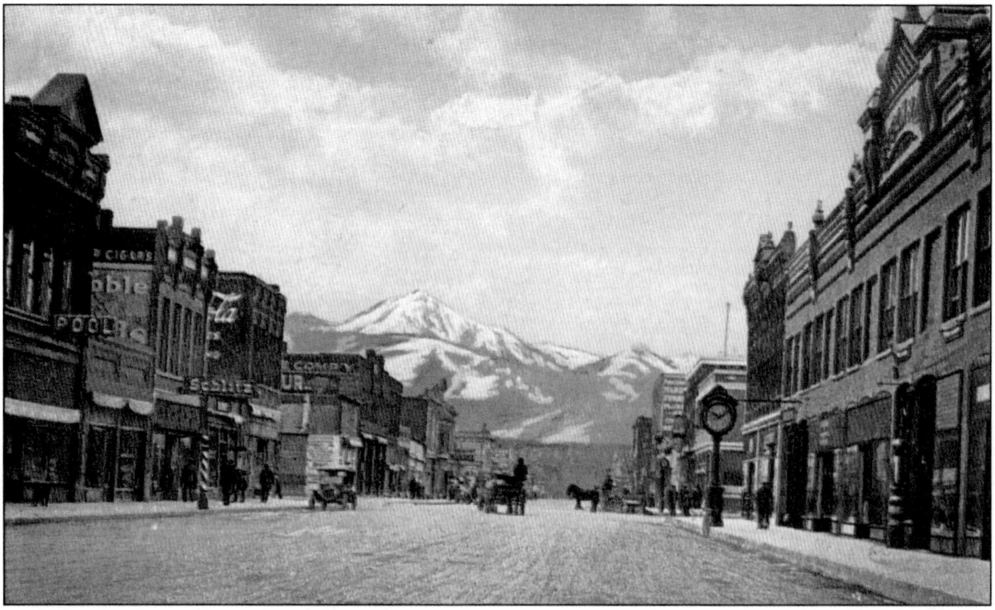

Livingston's Main Street accommodated many notable brick blocks of buildings. To the east stood the 1890s Harvat Block, the Danforth Block, and Hefferlin Block No. 2. Hefferlin Block No. 4 and the newly rebuilt Miles Block, which originally housed the elegantly appointed 1889 Miles building before its destruction in a 1913 fire, dominated the west side, while J. L. Murphy's clock, the lone street sentinel, enumerated the passage of time. (Goss Collection.)

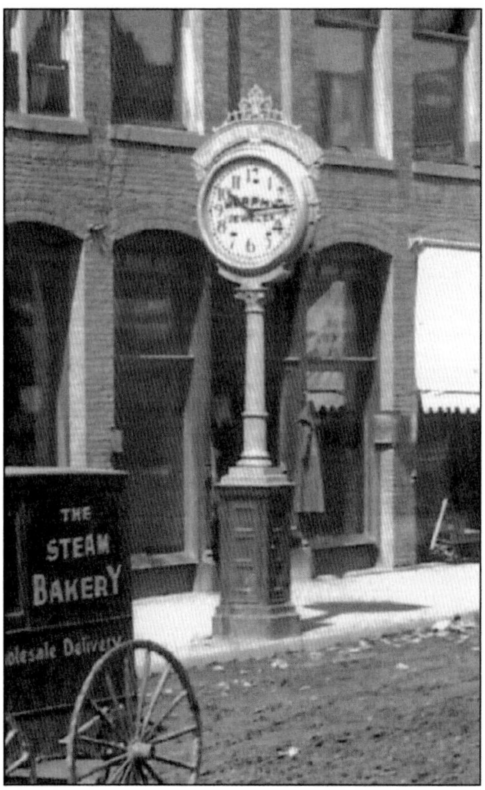

This Seth Thomas post clock originally garnered a significant location at 105 North Main Street in front of J. L. Murphy's jewelry store in the 1900s. The decorative clock remained on Main Street well into the 1920s but was moved onto Callender Street across from Sax & Fryer's bookstore at an unknown point in time. The clock was sold and moved to California sometime after 1950. (Private collection.)

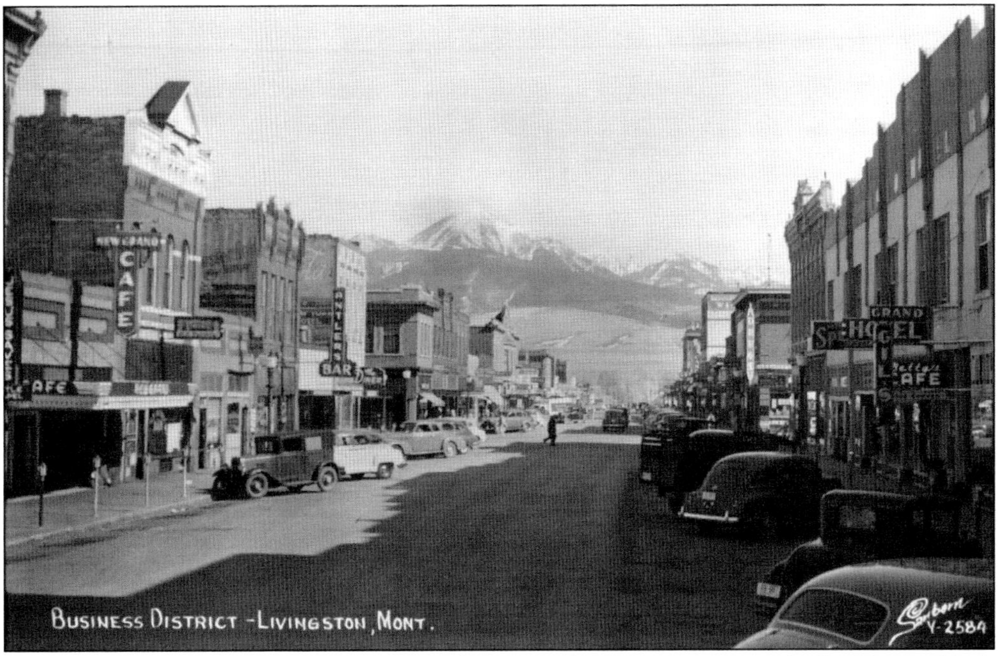

Looking south down Main Street from Park Street, this 1940s view reveals the Harvat Block building, with 1890 emblazoned on its pitched roof facade, still standing on the east side of the street. The Grand Hotel, visible in the center of the west side of the street, was destroyed with several other buildings in a 1969 fire. (Goss Collection.)

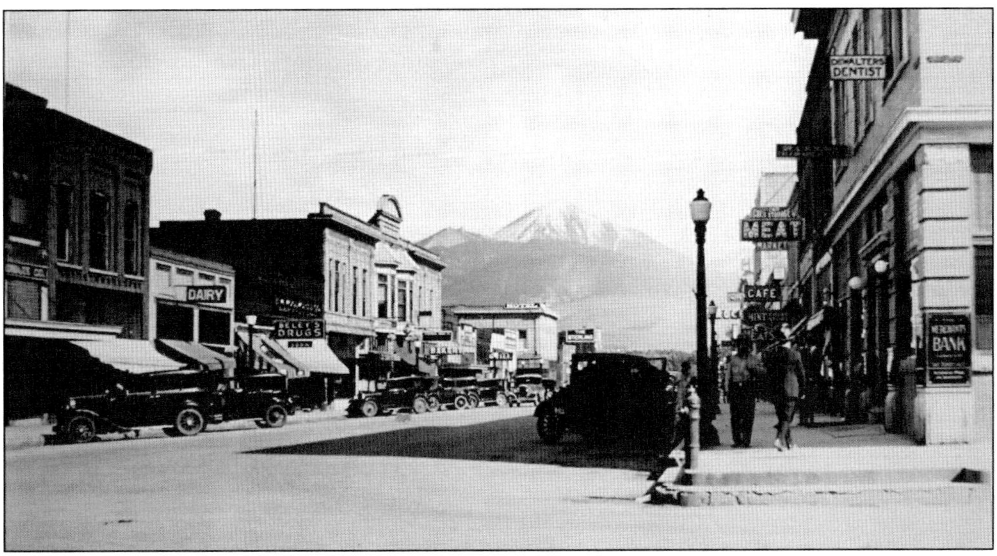

The Merchants' Bank, former resident in the stately Hefferlin Opera House, is now located on the corner of South Main and Callender Streets in this *c.* 1930 view. Next door is the Cold Storage Meat Market, originally established by William Hruza. Across the street is the drugstore of former mayor Frank Beley, whose son Fred went on to establish a drugstore in Billings. (Private collection.)

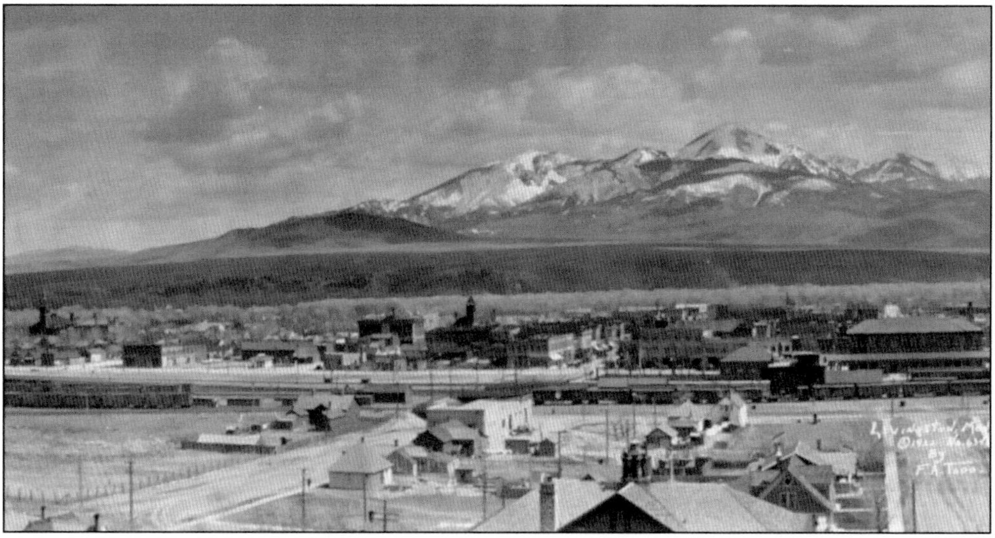

Overlooking Livingston from the hill north of town, Frederick A. Todd captured this panoramic view in 1922. Todd apparently lived in Livingston on a part-time basis around the early 1900s and captured scenes locally and in Yellowstone Park with both still and moving picture cameras. In the early 1920s, he arranged horseback camping parties into Yellowstone and directed a moving picture studio in Salt Lake City. (Library of Congress.)

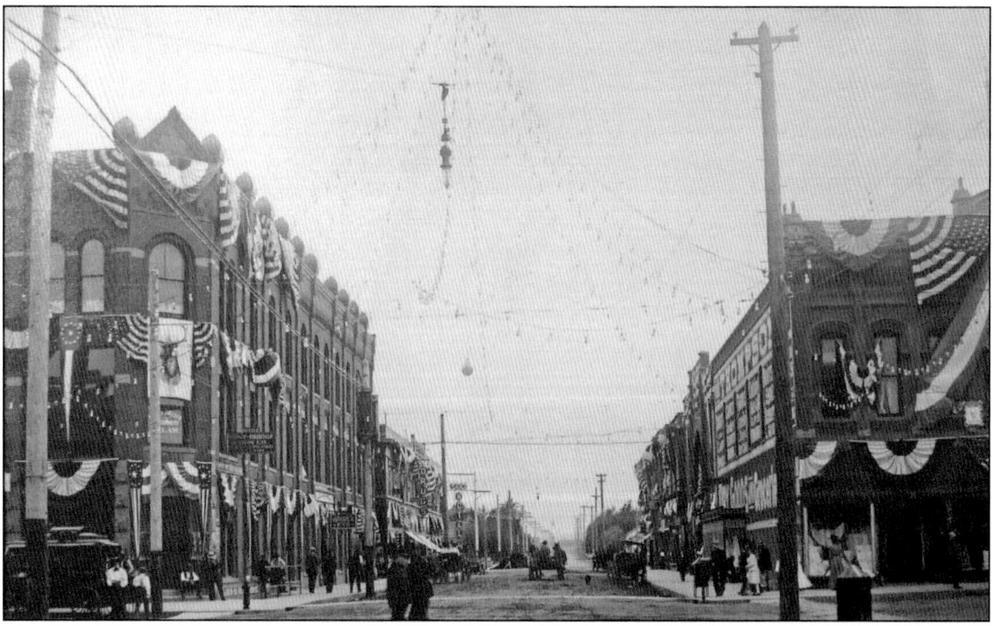

It seems Livingston was constantly celebrating in 1910 as the Montana Elks also held their annual convention here. Shown at right foreground is the Thompson Brothers Mercantile constructed in the early 1890s, while at left is the stately Miles Block, erected in 1889. The Miles building housed numerous businesses, including Miles Hardware, the First State Bank, and various other offices. A 1913 fire destroyed this magnificent building. (Private collection.)

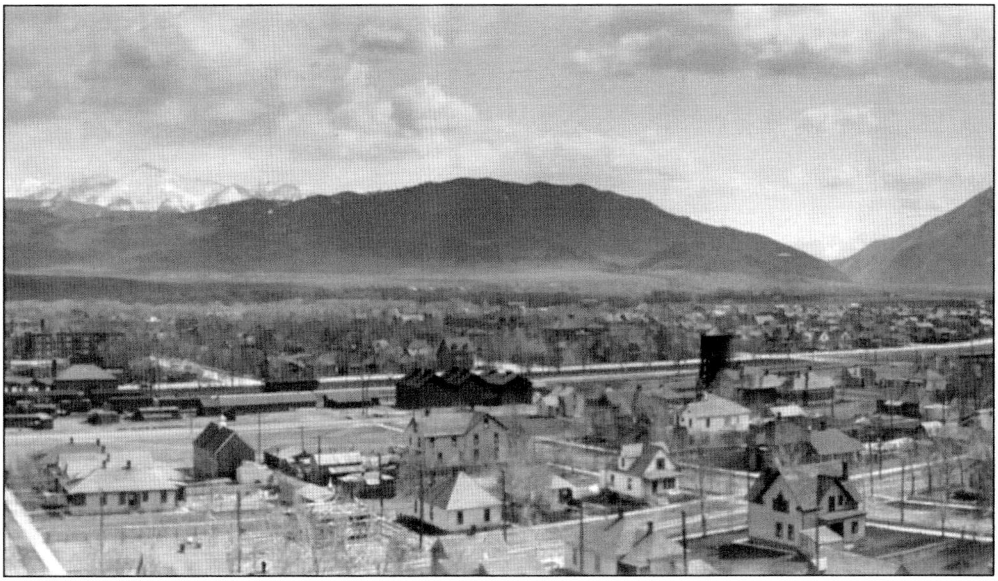

Continuing the panorama, this Todd photograph documented the extensive growth of the city west of town and the still relative sparseness of the north side. The Yellowstone River gushed forth through the narrow mountain canyon shown on the far right and flowed along the south side of town, as evidenced by the luxurious growth of trees. The railroad and highway shared access through this narrow defile. (Library of Congress.)

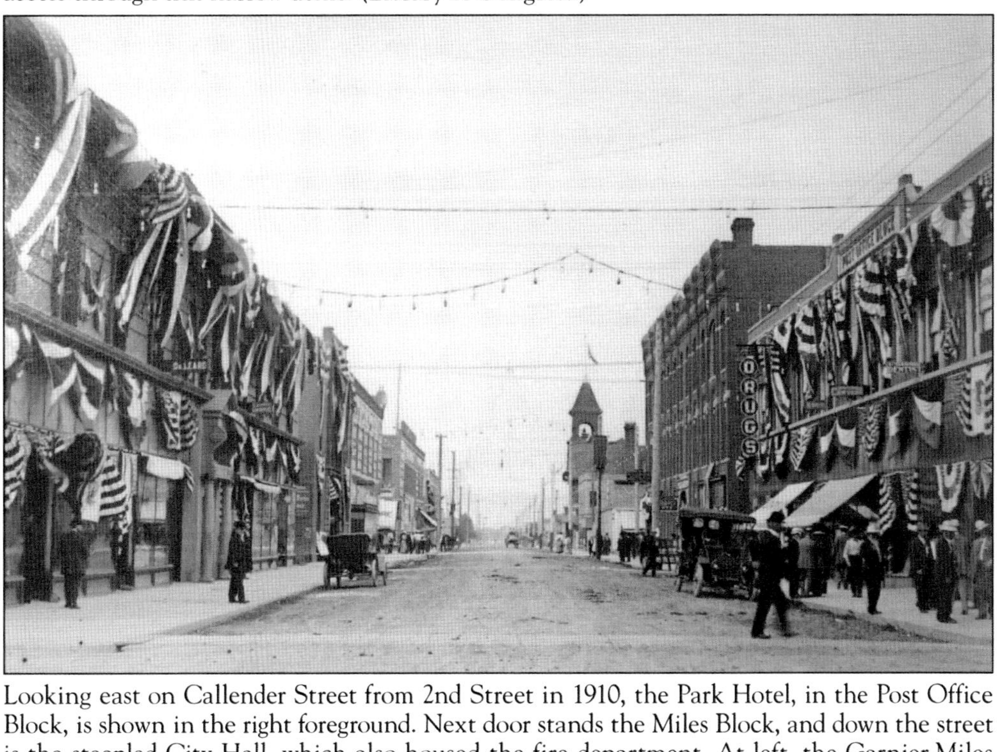

Looking east on Callender Street from 2nd Street in 1910, the Park Hotel, in the Post Office Block, is shown in the right foreground. Next door stands the Miles Block, and down the street is the steepled City Hall, which also housed the fire department. At left, the Garnier-Miles Block adjoins the Thompson building, located on the corner of Callender and Main Streets. Hefferlin Mercantile is across the street on Main. (Private collection.)

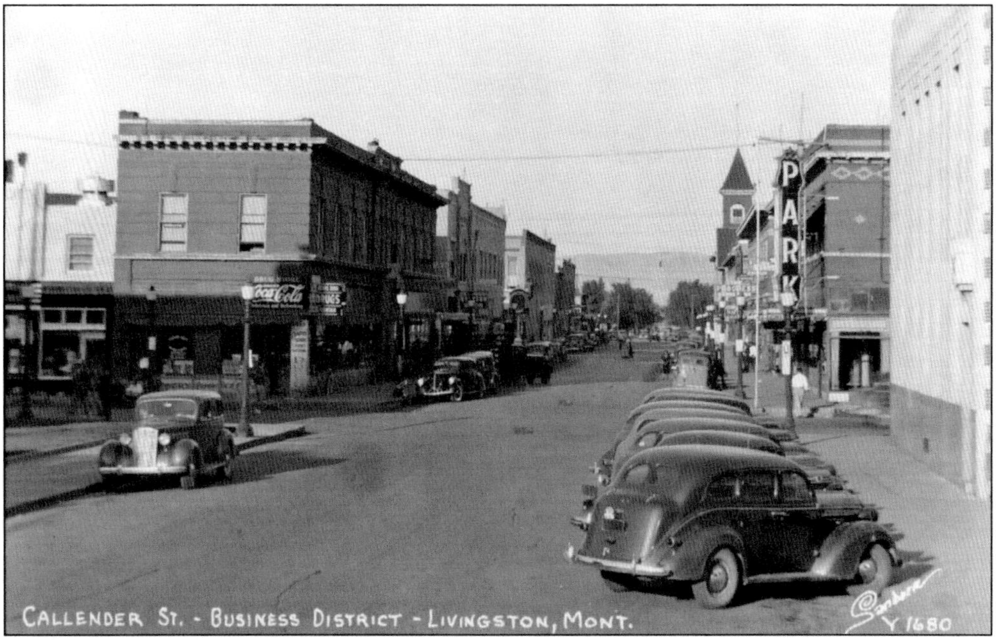

Livingston appeared a bustling metropolis in this view looking east on Callender Street around 1935. Many businesses had come and gone since the turn of the century, but a few standards remained, including the Park Hotel, rebuilt in 1904 after a disastrous fire, and James Vicar's Drug Store, a fixture since 1906. In the next decade, the classic bell tower of City Hall would be removed, forever changing the skyline. (Goss Collection.)

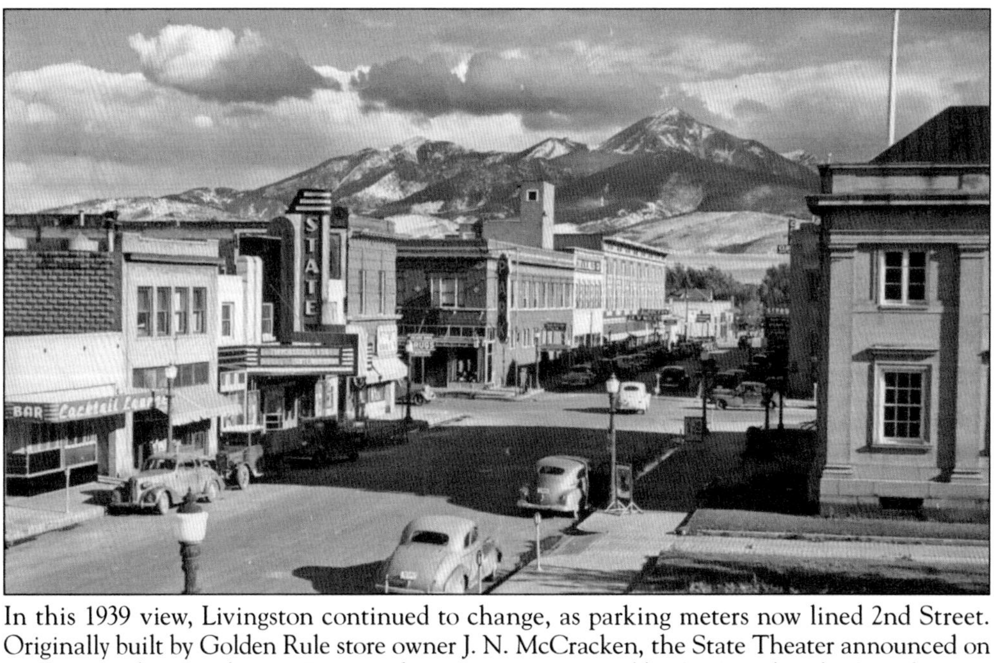

In this 1939 view, Livingston continued to change, as parking meters now lined 2nd Street. Originally built by Golden Rule store owner J. N. McCracken, the State Theater announced on its marquee the 1939 feature *Topper Takes a Trip*. Later owned by A. W. Miles, the State became the Empire Theater in 1954. The competing Strand Theater, built by Miles in 1914, is shown across from the A. W. Miles block. (Goss Collection.)

Six

A Most Desirable Residence City

As the NPRR railroad shops, the tourist traffic to Yellowstone, the coal and limestone mines, and the cattle and sheep industry all flourished, Livingston's residential population grew proportionately. Official census records through the next few decades reported continual population gains with 2,850 residents in 1890 and 6,311 by 1920. As Livingston's business district prospered, hundreds of homes were erected in every part of the city.

The Eastside residential area reflected a modest assortment of homes that exhibited economy and practicality. With the expansion of the railroad repair facilities between 1901 and 1907, contractors quickly erected simple four-square wood-frame and hip-roofed structures to accommodate the influx of railroad workers.

Livingston's Westside residential area reflected a variety of early-20th-century architectural styles. Yellowstone Avenue, known as "Bankers Row" with its array of stunning homes, became the residential showcase of Livingston's prominent populace. As Livingston's population and residential areas grew, the milieu of the Westside residential area became an eclectic mingling of architectural designs from simple to Prairie style to the ornamental Victorian. A host of neighborhood churches completed the picturesque appearance of this most desirable residence city.

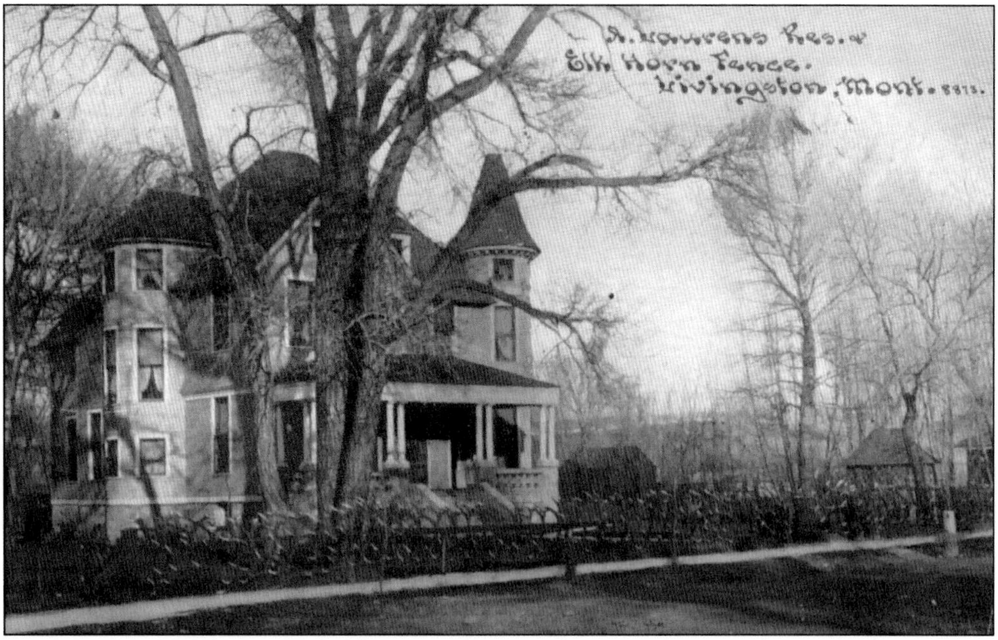

Photographer Alfred Laurens and his wife, Mary, lived in this distinctive house that featured an elk antler fence. Laurens operated the Park Street Studio by 1890, catering to the Yellowstone and local trade. Laurens probably began practicing his art in Fargo, Dakota Territory, in the 1880s. The 1910 census listed his primary occupation as real estate agent. By 1920, the family had moved to Seattle, where Laurens continued in real estate. (Goss Collection.)

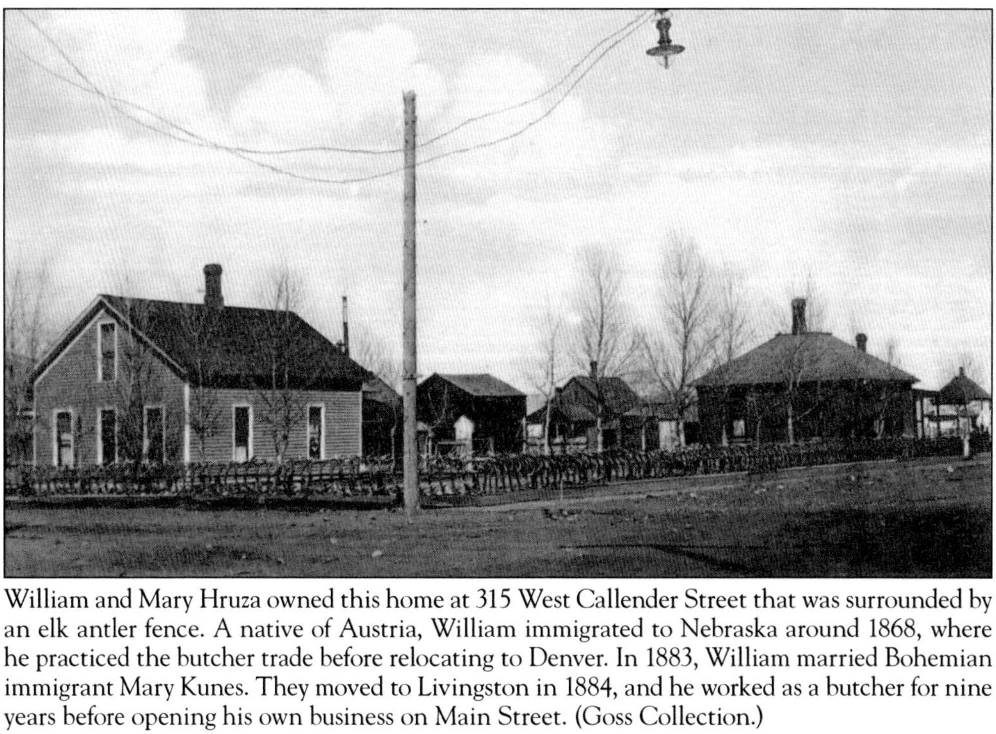

William and Mary Hruza owned this home at 315 West Callender Street that was surrounded by an elk antler fence. A native of Austria, William immigrated to Nebraska around 1868, where he practiced the butcher trade before relocating to Denver. In 1883, William married Bohemian immigrant Mary Kunes. They moved to Livingston in 1884, and he worked as a butcher for nine years before opening his own business on Main Street. (Goss Collection.)

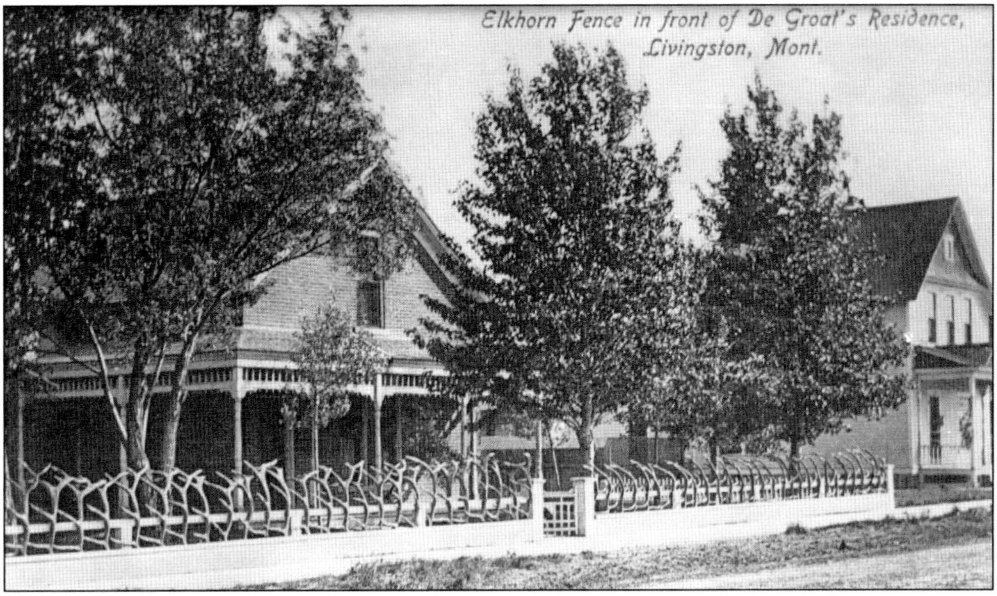

Charles and Emma DeGroat lived in this quaint residence at 417 West Park Street. It was one of several homes in Livingston that featured a fence made out of elk antlers. Charles was a traveling engineering on the Montana Division of the NPRR. Both New York natives, the couple moved to Livingston during its earliest days. (Yellowstone Gateway Museum.)

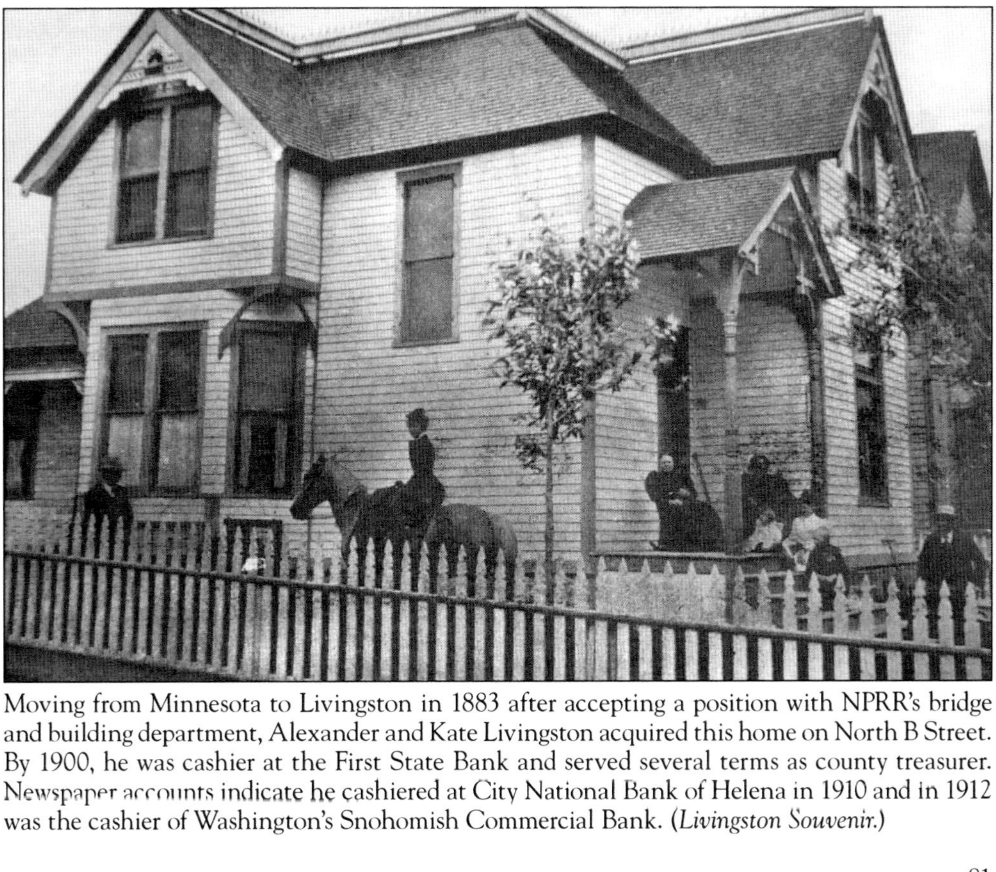
Moving from Minnesota to Livingston in 1883 after accepting a position with NPRR's bridge and building department, Alexander and Kate Livingston acquired this home on North B Street. By 1900, he was cashier at the First State Bank and served several terms as county treasurer. Newspaper accounts indicate he cashiered at City National Bank of Helena in 1910 and in 1912 was the cashier of Washington's Snohomish Commercial Bank. (*Livingston Souvenir.*)

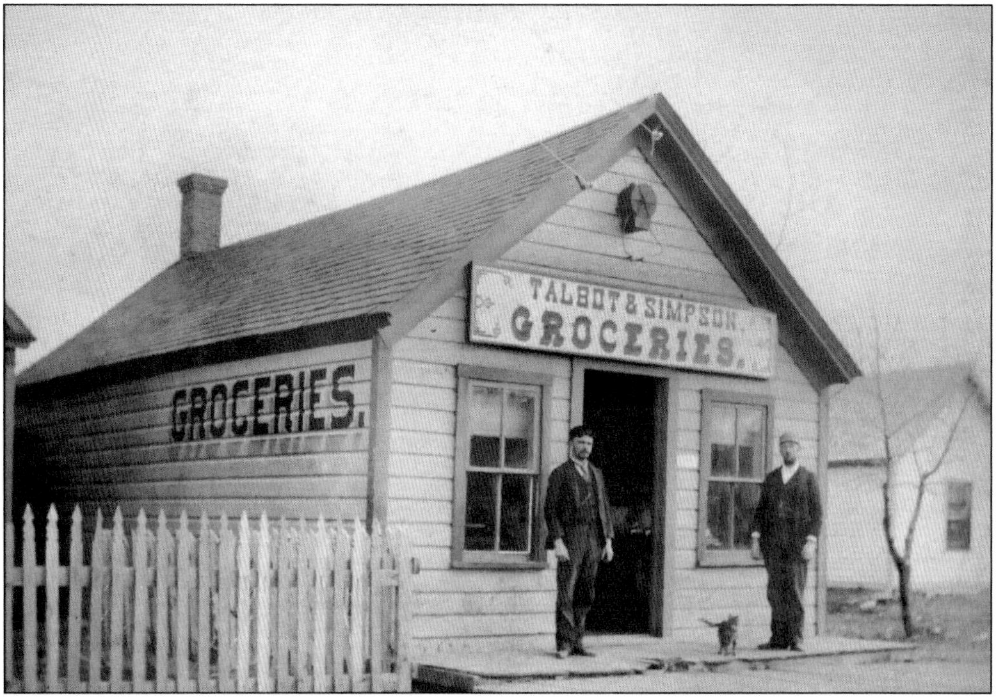

Talbot & Simpson Groceries represented one of Livingston's first suburban grocery stores. Reportedly located on South F Street, just south of Clark Street, the store was in operation in 1895. C. A. Talbot apparently moved on to greener pastures in the early 1900s, as he does not appear in the 1906–1907 Polk Livingston City Directory. (Private collection.)

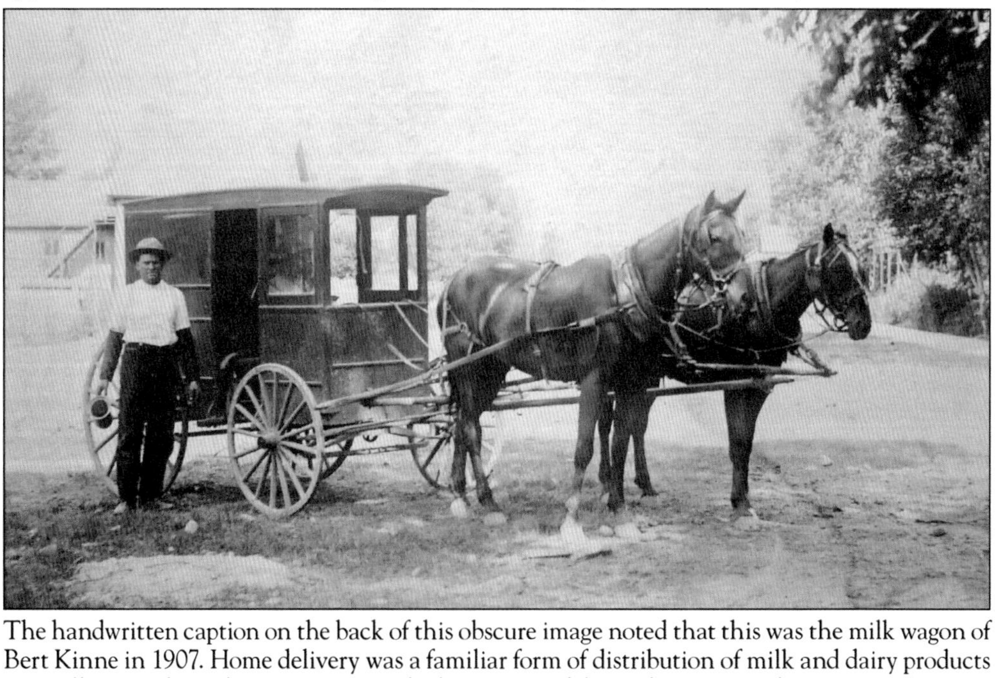

The handwritten caption on the back of this obscure image noted that this was the milk wagon of Bert Kinne in 1907. Home delivery was a familiar form of distribution of milk and dairy products in small towns throughout America at the beginning of the 20th century. This common practice survived in many rural areas until the late 1960s. (Private collection.)

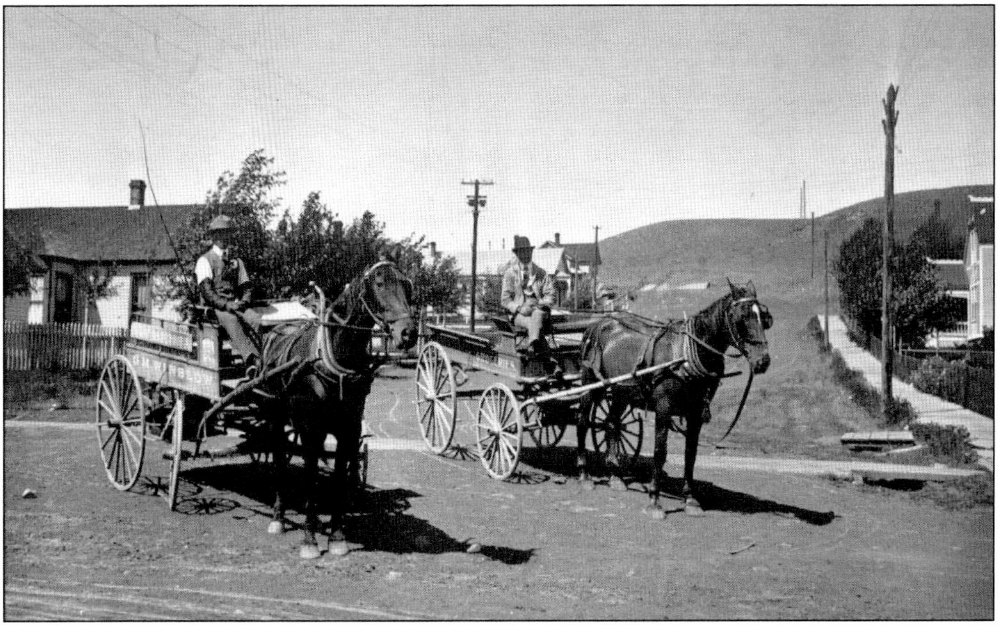

Another entrepreneur offering home delivery was Winslow Mercantile on 103–105 South Main Street. George and Anna Winslow established their enterprise around 1900 and employed future grocer Glen Blakeslee as delivery driver in 1901. Selling in 1906, the Winslows resided in Tacoma and Billings before retiring in Casper, Wyoming, where George died in 1938. Anna passed on two years later in Livingston. (Yellowstone Gateway Museum.)

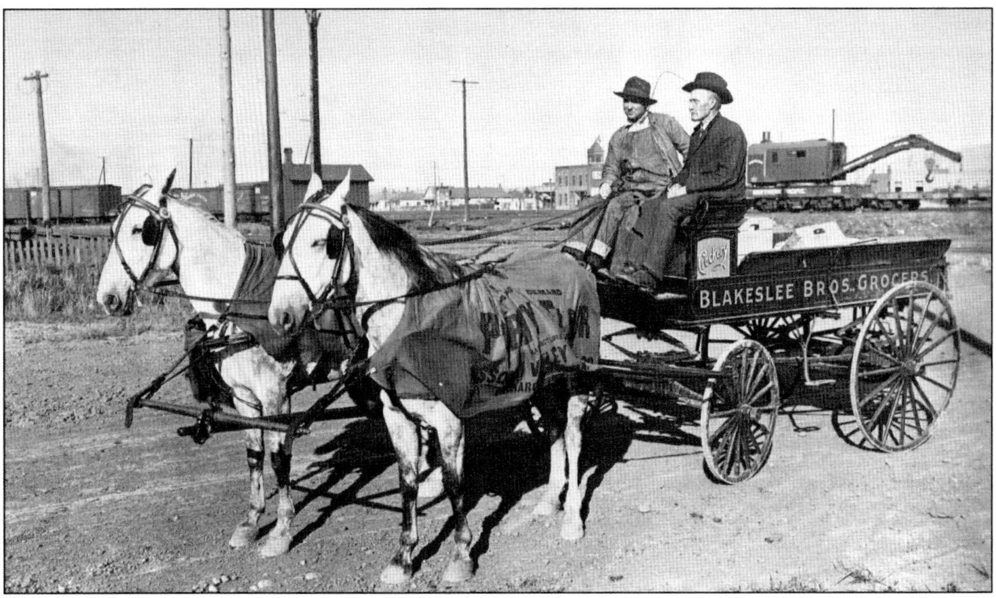

Shortly after Glenn Blakeslee's move to Livingston in 1901, his brother Harry also relocated. Glenn left Winslow's employment, and both men became employed by James Thompson. Harry then purchased a grocery store on Main and Lewis Streets with Harry Huston. After Glenn bought out Huston's interest in 1902, the two siblings formed Blakeslee Brothers grocers. Like his earliest mentor, Blakeslee offered home grocery delivery. Glenn died at age 93. (Yellowstone Gateway Museum.)

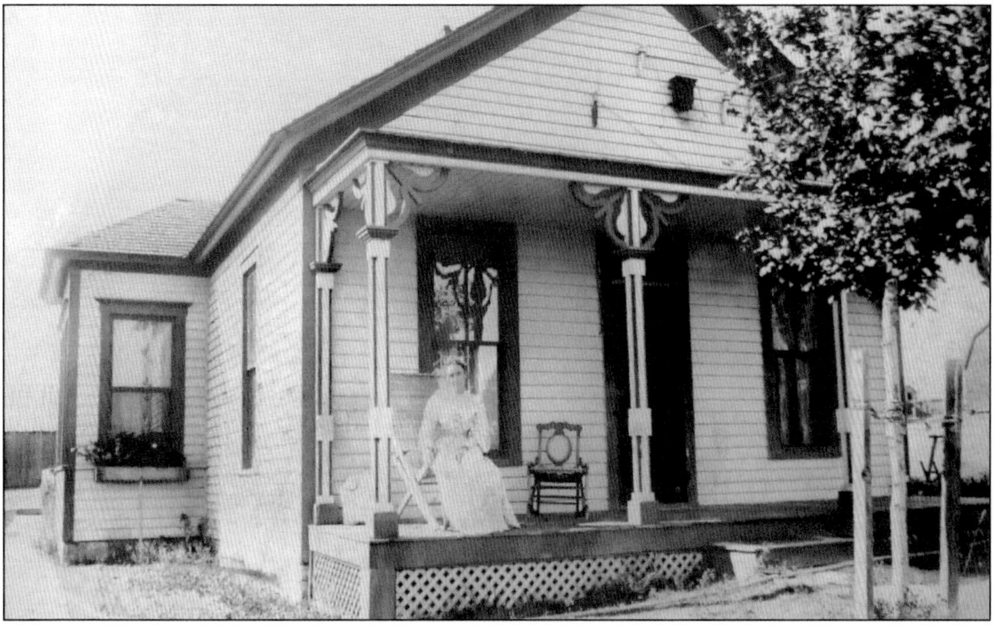

This cozy cottage on North 3rd Street near Chinook Street was the home of Mentor Wetzstein, who in 1883 established a wholesale and retail liquor business. In 1886, Wetzstein married Sophia Mae Harmon of Ohio, and in May of that year, the couple purchased this home from carpenter D. K. Buchanan. Sophia is shown sitting on the porch in this undated photograph. (Private collection.)

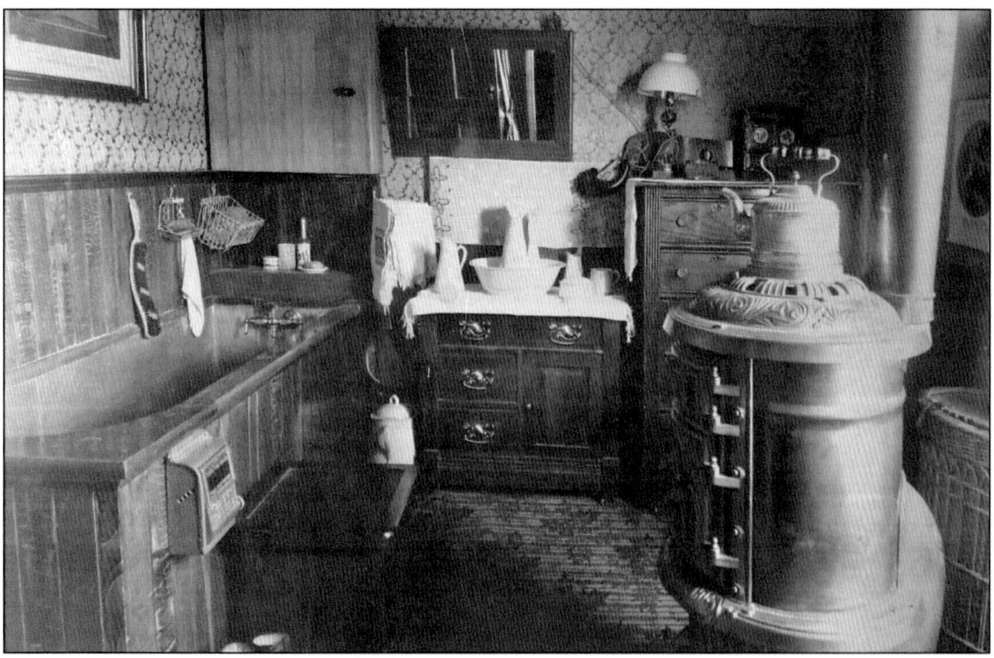

Although appearing simple from the outside, the Wetzstein house was tastefully decorated with many "modern" conveniences. In this photograph, a coal stove stands ready to heat water in the latest style bathroom that allowed the Wetzsteins to enjoy a hot soak in what was reportedly the first completely copper bathtub in Livingston. (Private collection.)

This pre-1900 view of the second parlor of the Wetzstein residence shows the construction and furnishings typical of the era, including the high ceilings, dark wood trim, and decorative wallpaper-covered plaster walls. A freestanding coal stove afforded heat, while electric lights provided illumination. The town's first telephone was on the wall behind the stovepipe, although it was only connected to his business establishment. (Private collection.)

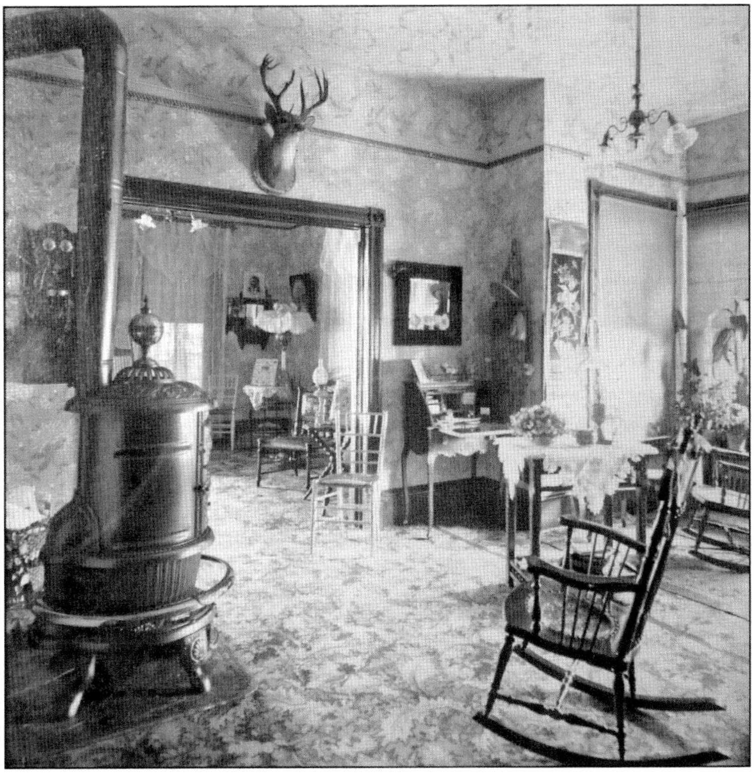

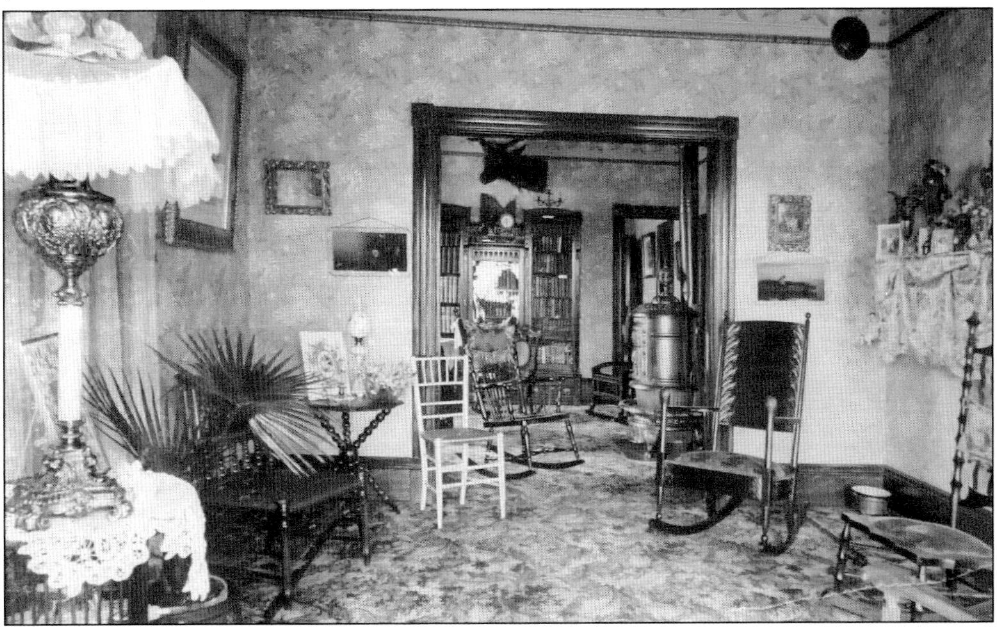

The main parlor opened into the second parlor and library, which displayed trophies from Mentor's successful hunting forays. The Wetzsteins enjoyed this comfortable home until 1903, when they departed Livingston and moved to South Bend, Indiana, where Mentor became president of the Ideal Concrete Machinery Company. Sophia died there in 1940 at age 80, and Mentor followed in 1951 at age 95. (Private collection.)

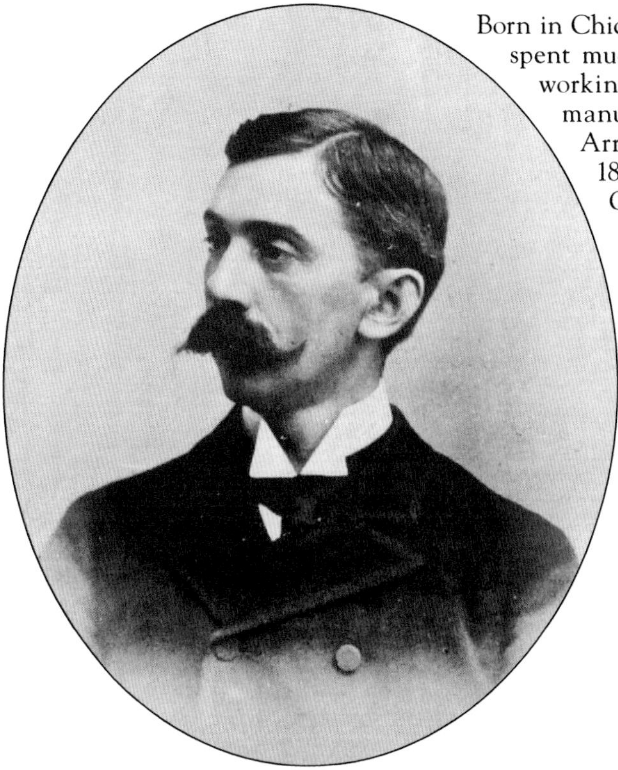

Born in Chicago in 1859, Edward Hart Talcott spent much of his youth in Connecticut, working for a time in a family woolen manufacturing plant in Talcottville. Arriving in Livingston in December 1883, he was recruited to manage the Carver Mercantile emporium. In 1887, he accepted the position of assistant cashier with the newly reorganized National Park Bank and after two years was promoted to cashier. (*Livingston Souvenir.*)

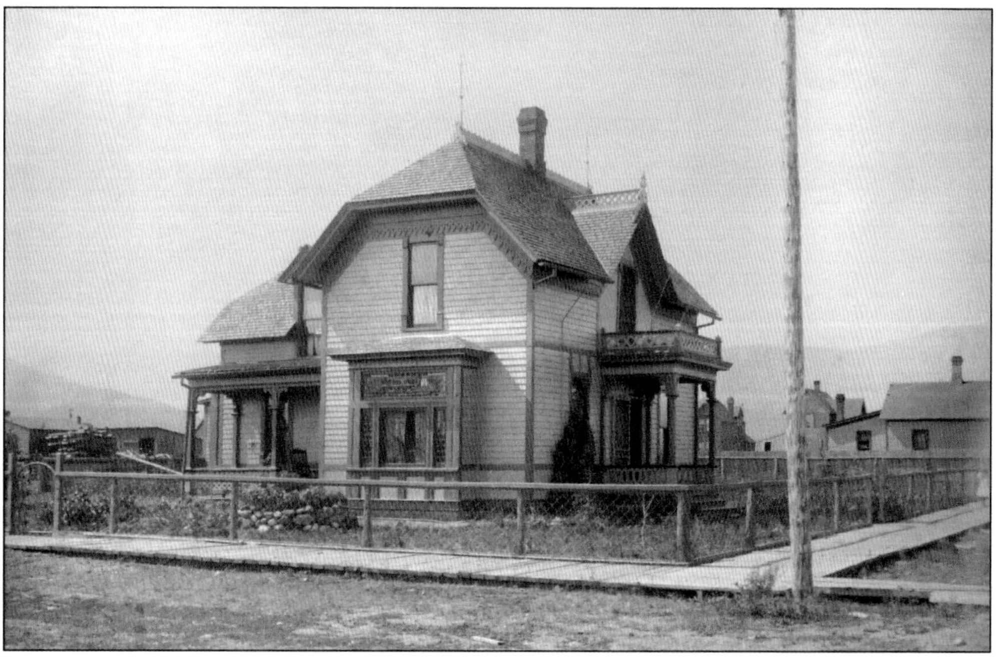

Born around 1866 in Illinois, Eliza Ballinger moved with her family to Montana in 1880. On January 21, 1886, Edward Talcott married Eliza, one of five daughters of Merrill Ballinger. This house is purportedly Edward and Eliza's first house in Livingston. The couple raised three sons, Robert, Warren, and Kenyon. (Private collection.)

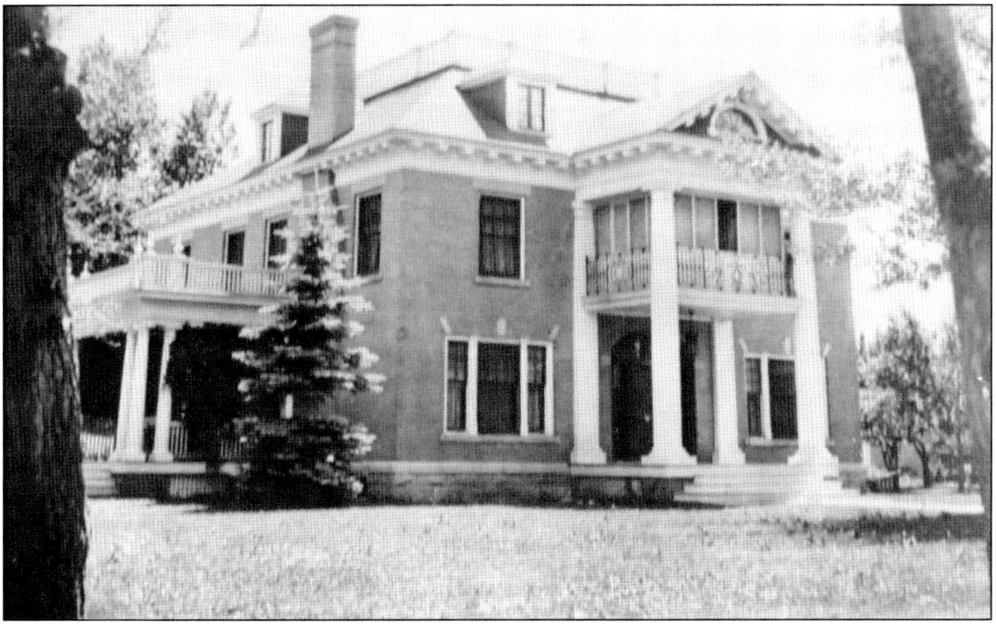

Continuing to move up the ladder of success, Edward Talcott was elected president of the National Park Bank in 1891, a position he held for the remainder of his life. He served two terms as mayor and was a member of the first executive board of Bozeman State Agricultural College. These achievements allowed Talcott to build this stately manor in 1903 on Livingston's prestigious South Yellowstone Street. (Private collection.)

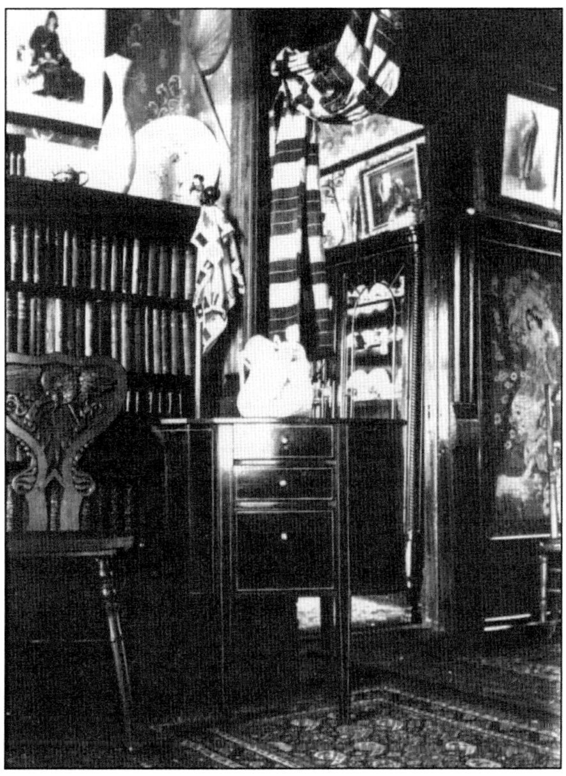

Filled with books, artwork, and fine furniture, the Talcott house was a showcase of social culture in the community. *Progressive Men of Montana* remarked their home was "a center of gracious and refined hospitality." Unfortunately this success ended all too soon as in 1908 at age 48, life ended for Edward Talcott. Eliza lived on for almost another half century, passing away in 1954. (Goss Collection.)

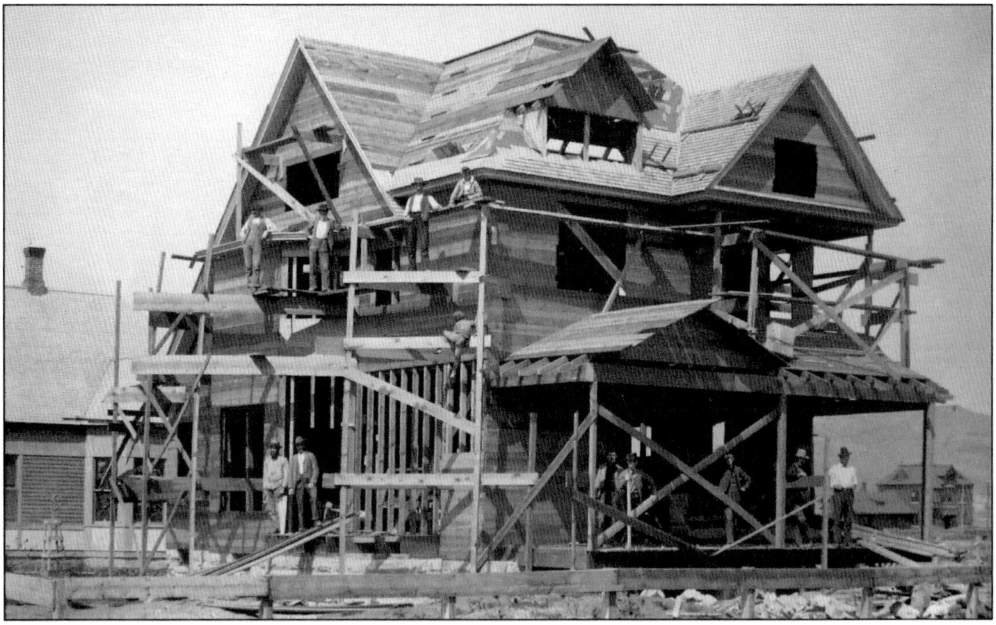

Moving to Livingston in 1883 to continue his legal profession, Frank Henry became the first city attorney upon the town's incorporation in 1888. Elected judge for the sixth judicial district in 1889, he was later characterized as a man of "marvelous judicial ability." This Queen Anne–style residence under construction in 1895 at Callender and Yellowstone Streets became the home of Frank, his wife, Julia (née Ballinger), and son Merrill. (Private collection.)

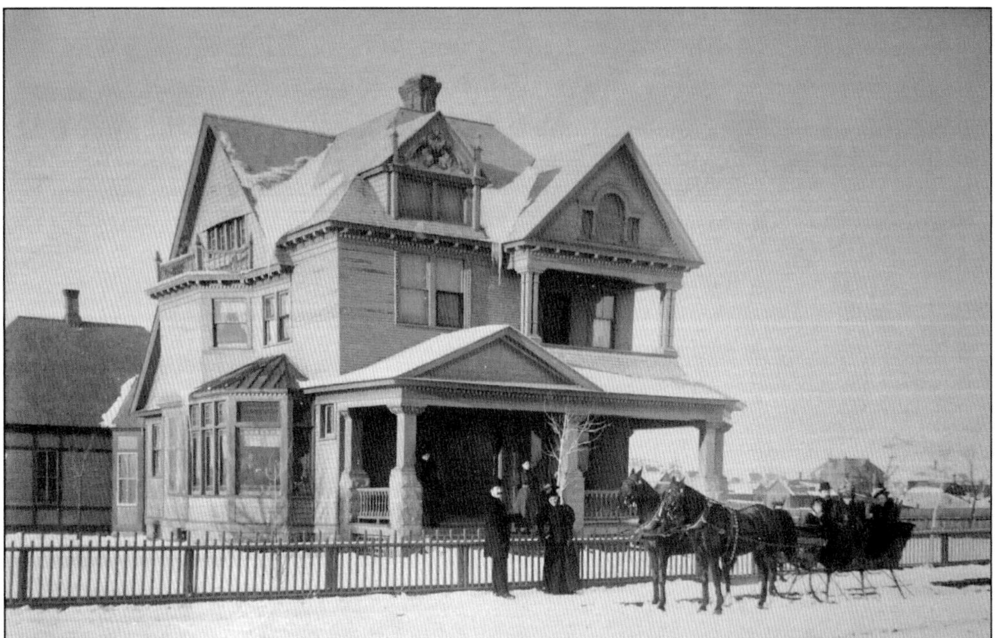

Family and friends gather together for a winter sleigh ride in this wonderful winter scene captured in front of Judge Henry's house. Julia Henry looks on from the center of the porch while sister Florence Ballinger stands by the fence. Sister Eliza is hidden from view, but her husband, E. H. Talcott, and son Kenyon prepare to drive the sleigh. (Private collection.)

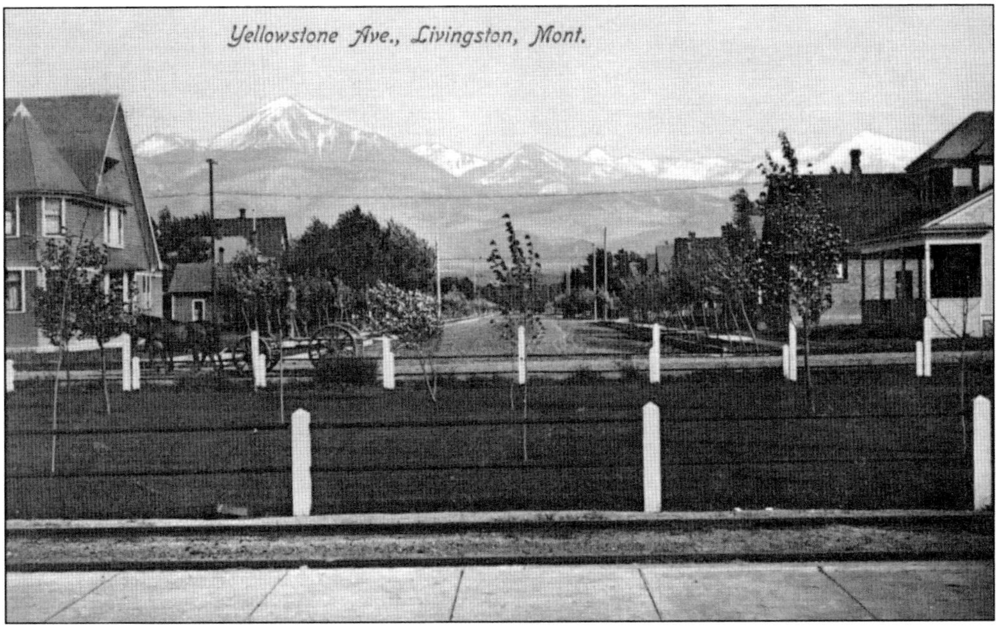

This view from c. 1908 looks south across the railroad tracks and down prestigious Yellowstone Street. A number of Livingston's most prominent families lived on this street, including cigar maker Charles Garnier, banker E. H. Talcott, sheep rancher John Harvat, physician/surgeon Dr. Byron Lee Pampel, Ralph Babbitt of the Park Hotel, photographer Alfred Laurens, and Judge Frank Henry. (Goss Collection.)

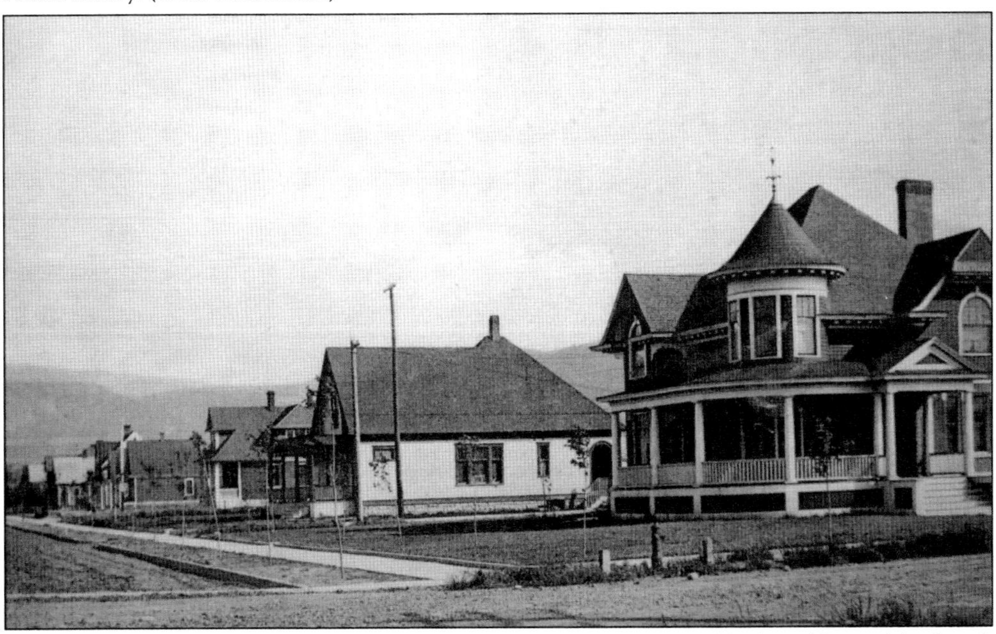

Located just west of Yellowstone Avenue, 5th Street was another socially desirable neighborhood. The presence of the Congregational Church, West Side School, and the high school attracted residents such as druggist Frank Scheuber, grocer Harry Blakeslee, and Yellowstone Camps man Edward Moorman. In this c. 1912 postcard, the Thomas Swindlehurst residence is displayed prominently on the still unpaved street corner of Park and 5th Streets. (Private collection.)

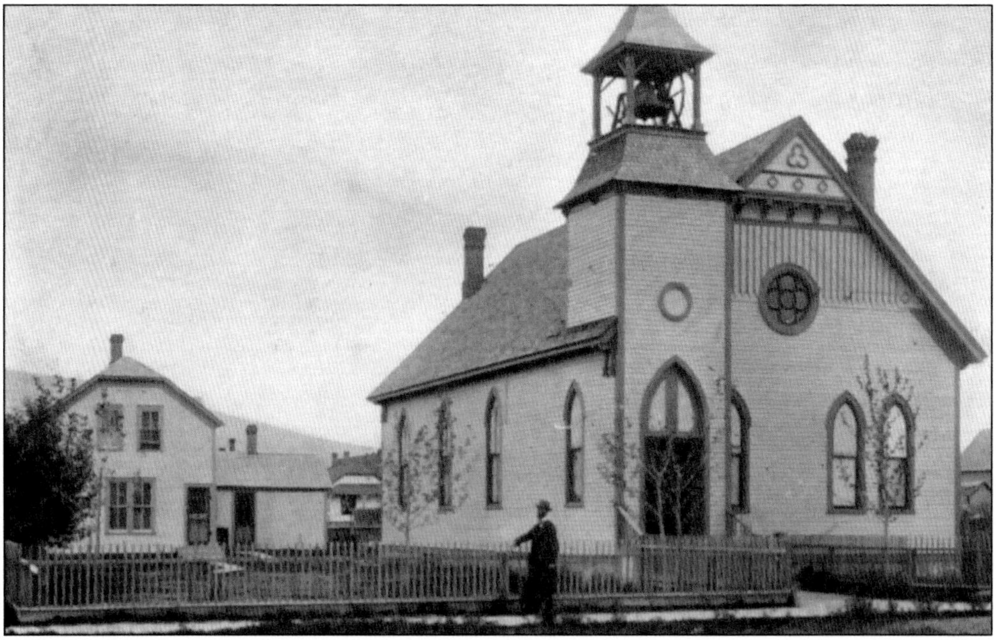

Although 1883 newspapers advertised nearly 30 saloons casting about to capture the spirits of men, the religious side of life was not neglected. On July 25, 1883, foundations for the Methodist Episcopal church (pre-1907 view) were laid by Rev. George Comfort. Located on Lewis and D Streets, it was the first church constructed in Livingston. In 1970, the church merged with the Holbrook Congregational Church. (Goss Collection.)

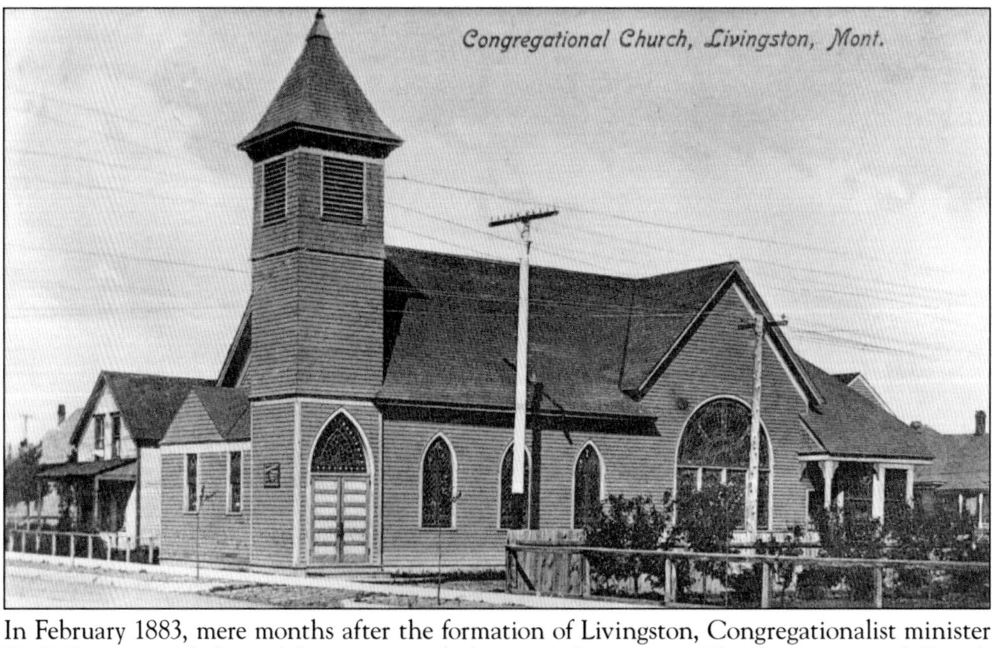

In February 1883, mere months after the formation of Livingston, Congregationalist minister H. C. Simmons enlightened the citizens with the town's first sermon. The Congregational Church was erected in the fall of 1884 and enlarged between 1896 and 1907. Located on Lewis Street between Yellowstone Avenue and 5th Street, it served the parishioners until 1933, when a new house of worship was raised nearby. (Yellowstone Gateway Museum.)

Seven

THE SOCIAL SIDE

A marker of refinement and style, Livingston's social and entertainment venues took shape nearly as quickly as the development of the city. From huge traveling circus performances to annual Fourth of July parades and rodeos to horse, car, and motorcycle races to a nine-hole golf course and an opera house, Livingston by the early 1900s exhibited all the elements of a cultivated city.

Livingston, like most American cities, celebrated the Fourth of July with flair and flourish. Buildings were festooned with red, white, and blue bunting from curb to rooftop, and celebratory parades pranced and strode down the main boulevards while excited parade watchers thronged the city's streets. The Livingston Roundup provided the highlight of the Fourth of July celebration for most residents and visitors alike. This three-day event began informally early on but developed into the officially organized Livingston Roundup in the mid-1920s. The events offered something for everyone, with trick ropers and riders, dude and relay races, stagecoach races, bronc riding contests, and a famous clown. Attendees were promised "3 Wild Days and Wilder Nights."

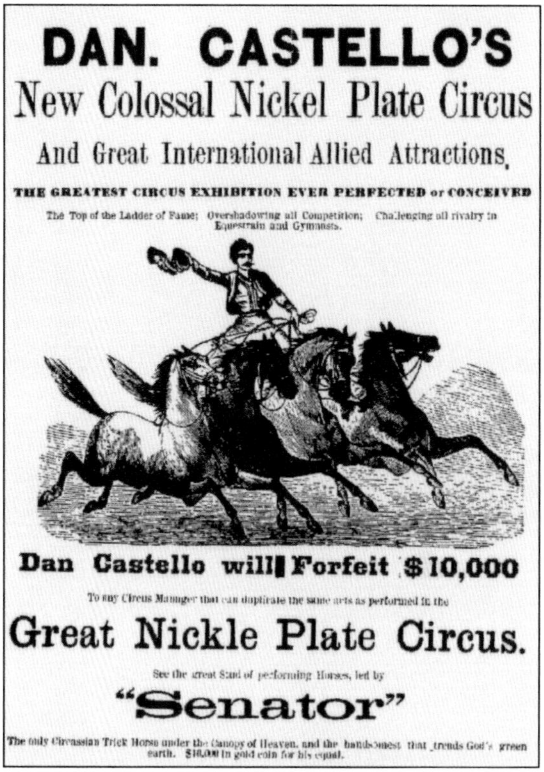

Railroad access allowed entertainment-starved residents a luxury not readily available to other rural Montana communities. Dan Castello's Circus performed in Livingston on June 27, 1883, less than a year after the town was established. Castello, founder of the famed Riding Castello Family of bareback riders, had been part of Barnum and Bailey's Circus in 1871. Livingston also entertained W. W. Cole's circus in 1886, which included Dr. Carver's Wild West Show. (*Livingston Enterprise.*)

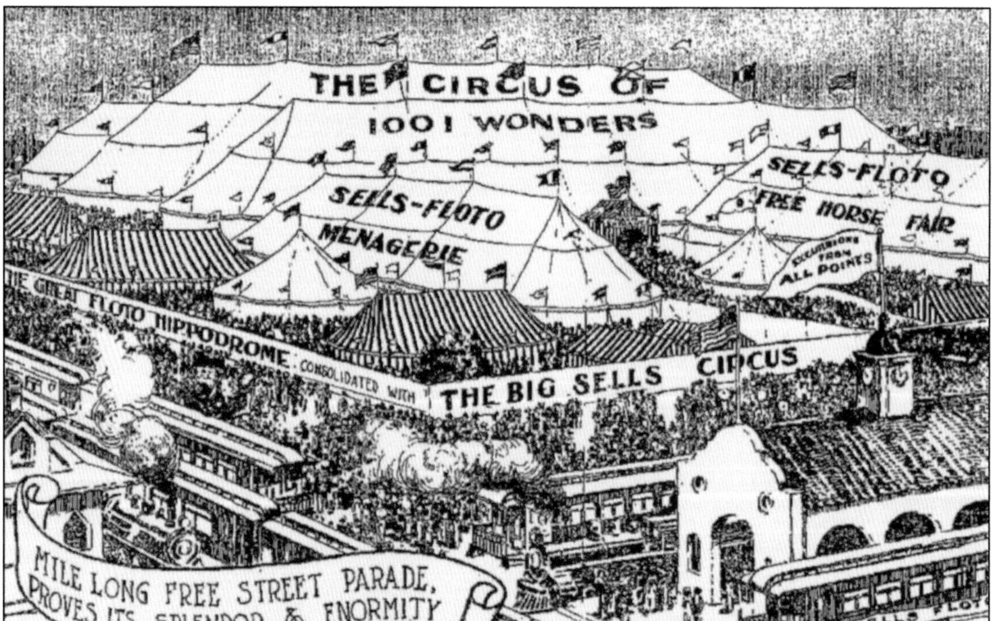

Circus performances were a recurrent form of entertainment in Livingston and other towns along the rail line. According to the June 12, 1912, *Anaconda Standard*, a mere 25¢ admission granted access to the Sells-Floto circus that boasted "1001 Wonders," menageries, hippodrome, chariot races, aerial gymnastics, and a free mile-long street parade. (*Anaconda Standard.*)

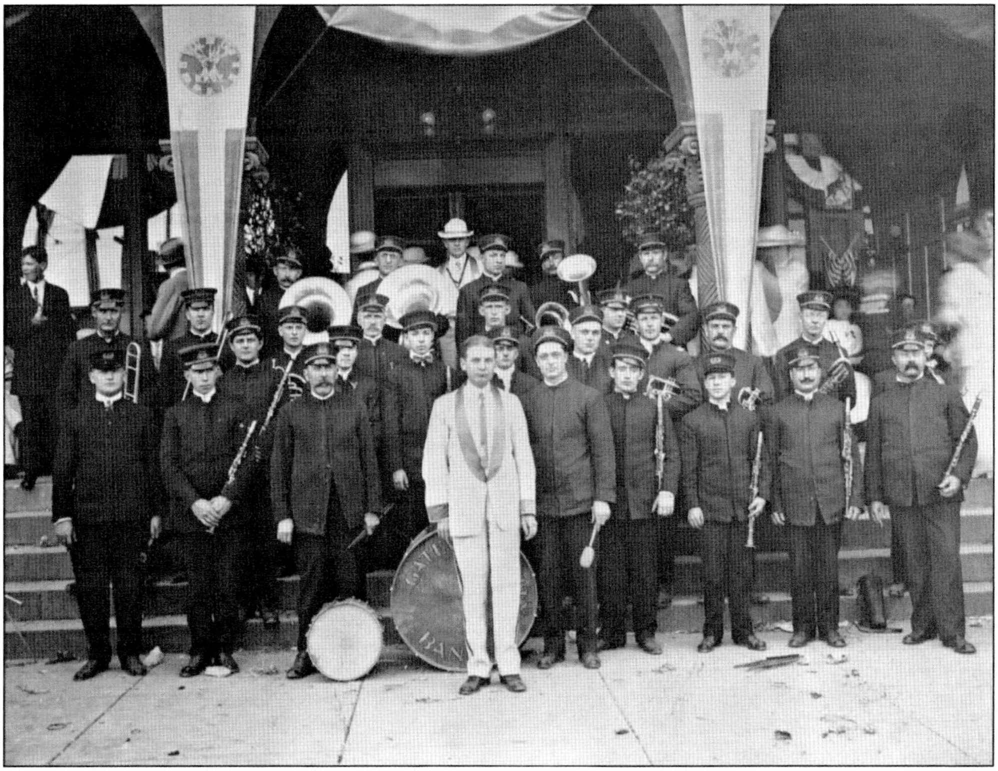

Pride of the community and well known throughout Montana, the Gateway City Band was on-call to entertain at the myriad of local social functions and festivities. Incorporated in 1903, the band purchased new uniforms in 1907 and was one of the two oldest such organizations in Montana. Led by Joe Brooks, they played at functions held throughout the state and later performed regularly at the Montana State Fair. (Yellowstone Gateway Museum.)

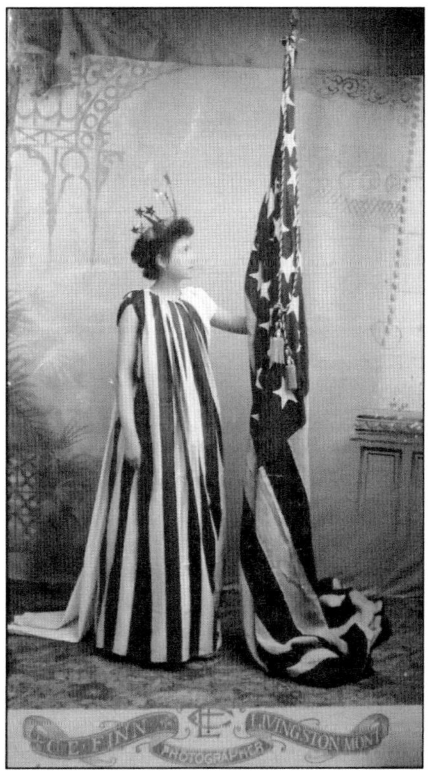

Lucy "Lulu" Ballinger, a schoolteacher, apparently represented Miss Liberty for a Fourth of July celebration pageant in 1893. One of five sisters, Lulu moved with her family to Montana in 1880. She married banker Wells Davidson in 1895 at age 26 and was living in Bozeman by 1900. Her sister Eliza married banker E. H. Talcott, and her sister Florence wed James Hamilton, dean of men at the state college in Bozeman. (Private collection.)

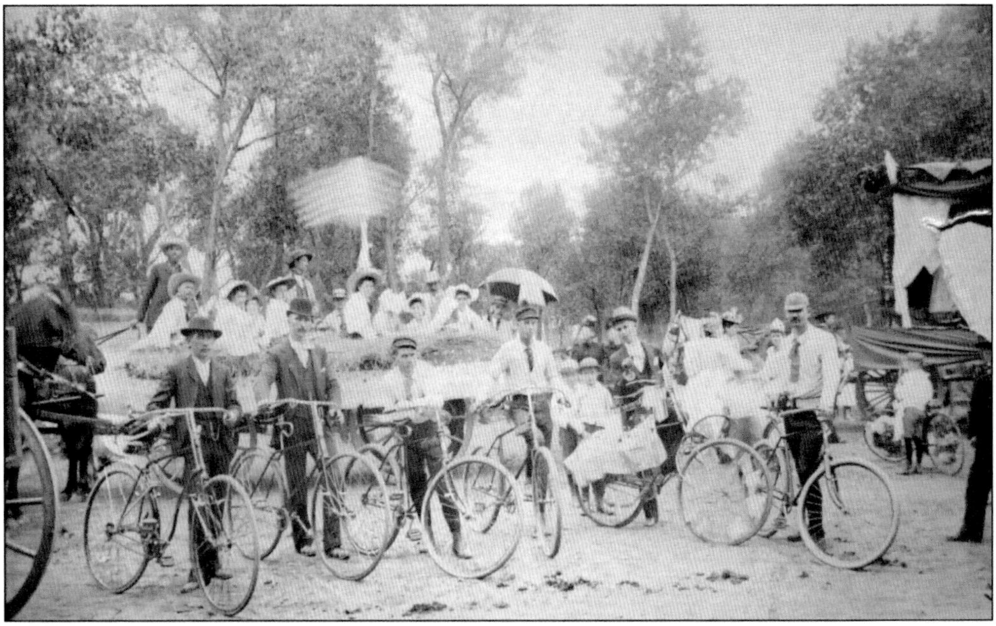

Bicyclists as well as horse drawn-floats, drivers, and riders were captured in this unique image in Miles Park as they assembled for an annual Fourth of July Parade in the 1890s. Almost all of Livingston's businesses and organizations displayed a float on this festive occasion. Historically, floats were gaily decorated barges towed with ropes along canals and waterways by equally decorated parade marchers. (Private collection.)

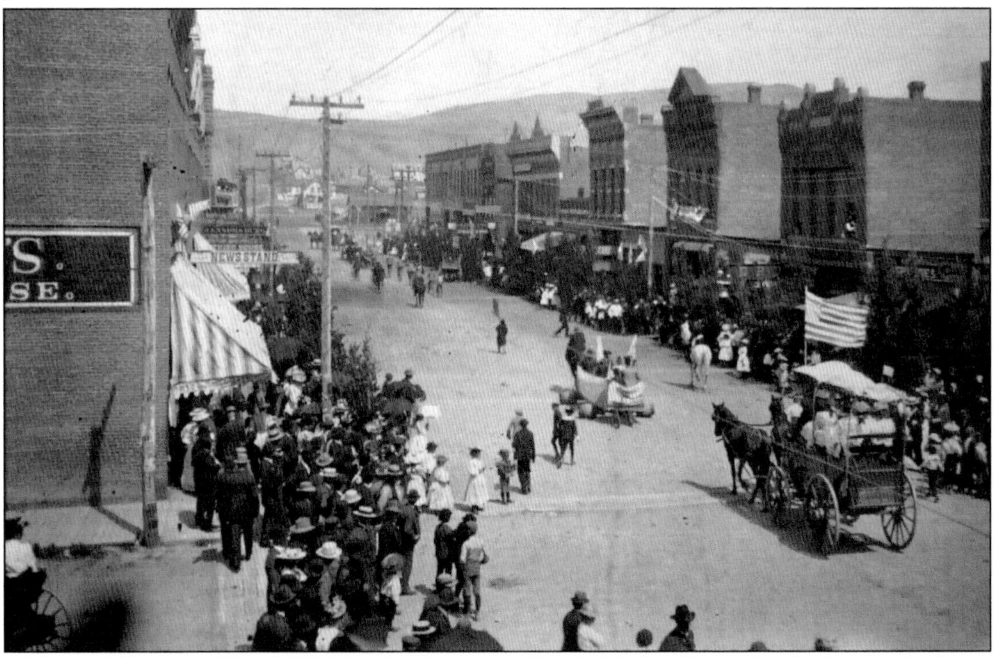

This rooftop view offered the best seat in town for watching a Fourth of July parade down Livingston's Main Street in the mid-1890s. Lined with brick buildings and wooden sidewalks as well as fashionably dressed parade watchers, Livingston's downtown displayed a progressive tone on this observance of America's Independence Day. (Private collection.)

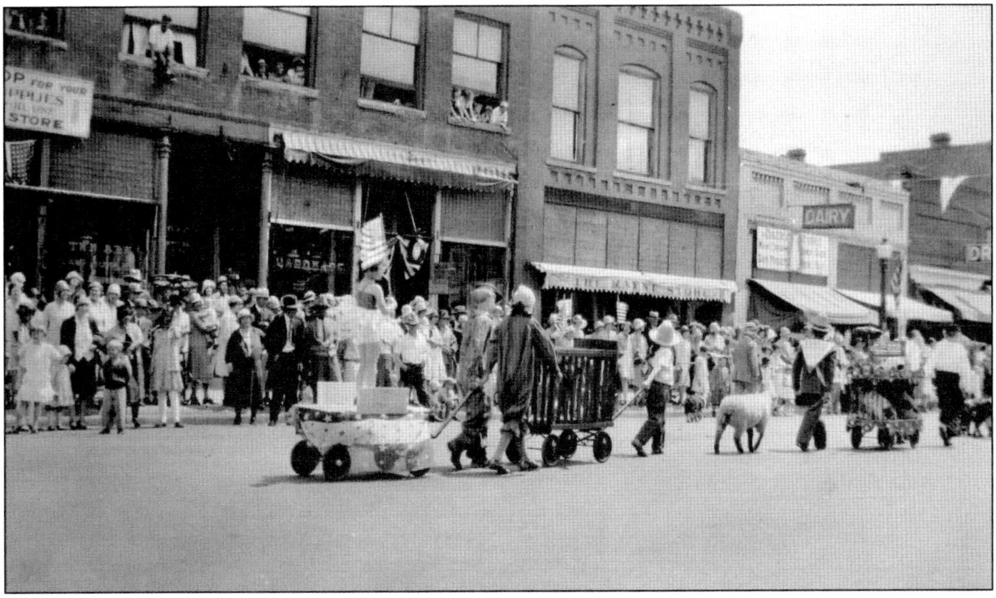

A *Park County News* advertisement in June 1926 publicized the Kiddies Parade as "an added feature" to the upcoming Fourth of July festivities. Calling all boys and girls under 16 years of age, the newspaper listing of prizes and categories included most beautiful $10, most comical $10, most original $10, and seemingly this group's entry, best trained animals $10. By 1930, this special pageant had become the "famous" Kiddies Parade. (Private collection.)

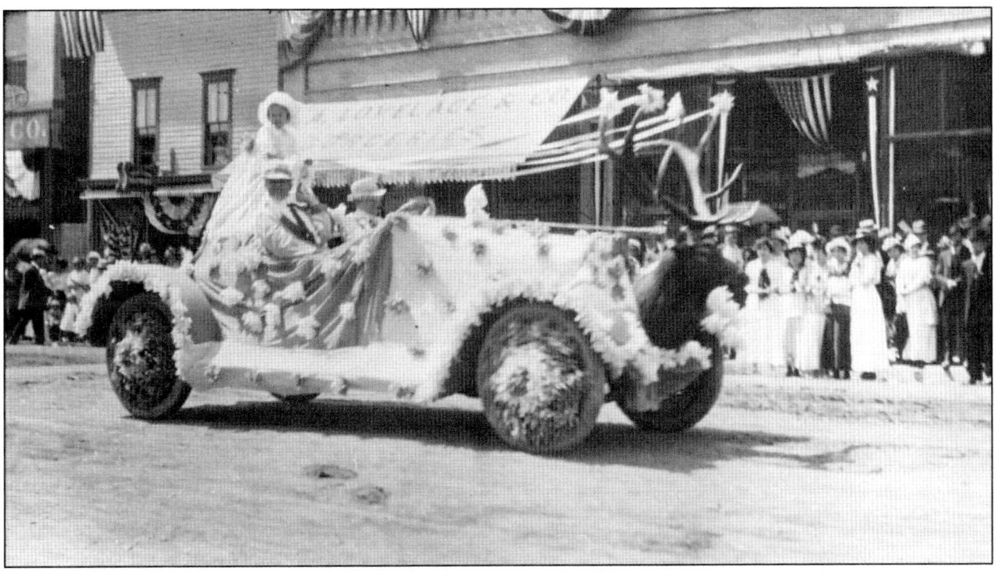

Sporting an elk head complete with a six-point rack of antlers as a festive hood ornament, Dr. George Windsor's vividly decorated car represented Livingston's Order of Elks in this 1915 Fourth of July parade. When not contributing his car as a parade entry, Dr. Windsor provided health care services in Livingston as well as Mammoth Hot Springs, located 59 miles south in Yellowstone National Park. (Yellowstone Gateway Museum.)

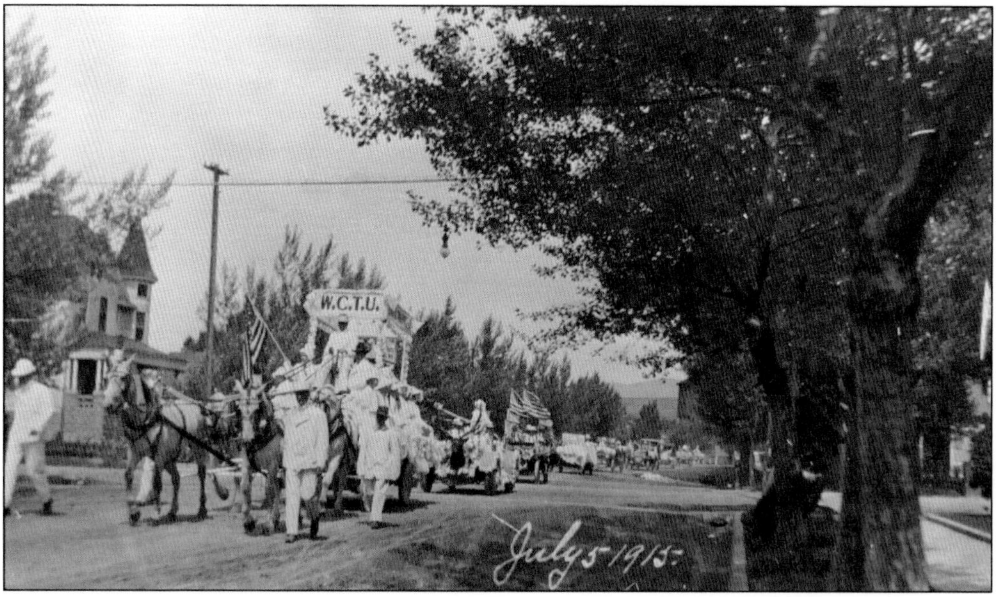

Activated in 1883, the Montana chapter of the Women's Christian Temperance Union campaigned not only for temperance, but also for women's suffrage. Involvement in issues such as these transformed many women's clubs from local civic improvement groups into strong national political alliances, especially after gaining the right to vote in 1914. Public displays such as this 1915 parade, brought their mission of social reform to the streets. (Yellowstone Gateway Museum.)

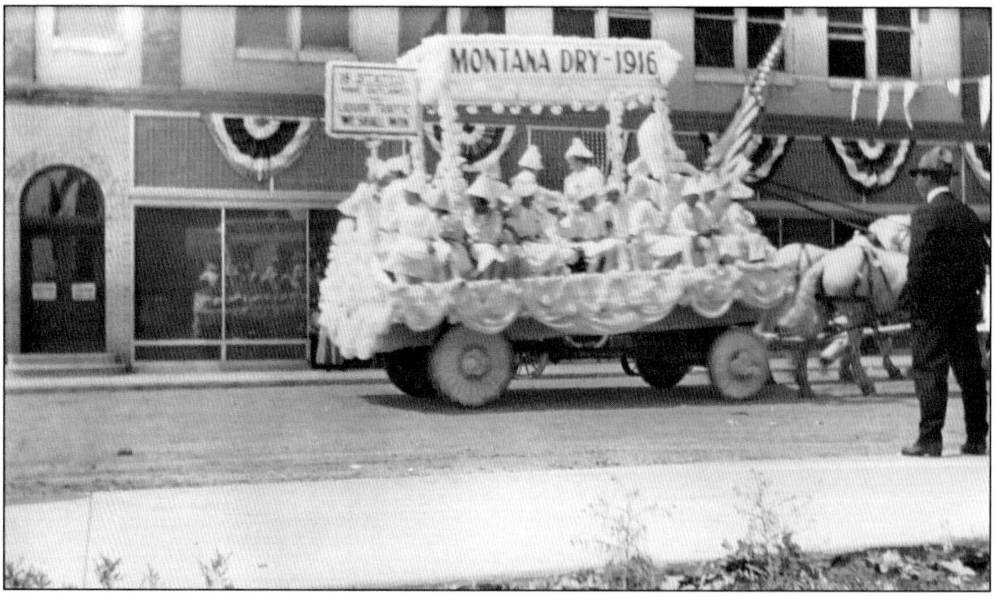

In 1916, the question of public morals as well as the benefits of a dry society was once again paraded through the streets of Livingston. Montana's WCTU membership increased from 1,000 temperance and suffrage activists in 1903 to more than 4,000 anti-saloon crusaders by 1916. On November 7, 1916, Montana overwhelmingly voted in favor of prohibition. Effective December 31, 1918, Montana "went dry" two years ahead of national Prohibition. (Yellowstone Gateway Museum.)

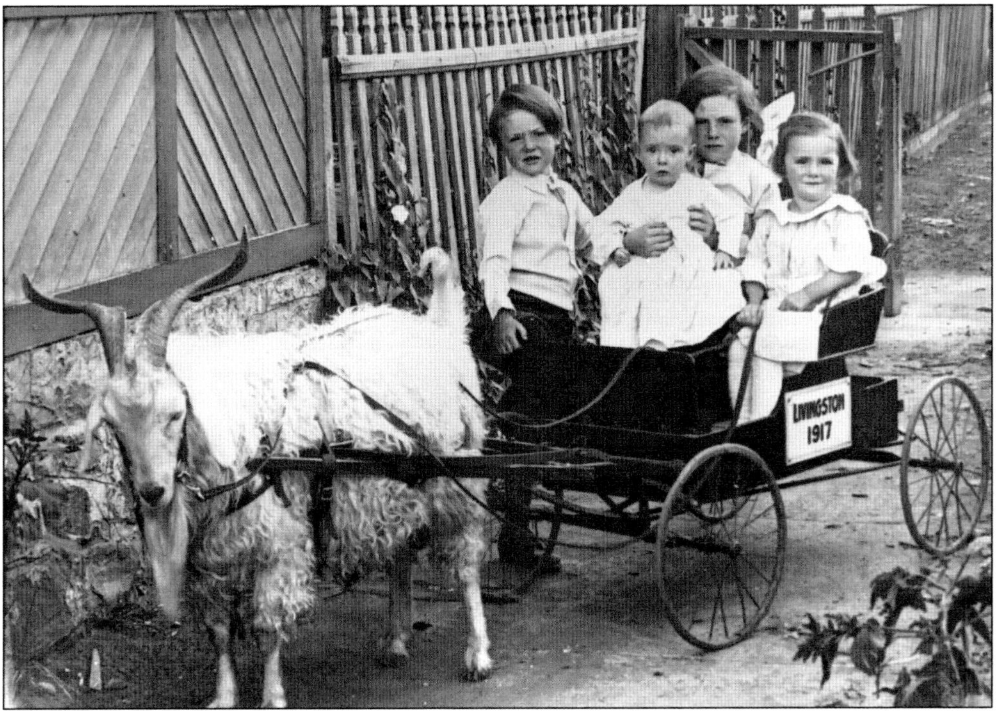

Children riding in wagons pulled by goats appeared in many Fourth of July parade photographs in small towns like Livingston as well as larger cities such as Great Falls in 1917. While the Kiddies Parade was a feature of the celebrated Livingston Roundup, this type of parade entry seemed to present a more significantly themed message, which has apparently escaped the annals of history. (Yellowstone Gateway Museum.)

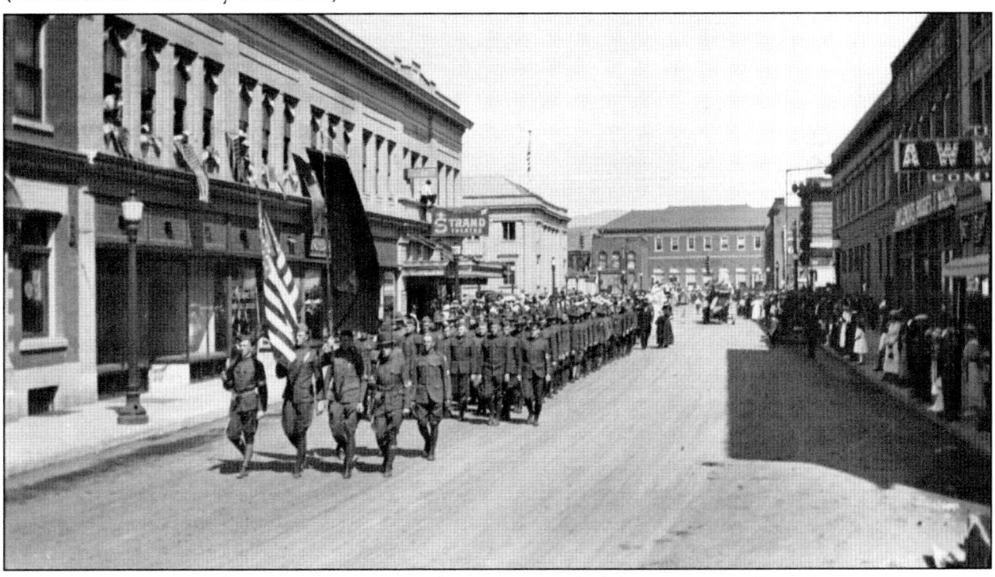

Like thousands of other towns in 1918, this scene probably represented an American victory parade following the end of World War I. Victory parades have been a popular show of American patriotism as well as public demonstration of admiration for the men and women who risked their lives to fight for freedom and democracy since 1776. (Yellowstone Gateway Museum.)

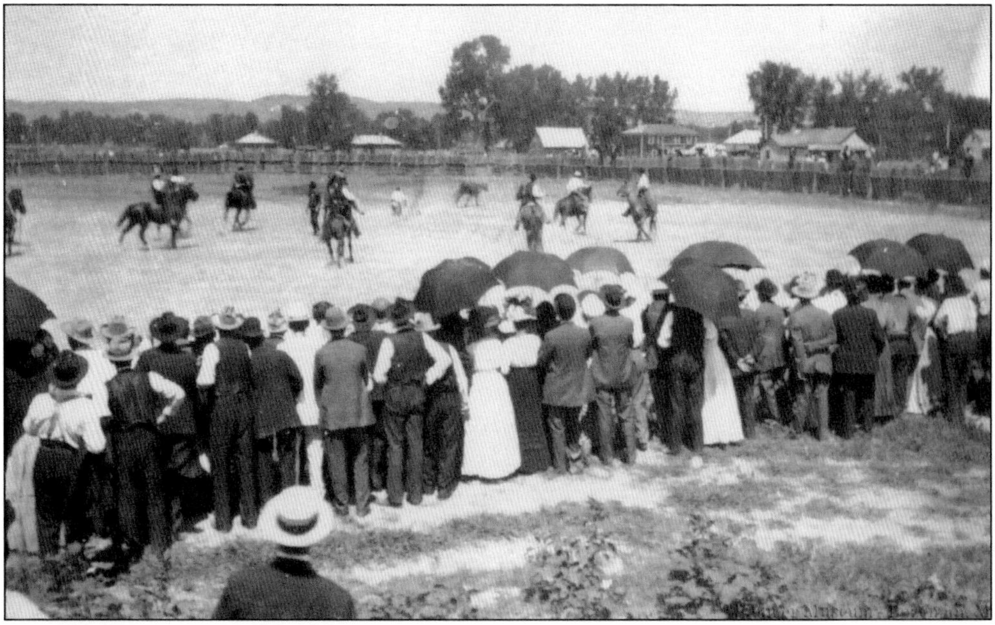

Derived from the Spanish *rodear*, meaning to "go around" or "surround," rodeos originally represented actual working skills of early-day cowboys on the range. These "round-ups" evolved into public exhibitions as early as the 1860s. This 1910 photograph of an early rodeo in Livingston represented part of the evolution that had already established formal rodeos, such as the Calgary Stampede and Cheyenne Frontier Days. (Pioneer Museum, Bozeman, Montana.)

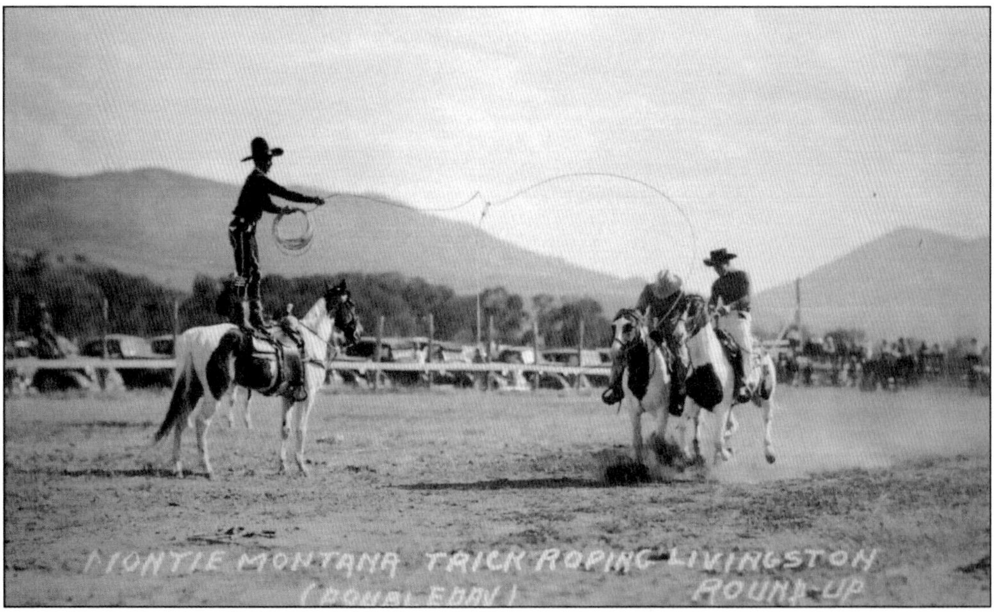

Montie Montana performed his specialty, trick riding and roping, at the Livingston Roundup in this c. 1930 postcard. Born Owen Mickels near Wolf Point, Montana, in 1910, Montie participated in rodeos and parades across the country from 1925 until 1997, just one year before his death at age 87. Also performing in movies, he appeared with John Wayne, Tom Mix, Roy Rogers, Gene Autry, and Joel McCrea. (Private collection.)

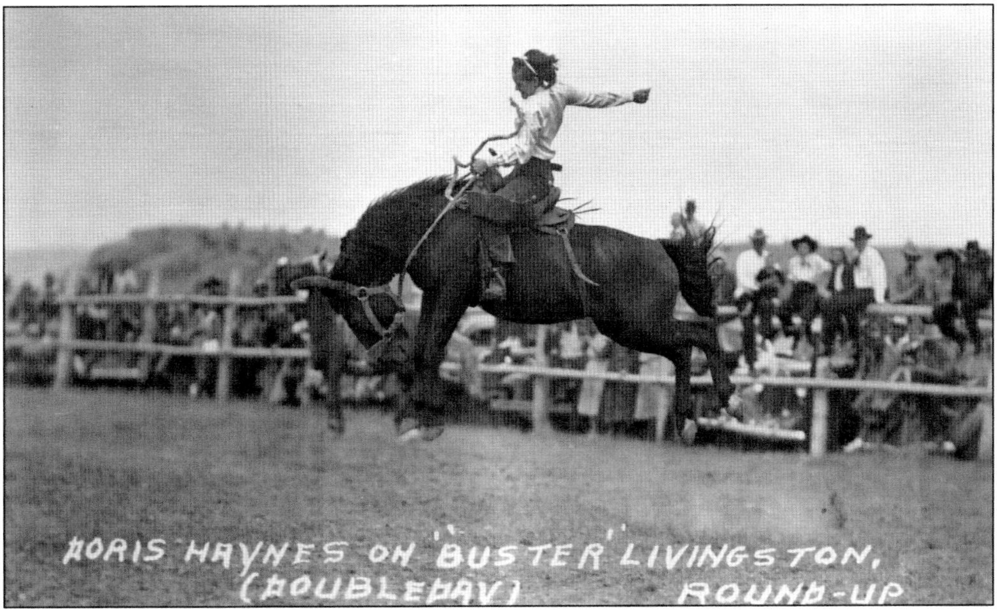

Involvement of women during 1880s Wild West shows spurred participation of cowgirls in early-20th-century rodeos, where they challenged cowboys head-to-head in events such as bronc riding. When rodeo cowboys unionized in 1936, they excluded women from competing against them, declaring these events too dangerous for the fairer sex. Doris Haynes, riding "Buster" in this 1930s postcard, was once advertised as "America's greatest cowgirl bronc rider." (Yellowstone Gateway Museum.)

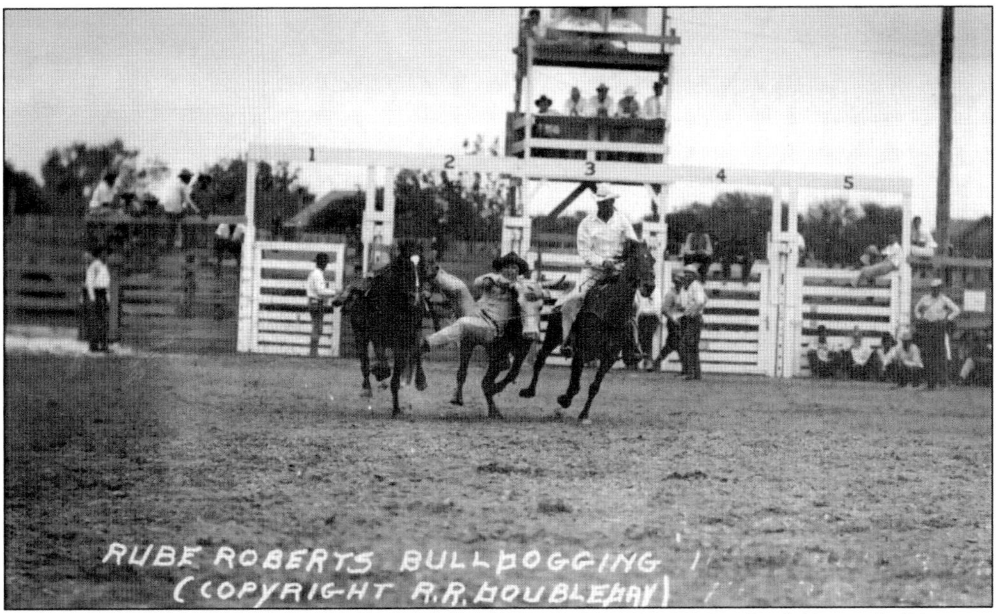

Cowboy Rube Roberts, from the Badlands of South Dakota, was doing what he did best—bulldogging steers—in this 1930s Livingston Rodeo postcard. A 1933 newspaper described him as "stocky, muscular, right good looking" with "quite a bit of good Oklahoma Indian in him." He became the World Champion Bulldogger in a 1930 Fort Worth rodeo with a time of four seconds flat. (Goss Collection.)

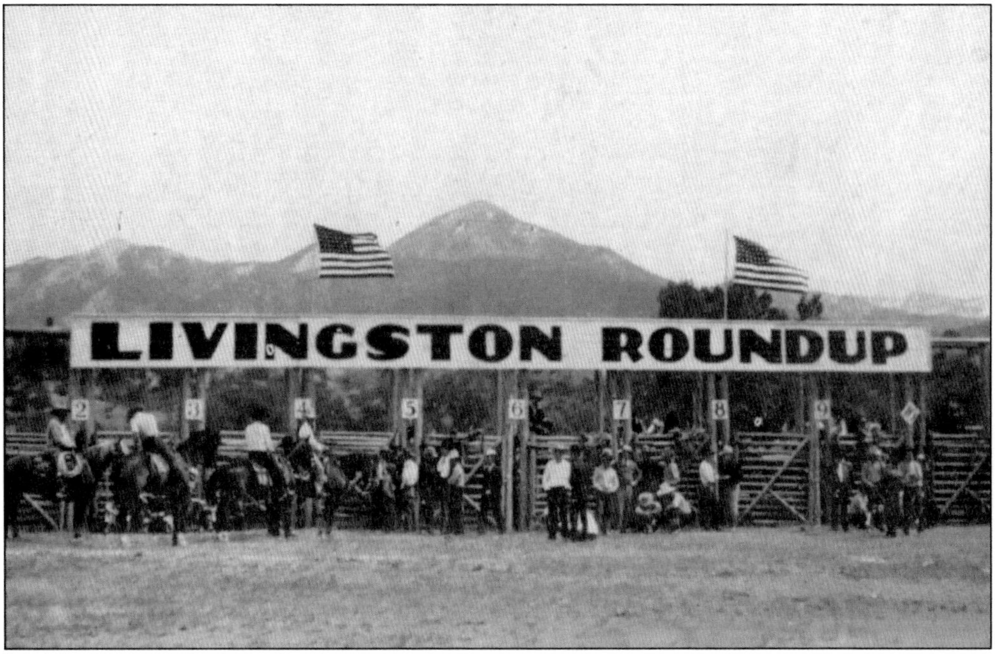

The Livingston Roundup, held every July 2, 3, and 4, has been an annual tradition lasting over 80 years. This three-day extravaganza continues to present, as this 1940s brochure declares, "Three High Fallutin', Rip Snortin', Hell Roarin' Days." Don't miss out on the fun! (Goss Collection.)

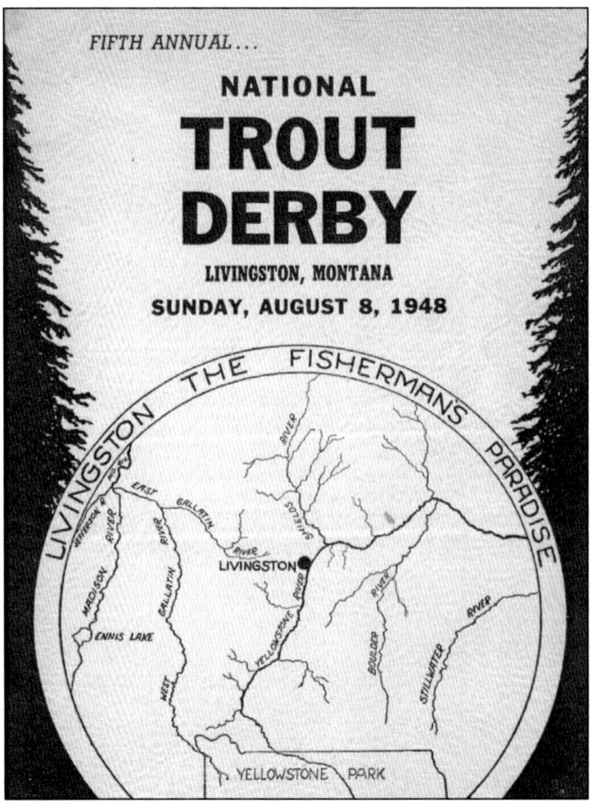

The Annual National Trout Derby was initiated in 1941 as a means to provide entertainment and to entice visitors to the Livingston area, while creating a boost to the economy. Held in early August, the event offered $1,000 prize money to the person catching the largest trout in the Yellowstone River. The derby was held almost yearly until 1977. (Goss Collection.)

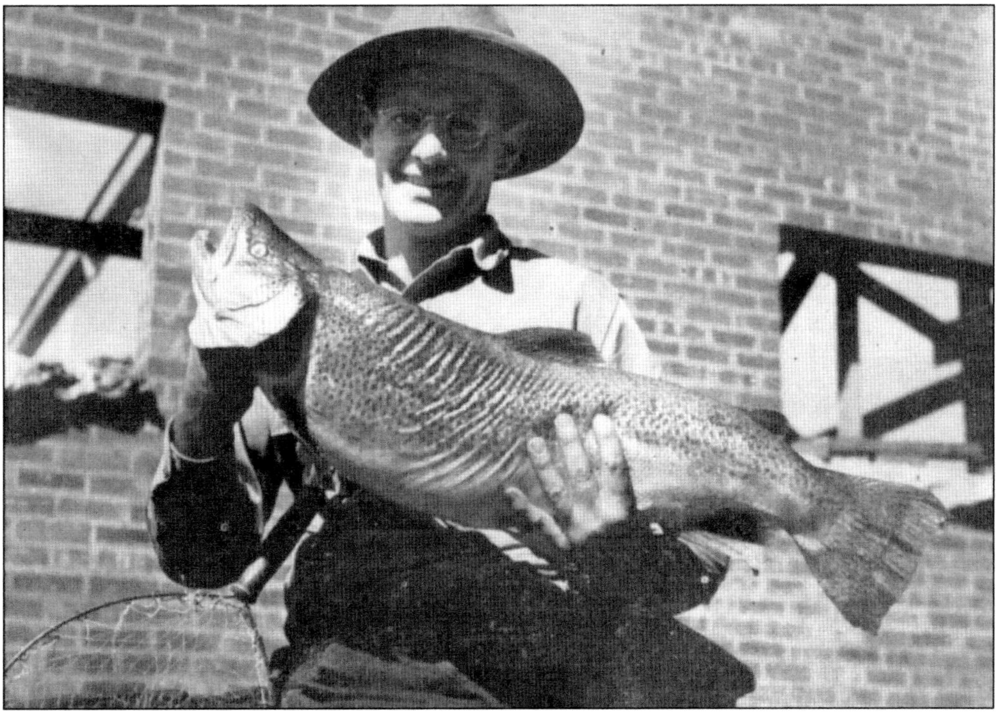

This 14-pound German brown trout was caught in the Yellowstone River in the 1940s within a mile of Livingston's business district. Unfortunately, it was not caught during the official Trout Derby and this unlucky man missed out on $1,000. Still, a catch like this made a great "fishing story" to tell his buddies. (Goss Collection.)

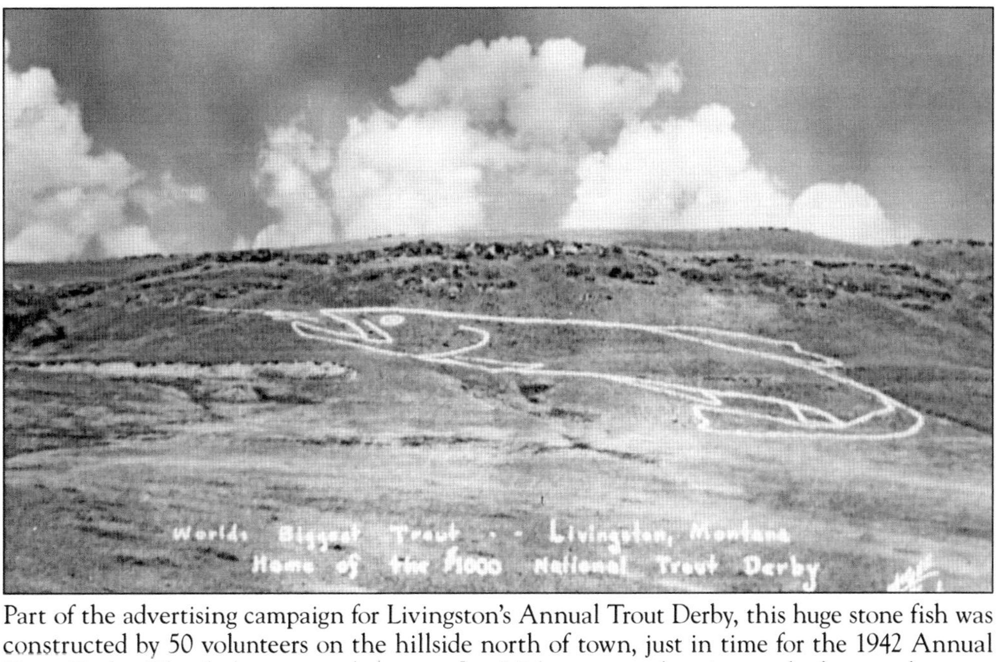

Part of the advertising campaign for Livingston's Annual Trout Derby, this huge stone fish was constructed by 50 volunteers on the hillside north of town, just in time for the 1942 Annual Trout Derby. The derby attracted thousands of fishermen and curious onlookers to the area. (Goss Collection.)

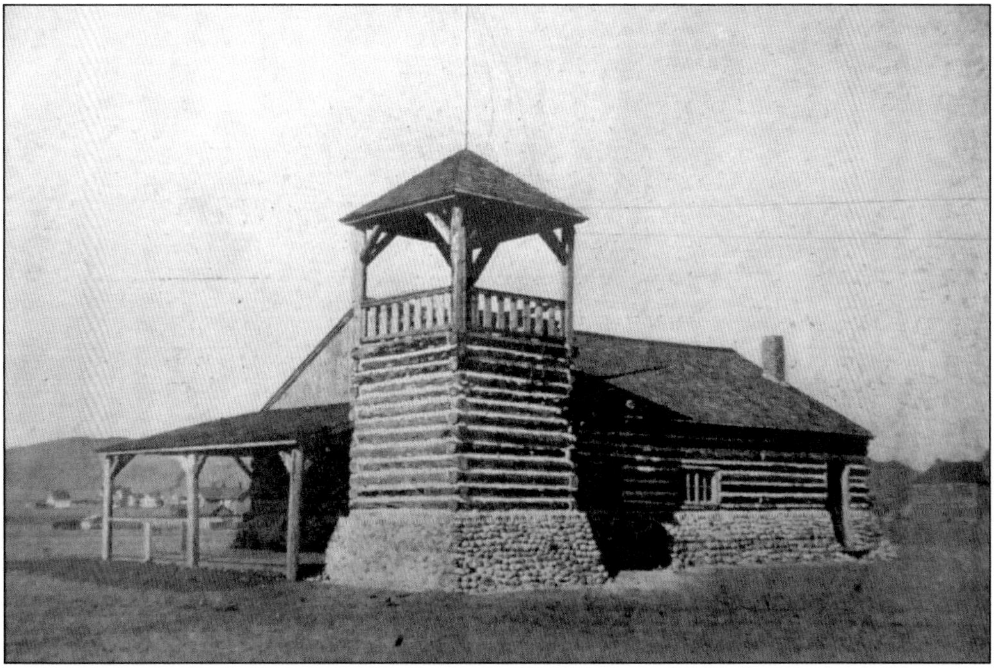

Livingston's quest for cosmopolitan status led to the establishment of the epitome of civilization, a golf course, in 1900. Mayor John Smith spearheaded the community drive to construct the course near the end of 8th Street. The *New York Times* in September 1900 described it "a sporty nine-hole course" and portrayed Livingston as "a progressive town." This log clubhouse was originally located at 124 South 7th Street. (*Rocky Mountain Magazine*.)

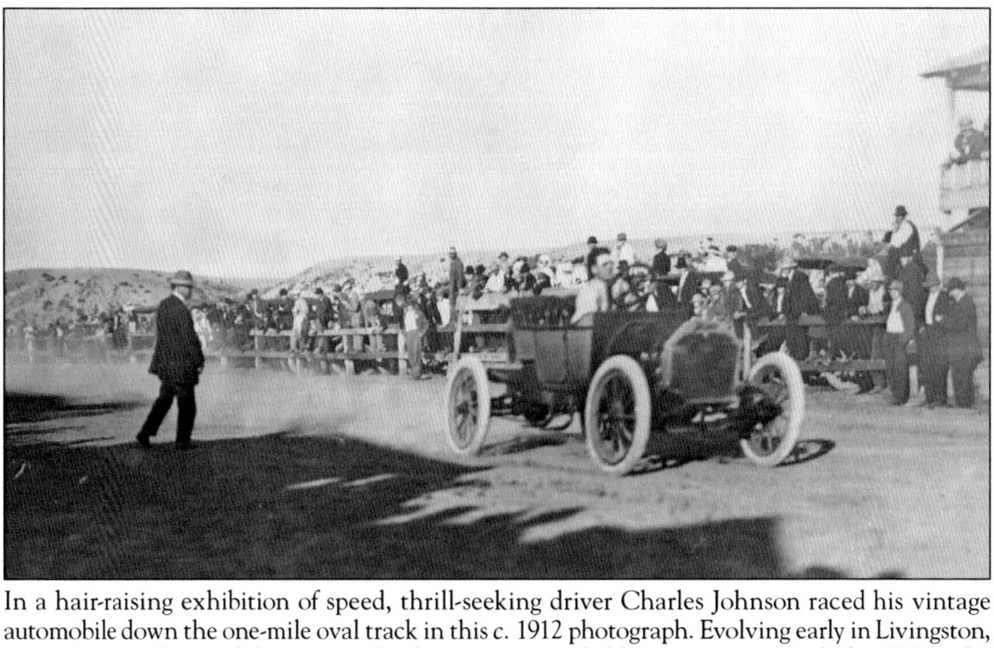

In a hair-raising exhibition of speed, thrill-seeking driver Charles Johnson raced his vintage automobile down the one-mile oval track in this *c.* 1912 photograph. Evolving early in Livingston, auto races complete with loving cups for the winners were held in conjunction with the 1910 Eagles Convention. By 1913, racing had become a regular event at the Park County Fair. (Yellowstone Gateway Museum.)

Eight

Playing Host

As the tourism gateway to Yellowstone National Park, Livingston and its convivial hostelries performed an important role in playing host to the Yellowstone traveler. The Albemarle Hotel became one of the most popular of Livingston's early hotels. An 1884 Sanborn map showed the Albemarle originally located on the corner of 2nd and Park Streets. Also depicted was the under-construction foundation for the future location of the Albemarle Hotel on the corner of Main and Park Streets, which opened in 1886. With an address of 203–207 Park Street, the Elite also commanded a prestigious location for capturing the tourist trade arriving by rail. In May 1903, an advertisement in the *Anaconda Standard* suggested that "when in Livingston stop in at the new Elite Hotel, opposite the depot." According to early maps of Livingston, the city contained dozens of early hotels for the transient trade from 1884 to 1921. Hotels such as the Brunswick, Metropolitan, Yellowstone, Winona, Callender, Sterling, Northern, Livingston, Windsor, and many others played host to thousands of travelers to Yellowstone, but their in-depth histories and extant photographs have yet to be uncovered.

Hunter's Hot Springs, approximately 10 miles east of Livingston, offered a different type of accommodation for travelers with its idyllic mountain resort setting, tennis courts, golf course, and its "remarkably curing" mineral baths. A three-day ticket with round-trip rail fare, two night accommodations, six meals, and bathing privileges sold for $6 for travelers from Bozeman and $10 from Butte.

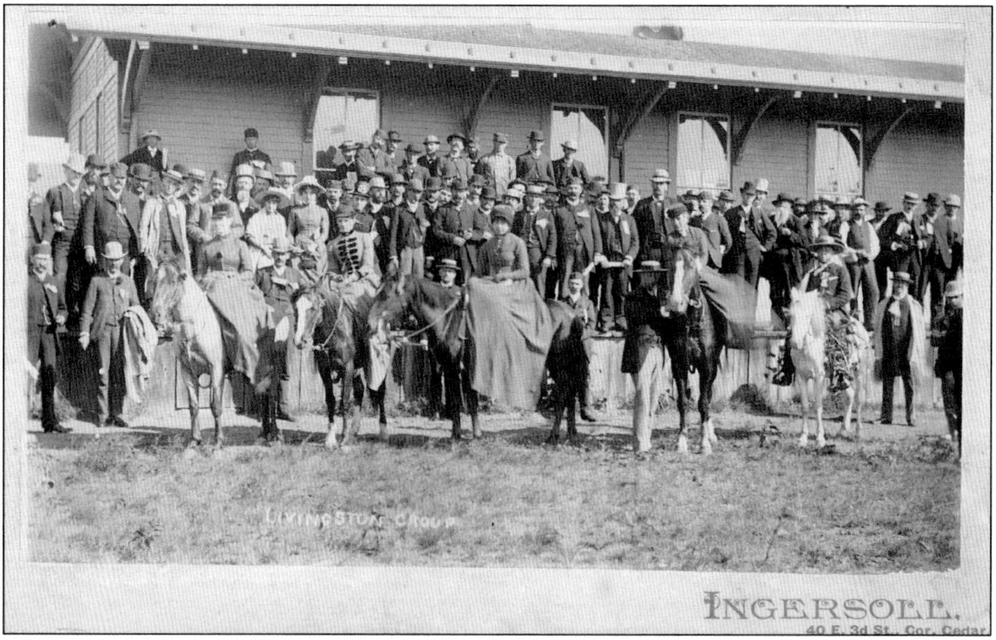

The reverse of this T. W. Ingersoll boudoir view includes a printed advertisement for views of the "Ice Palace," in St. Paul, which was not built until 1886, and a handwritten caption that states, "Livingston group at RR station, early days." If taken between 1886 and 1888 and the handwritten caption is correct, this could be a rare image of the first Livingston NPRR station. Research on this photograph to date has been inconclusive. (Yellowstone Gateway Museum.)

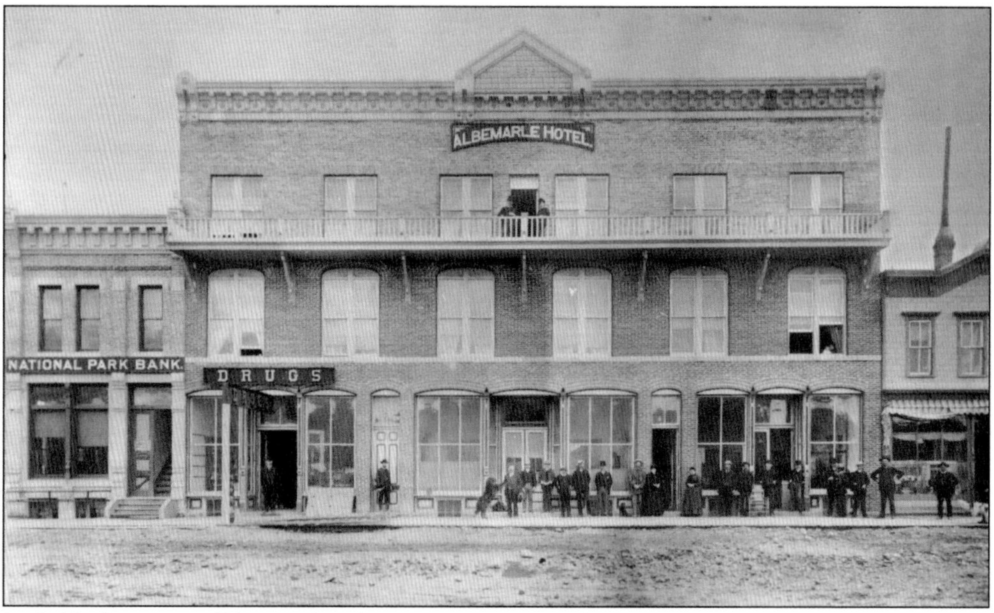

Probably the most well-known hotel in Livingston's early days was the Albemarle Hotel. Originally located on the corner of 2nd and Park Streets, that early building shared space with the Albemarle Sample Room and a bank. Shown a short time after construction in 1886, this impressive new brick edifice on Park and Main Streets replaced the old hotel. The National Park Bank erected the corner building that same year. (Yellowstone Gateway Museum.)

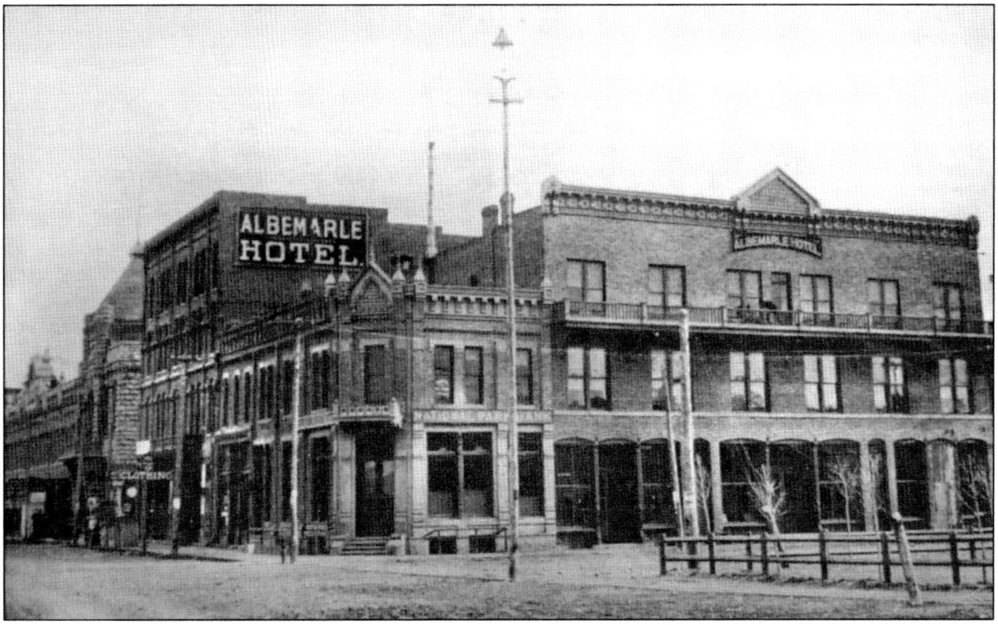

Conveniently located across from the railroad depot, the Albemarle Hotel was a customary stop for visitors to Livingston and Yellowstone. During its first 20 years, the Albemarle was owned or managed by a succession of businessmen that included C. W. Savage, George Wakefield, Benton Hatch, E. C. Waters, William Thompson, and A. O. Newton. The Albemarle Annex, positioned left of the bank, faced Main Street and was built around 1890. (*Livingston Souvenir.*)

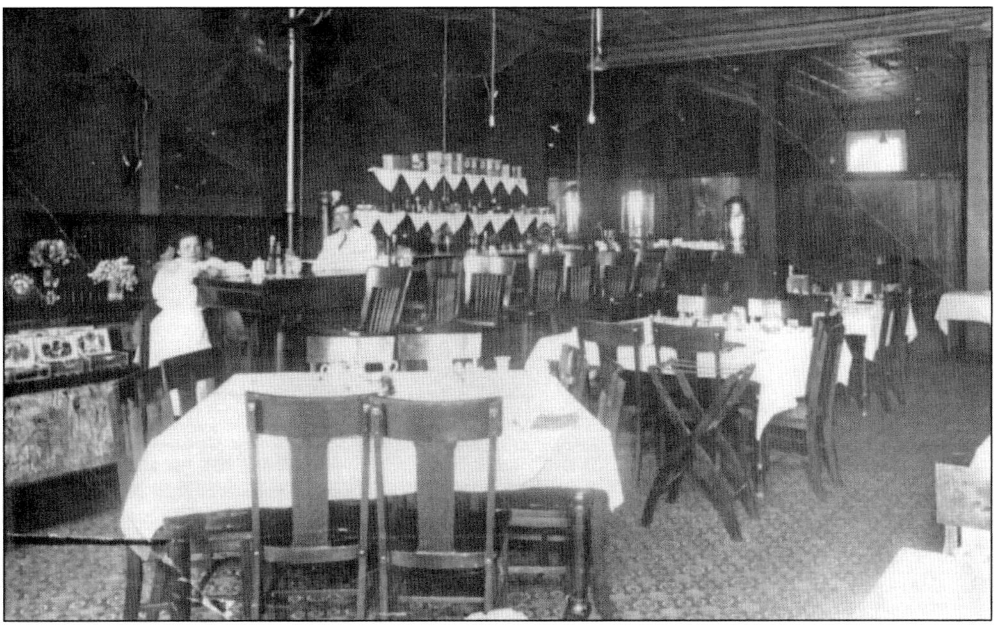

The Albemarle dining room, shown here in 1910 with proprietors Bill Wray and Jennie Sorenson, offered a fine dining experience to the local populace. In 1930, the National Park Bank moved to new quarters, and the following year, the Northern Pacific purchased the hotel for use by their rail passengers. This venerable landmark was demolished in 1958 to make room for the Guest House Motor Hotel. (Yellowstone Gateway Museum.)

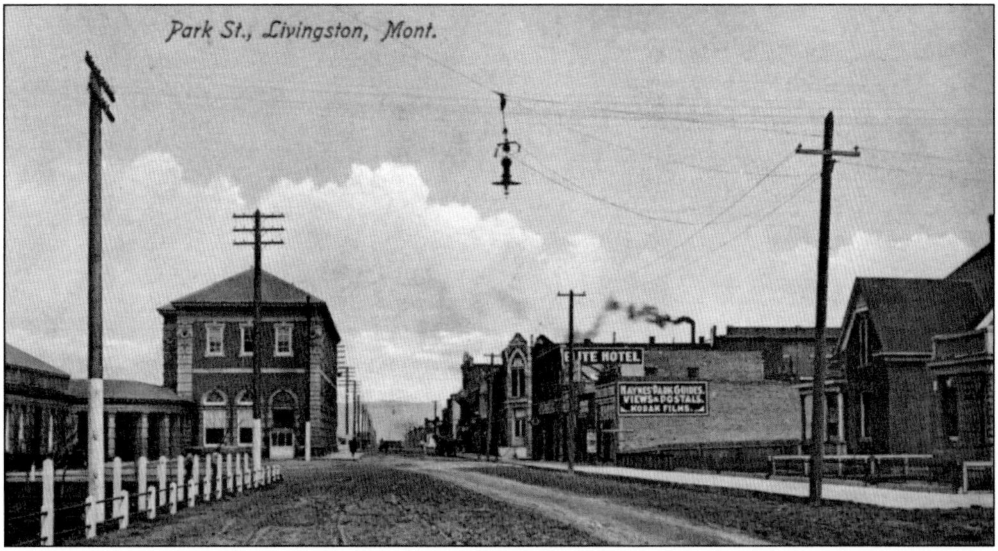

A year after the new depot was dedicated in May 1902, the *Livingston Enterprise* advised travelers to "stop at the new Elite Hotel, opposite the depot." Moving from Big Timber, Montana, around 1903, Josephine "Josie" Kline established this two-story hotel in the heart of the business district on Park Street. Next door, the *Livingston Enterprise* churned out the news, while a neighboring curio store peddled souvenirs to tourists. (Goss Collection.)

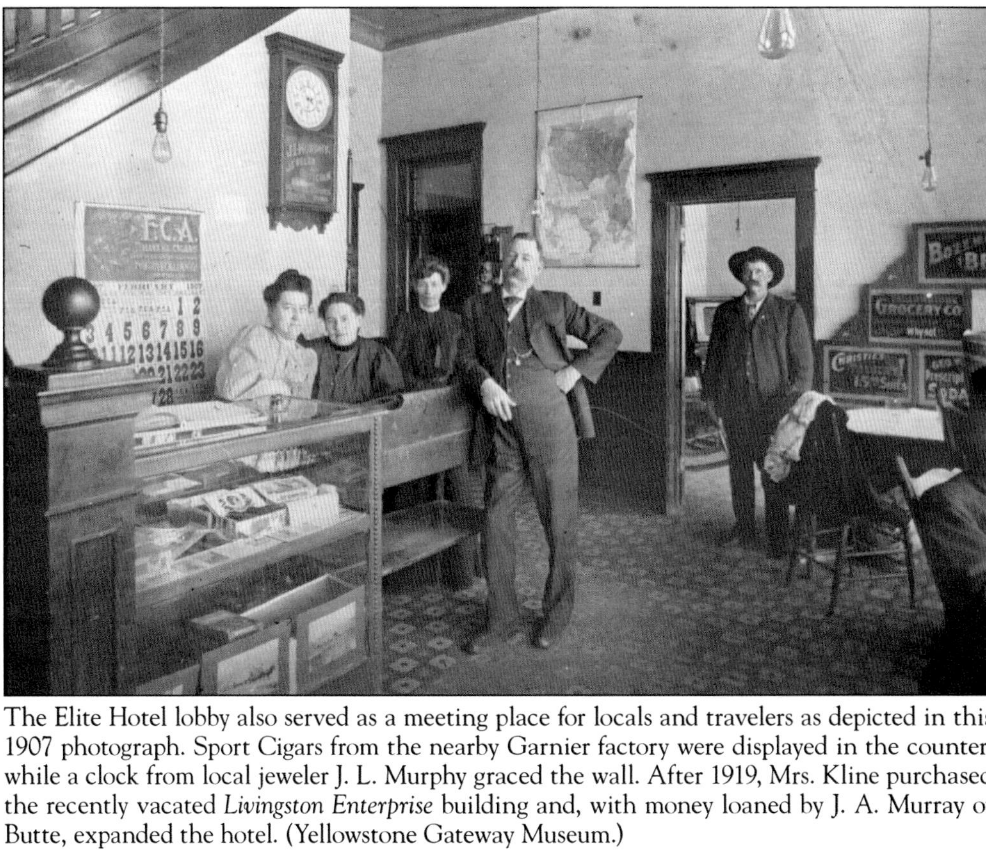

The Elite Hotel lobby also served as a meeting place for locals and travelers as depicted in this 1907 photograph. Sport Cigars from the nearby Garnier factory were displayed in the counter, while a clock from local jeweler J. L. Murphy graced the wall. After 1919, Mrs. Kline purchased the recently vacated *Livingston Enterprise* building and, with money loaned by J. A. Murray of Butte, expanded the hotel. (Yellowstone Gateway Museum.)

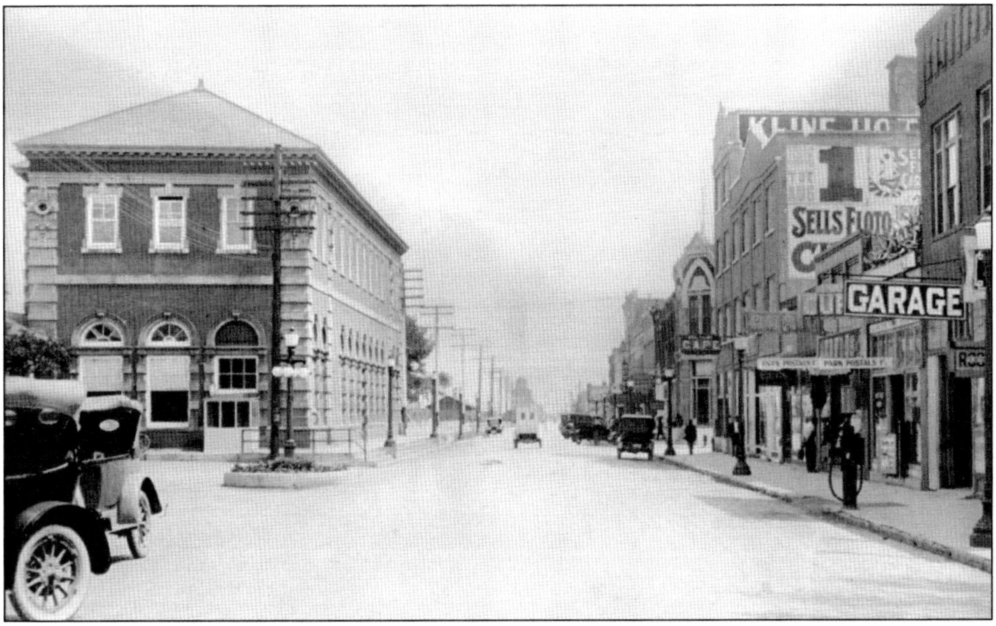

With borrowed money and architects Link & Haire of Bozeman, Josie Kline converted the old *Enterprise* building into hotel rooms and lobby area, added two floors, and boasted of the only elevator service in town. The Elite became the imposing Kline Hotel with the Kline Café located on the corner. However, success was short-lived when J. A. Murray died in 1921, and the debt passed to niece Mae Murray. (Goss Collection.)

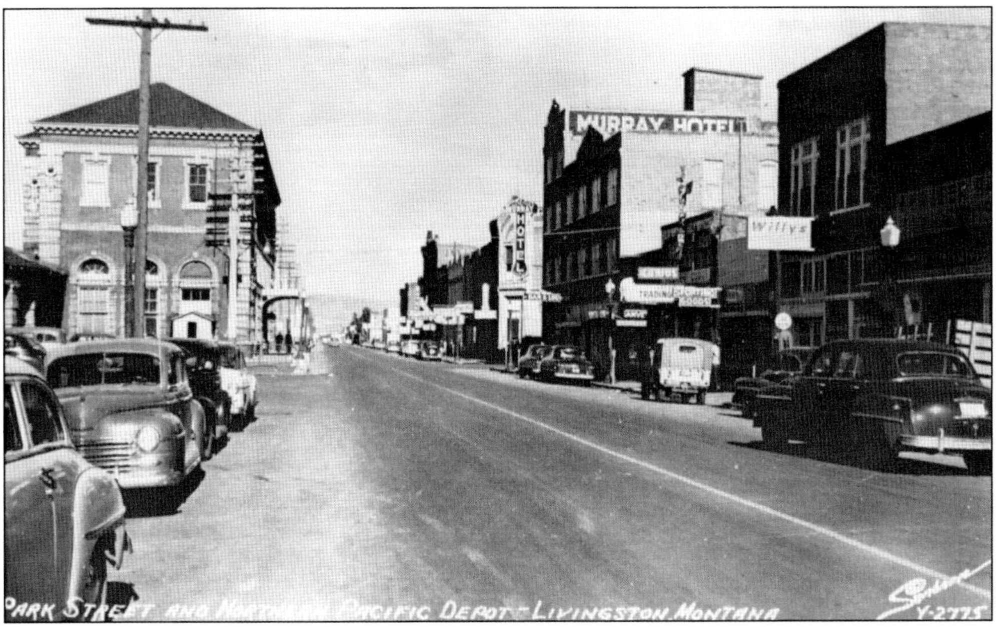

Through legal manipulation, Murray's heirs called in Kline's promissory notes and evicted her from her beloved hotel. In 1924, the "new" Murray Hotel was born. Kline battled for years, and in 1934 with a friend, the "two runaway kids from Montana," hitchhiked to Washington, D.C., to unsuccessfully plead her case. Attracting celebrities such as Will Rogers, Sam Peckinpah, and Warren Oates, the Murray remains a local landmark. (Yellowstone Gateway Museum.)

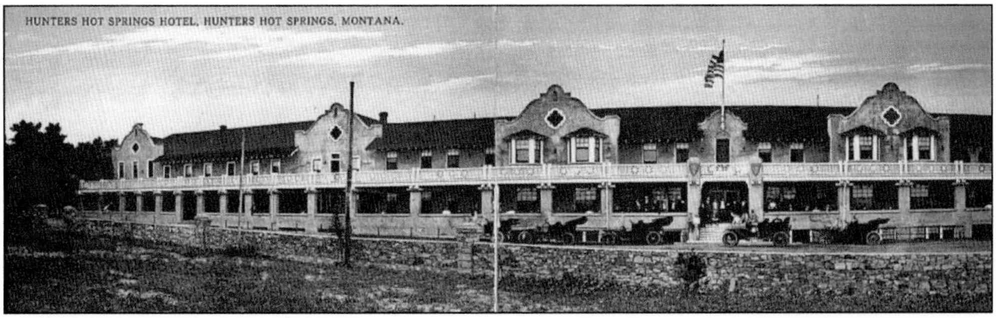

In 1884, A. J. Hunter, founder of Hunter's Hot Springs, was "desirous of disposing of them either by sale or on long lease [to someone] with means to develop the property." Unable to properly develop the area, the new proprietors passed ownership to J. A. Murray of Butte in 1899. Ten years in the planning, the grand Hotel Dakota became a reality in 1909. (Goss Collection.)

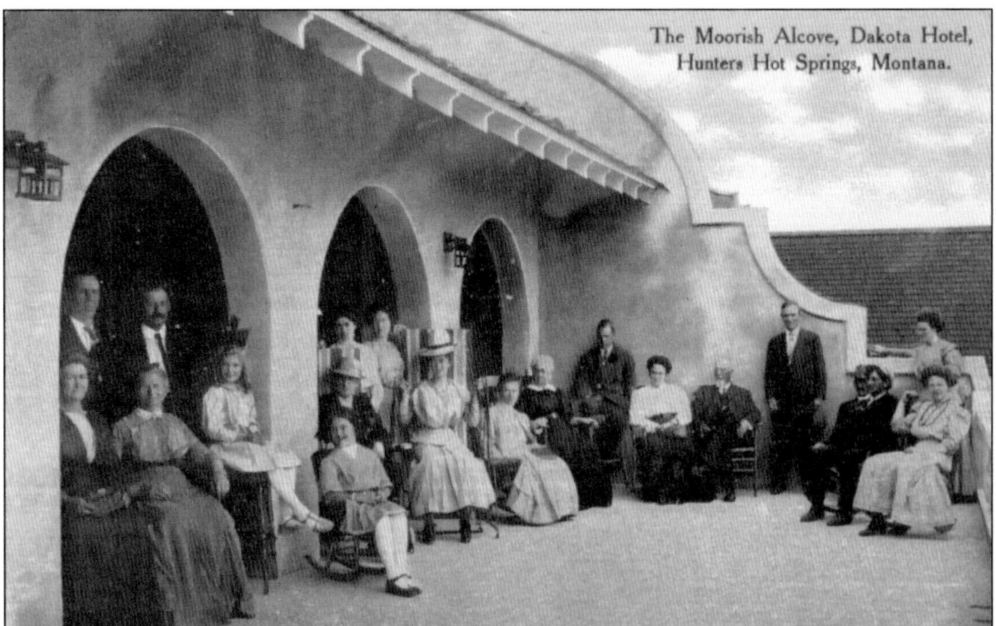

One of the popular social gathering spots at the Hotel Dakota both summer and winter was the Moorish Alcove. Located at the end of the long second-floor porch, this niche faced south and was well protected from the wind and elements. The lure of the curative waters and healthful surroundings attracted visitors from all parts of the country. (Goss Collection.)

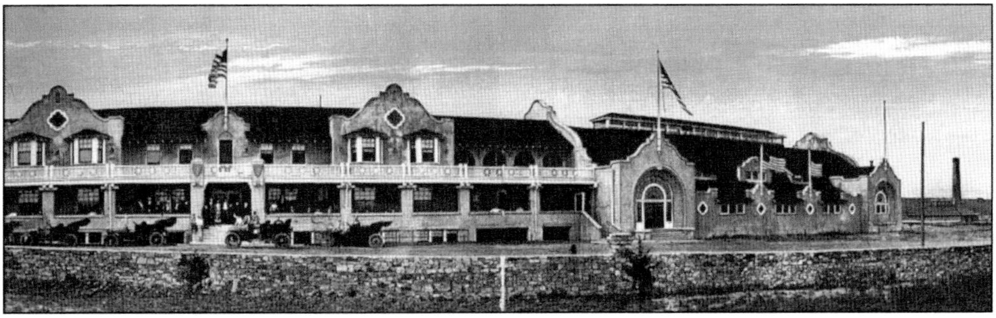

This Moorish-style hotel with its two-story, 400-foot veranda was indeed a marvel. Served by the NPRR at Springdale, the resort soon became the social hot spot of Montana. Guest rooms were equipped with electric lighting, steam heat, and hot and cold running water, while the swimming area included a 50-by-100-foot plunge, gymnasium, and private dressing rooms with attendants. The nearby solarium provided solace for reading, writing, or socializing. (Goss Collection.)

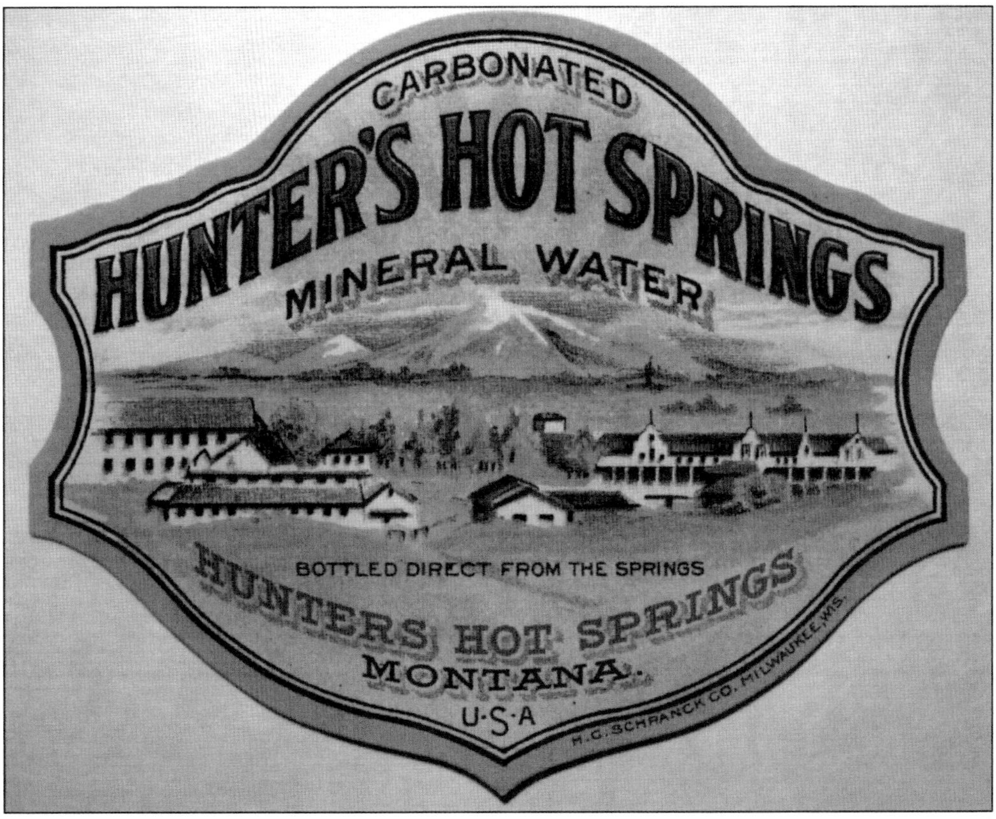

The springs at Hunter's consisted of 27 different springs of varying temperatures. The mineral content of the thermal waters was believed to have medicinal virtues that could aid in treatment of rheumatism, as well as skin, kidney, liver, stomach, and nervous diseases. A bottling plant was built nearby that produced plain and lemon-flavored carbonated mineral water that was marketed throughout the region. (Private collection.)

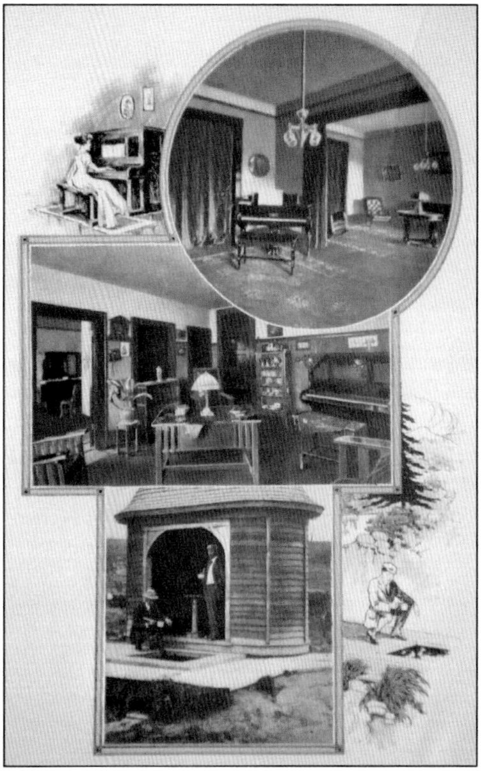

The Springs offered a variety of outdoor entertainment venues that included tennis, golf, dance pavilion, children's playground, gazebos, and fishing. Inside, the Hotel Dakota lobby featured beamed ceilings, wood-paneled walls, piano music, and mission oak furniture that provided a respite for weary travelers. Fine dining with local-grown produce and meat whetted appetites, while liquor flowed freely at the hotel bar. (1910 brochure, Livingston Library.)

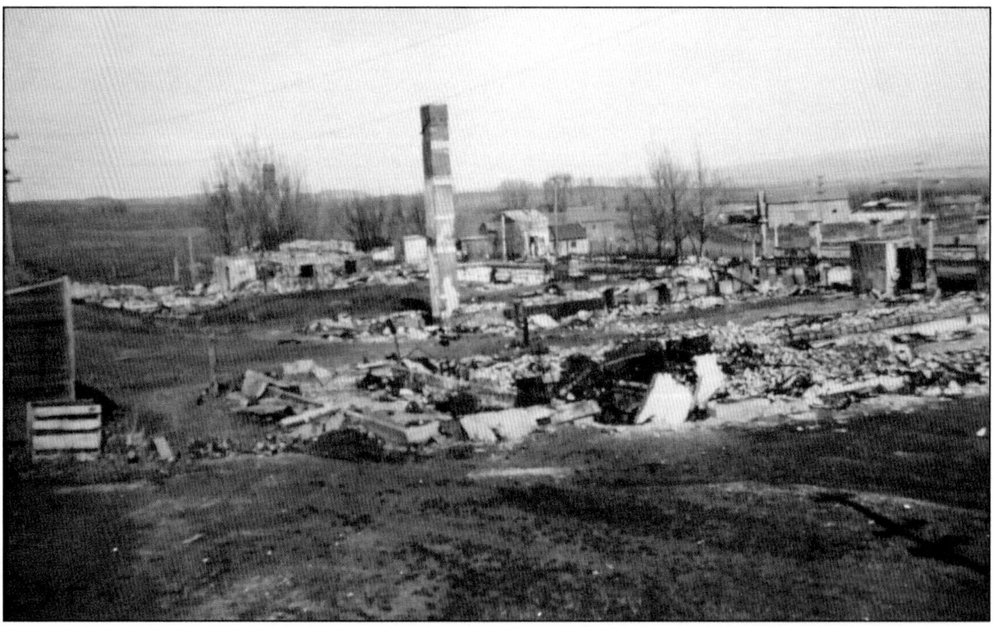

"Blaze Destroys Hunters Hot Springs. Flames Sweep Through Hotel at Dinner Hour. Popular State Resort Burns to Ground in Less Than an Hour." This headline from the *Billings Gazette* of November 4, 1932, spelled the doom of this historic and popular cultural landmark. The lure of the "Magic Waters" that entranced both Native Americans and Euro-Americans alike quickly disappeared and faded into the past, never to be resurrected. (Private collection.)

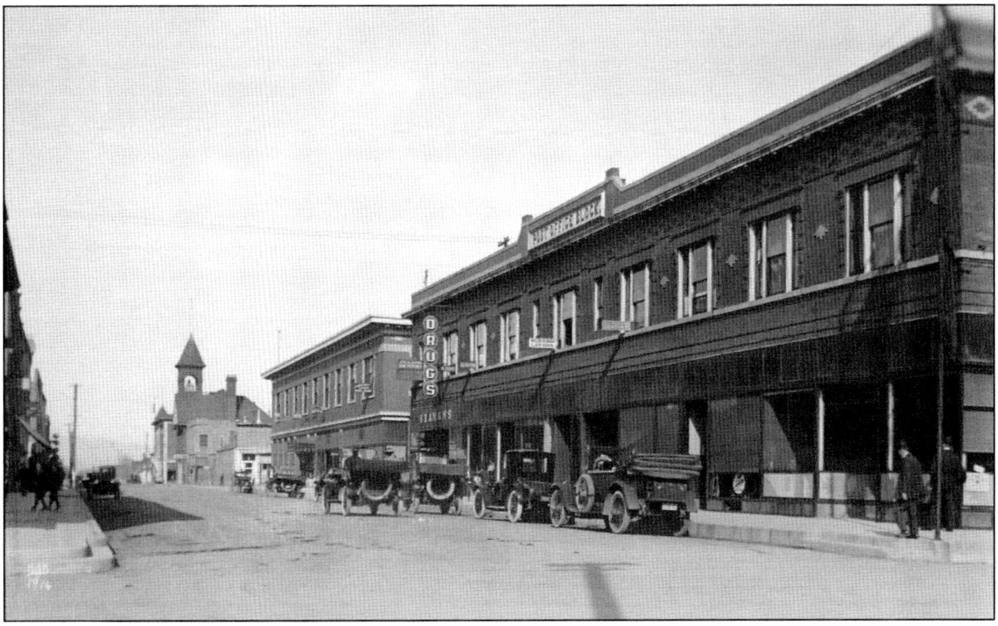

This was the second Park Hotel built on Callender Street after the original 1901 hotel was destroyed by fire in March 1904, along with the Golden Rule and Seaman Drug stores. Owner A. W. Miles immediately rebuilt. It was completed by summer, and George McCarn later took over management and engaged Arthur and Ralph Babbitt to run day-to-day operations. Leaving in 1913, McCarn took over the Hunter's Hot Springs hotel enterprise. (Private collection.)

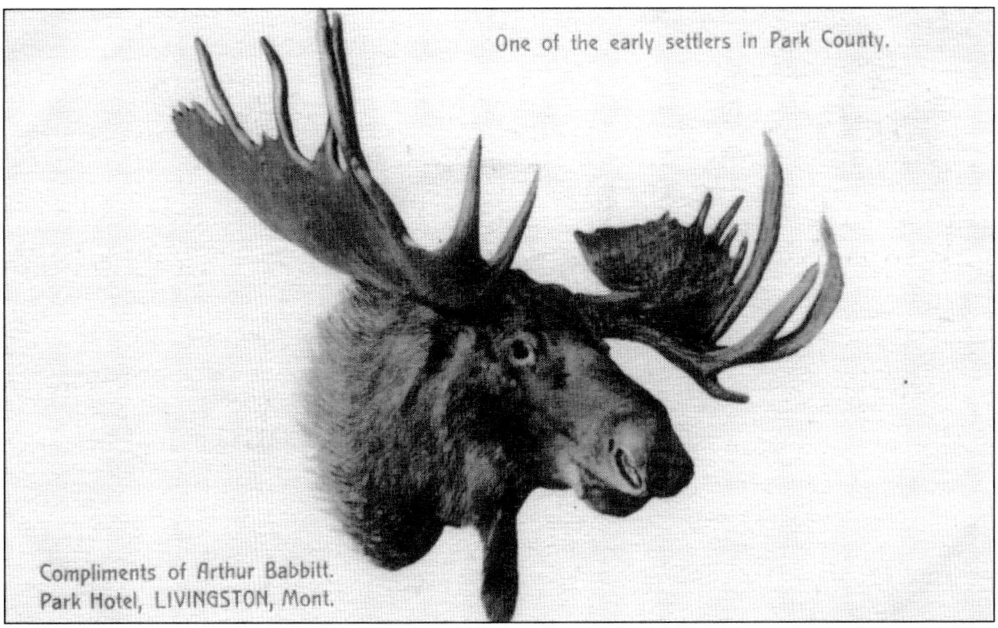

This whimsical postcard advertising the Park Hotel was characteristic of Arthur Babbitt's colorful character. Proprietor of the Park Hotel and dining room in the early 1900s, Babbitt's plaid pants and fancy vests were remembered as adding pizzazz to the dingy dining room. His "surprise plates" brought in traveling salesmen from around the state as he became famous for his unusual meals that served up a fun-filled dining adventure. (Goss Collection.)

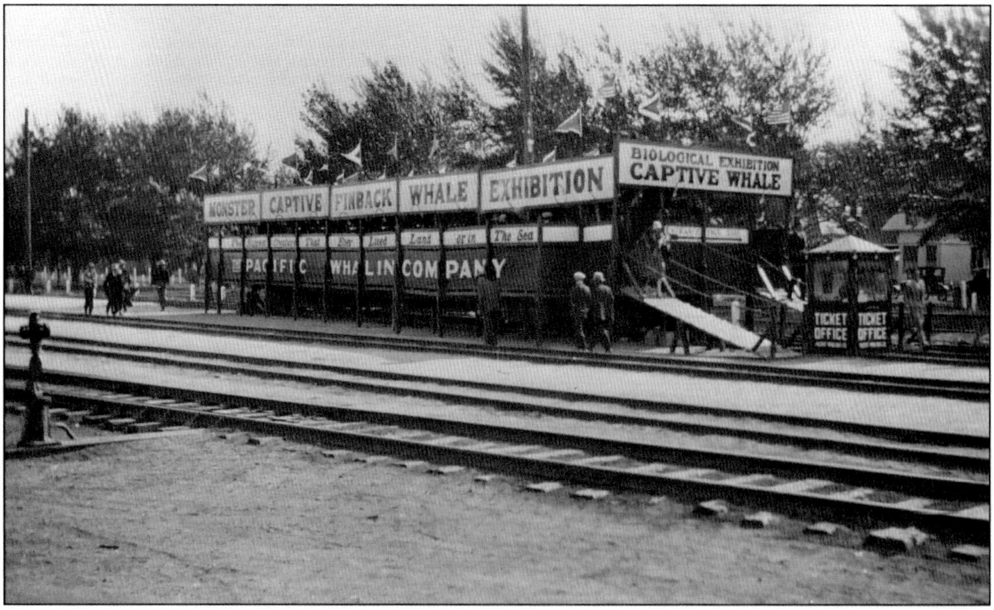

The *Livingston Enterprise* regaled readers on September 20, 1930, with "a whale of a tale" by announcing the upcoming exhibition of the largest fin-backed whale ever captured. This 65-foot preserved whale captivated Livingston audiences in its specially constructed 85-foot railroad car with glass viewing crypt September 27–28. This "whale of an exhibit" coincided with the release of the 1930 film *Moby Dick* starring John Barrymore. (Yellowstone Gateway Museum.)

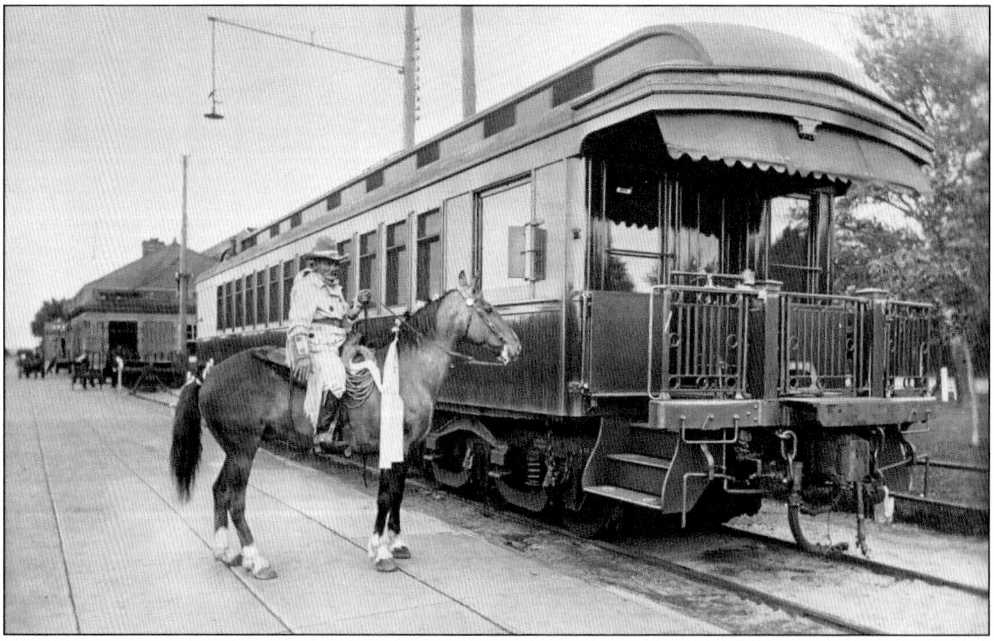

Observation cars such as this were originally built as emigrant sleepers by the Pullman Palace Car Company in 1884. Converted in 1913 to open-air "rubberneck cars" in St. Paul, Minnesota, these cars operated between Livingston and Gardiner on the NPRR Yellowstone Park Branch Line. Completely exposed to the scenery as well as the weather, these open-sided cars offered an unobstructed view from large cozy armchairs. (Yellowstone Gateway Museum.)

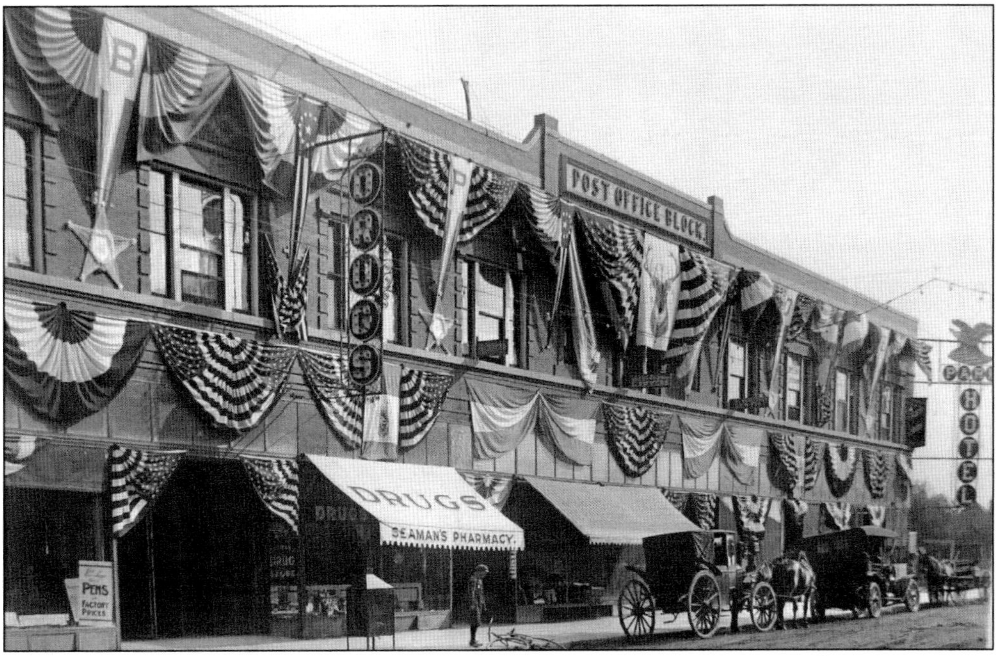

"Livingston welcomes the Elks of the Treasure state and their ladies," announced the *Anaconda Standard* newspaper on August 8, 1910, when Livingston hosted the statewide Elks Convention. The gaily decorated city featured activities that included parades, street pageants, band concerts, luncheons, ball games, and automobiles rides originating from the Park Hotel. Elks members were exhorted to bring "wives, sweethearts, sisters, mothers" to the grand ball that climaxed the three-day festivities. (Private collection.)

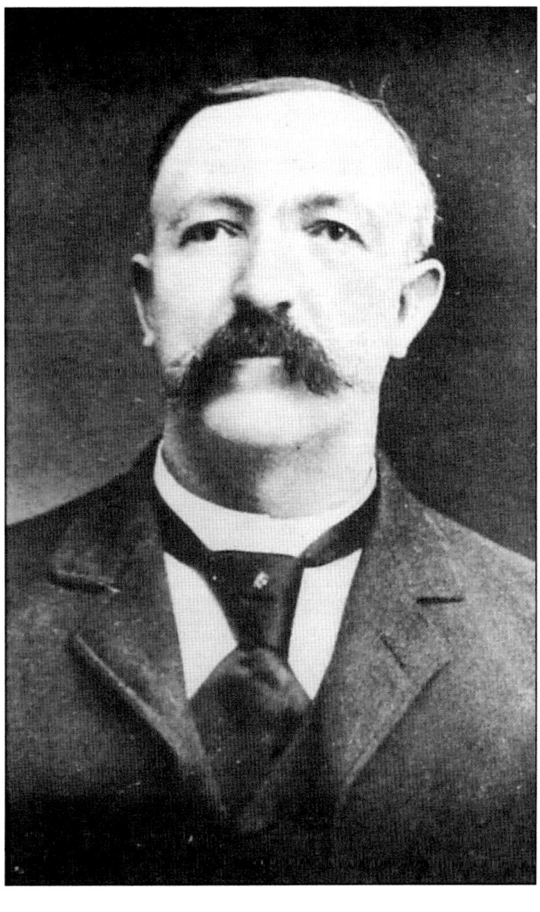

Emigrating from Germany in 1880, William Grabow arrived at Livingston in 1884. He labored six years before acquiring the wherewithal to establish the Tivoli Lodging House, which included restaurant and spirits. Early in 1911, William and his wife, Elizabeth, opened the three-story Grabow Hotel on East Callender Street, featuring café, bar, and mission-style lobby. William died unexpectedly during the 1918 flu epidemic, leaving Elizabeth and sons to manage the enterprise. (*Livingston Souvenir.*)

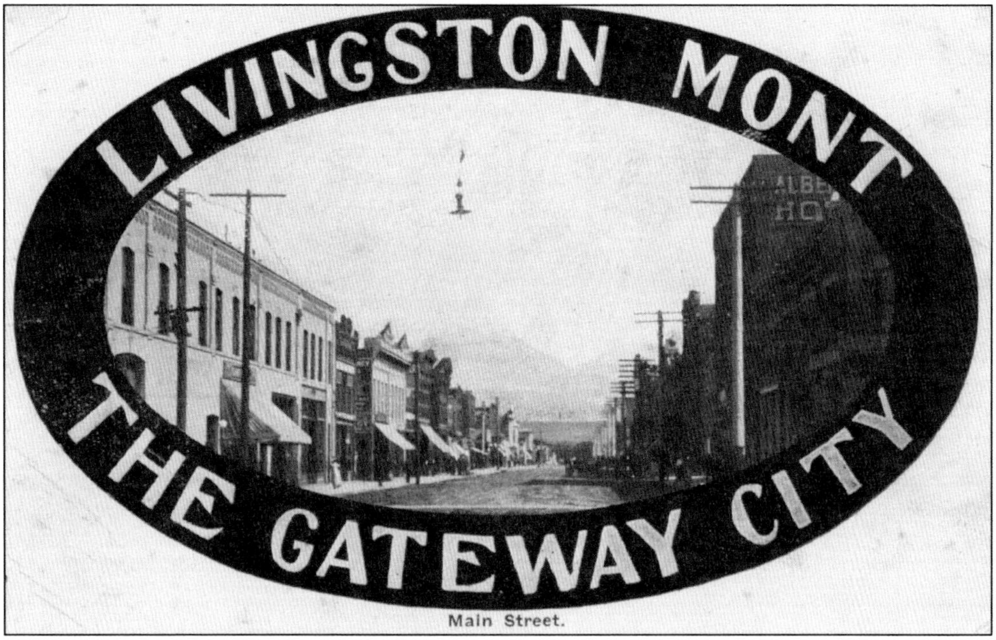

Situated at the junction of the NPRR's main line and the Yellowstone Park Branch Line, Livingston in 1883 became the Gateway City to America's first national park. Livingston's close proximity to world-class fly fishing, breathtaking scenic horseback rides, adventurous hiking trails, and spectacular wild game hunting bestowed another nuance to this postcard term as the town also became known as the gateway city of recreation. (Goss Collection.)

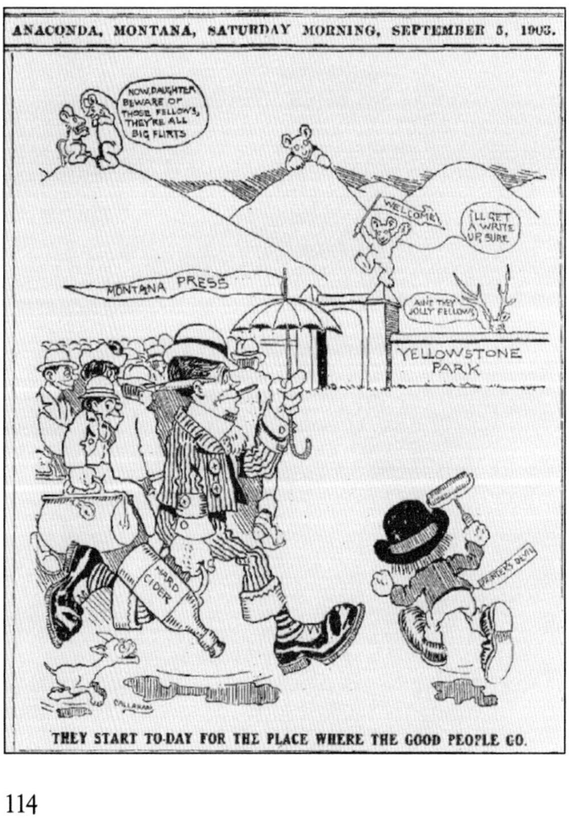

"They're in Livingston" and "They're Having Jolly Time" read the *Anaconda Standard* upon arrival of the Montana Press Association in Livingston on an annual pilgrimage that in September 1903 included a Yellowstone tour. The town rolled out the red carpet as the group made merry the first night in Livingston. While at Mammoth Hot Springs Hotel, the newspapermen and wives reveled to a Chicago orchestra at the Press Ball. (*Anaconda Standard*.)

Nine

All Aboard for Yellowstone

In late August 1883, the Northern Pacific Railroad completed its Yellowstone Park Branch Line to Cinnabar, Montana, 51 miles south of Livingston. From Livingston, Yellowstone's original gateway, passengers would travel along the Yellowstone River, making whistle-stops along the way in small rural communities such as Emigrant, Montana. Continuing through picturesque Paradise Valley and slinking along the craggy cliffs of Yankee Jim canyon, the train deposited passengers in Cinnabar from 1883 until 1902, and thereafter in Gardiner from 1903 until the 1950s.

Debarking passengers would then board the Yellowstone Park Transportation Company's six-horse Talley-Ho stagecoaches or the four-horse touring coaches of a myriad of independent touring operations. Outfits such as the Wylie Camping Company and the Shaw & Powell Camping Company offered economy as well as comfort with their complete transportation and tent-style accommodation packages. Closing a romantic era in Yellowstone's history in 1917, YPTCo traded their Talley-Ho coaches for auto stages manufactured by the White Motor Company. When passenger rail service to Gardiner ceased in the 1950s, these yellow buses transported rail passengers from Livingston.

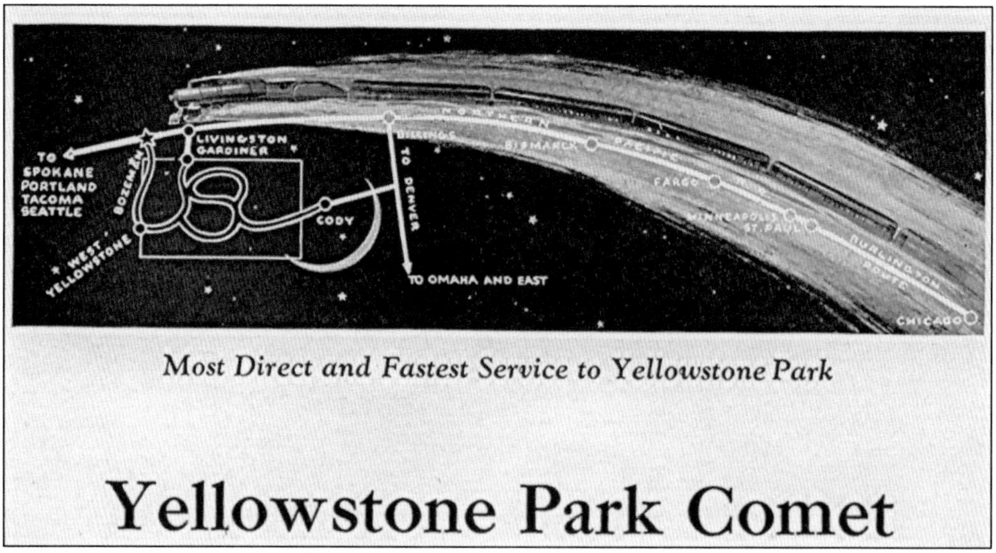

Whisking passengers along the Northern Pacific route from Minneapolis to Seattle, the train stopped in Livingston, where Wonderland-bound travelers transferred to the Yellowstone Park Branch Line. The railroad provided Pullman Sleeping Car Service to Livingston as early as 1890 and Cinnabar by 1895. It became known as the *Yellowstone Park Comet* in 1923, competing with the Union Pacific's *Yellowstone Special* to West Yellowstone. (1928 NPRR brochure.)

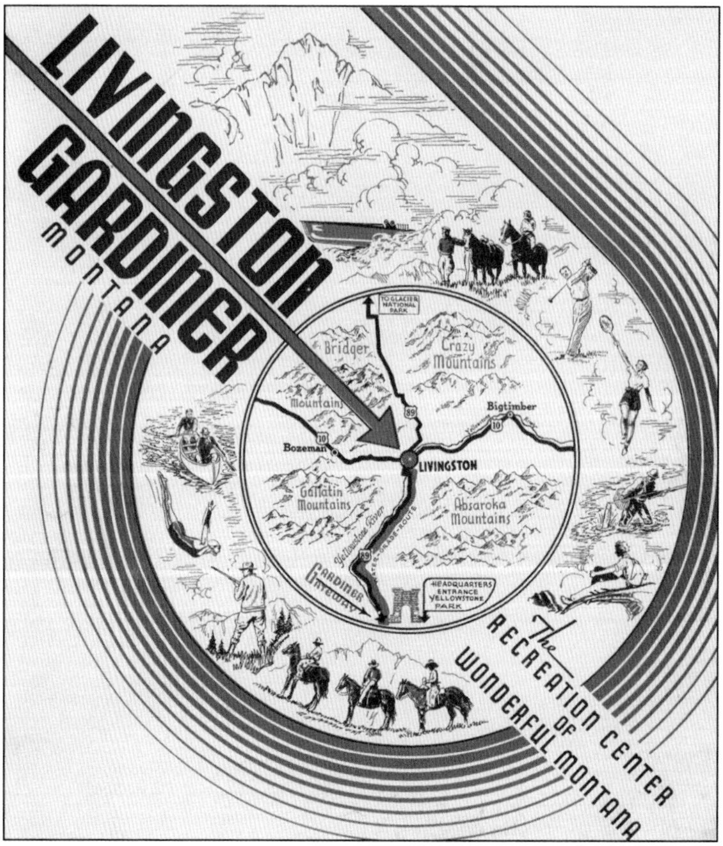

This 1940s brochure advertised Livingston as the "Recreation Center of Wonderful Montana" to help attract visitors. In addition to the well-known attractions in Yellowstone, Livingston drew on other lesser-known recreational opportunities that were available in Park County. These paradisiacal activities included boating, swimming, horseback riding, fishing, hunting, tennis, and golf. (Goss Collection.)

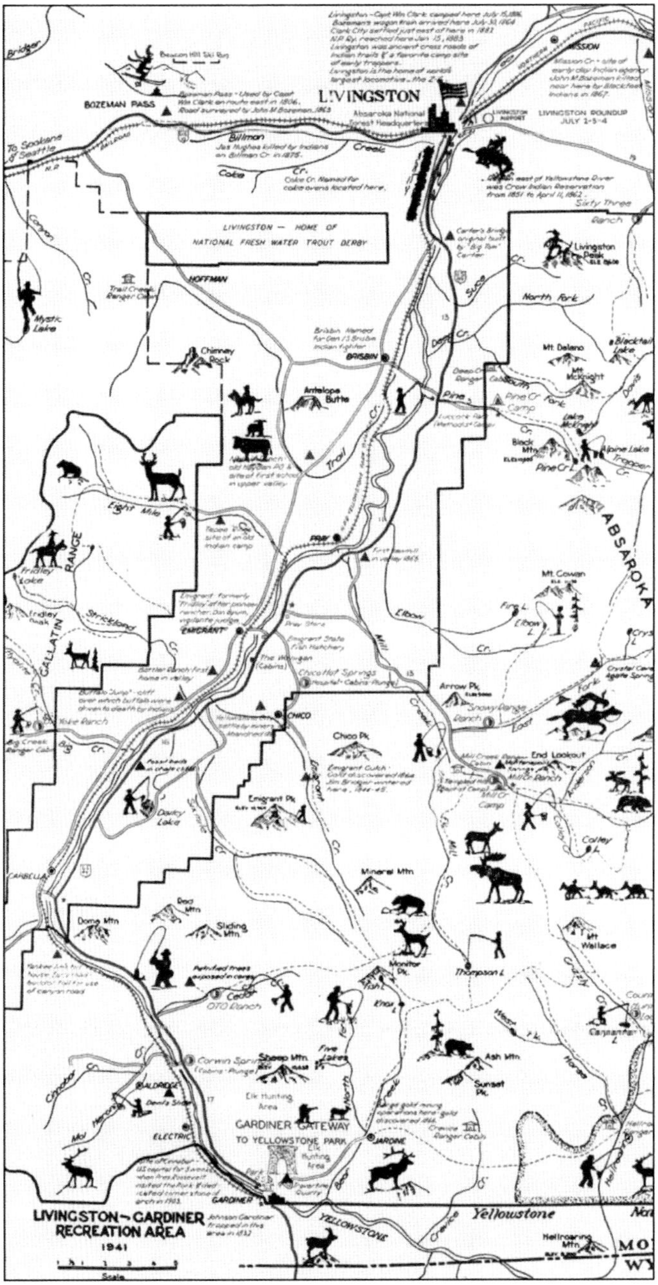

The route from Livingston to Gardiner was filled with historical and activity-laden enclaves to be explored by the adventurous tourist. The Yellowstone Park Branch Line of the Northern Pacific made stops along the way at Brisbin, Pray, Emigrant, Carbella, Corwin Springs, and Electric prior to reaching its final destination at Gardiner. Near Emigrant, one could soak in the invigorating waters of Chico Hot Springs, view buffalo jumps along the basalt cliffs, or look for fossils in the chalk cliffs above the Yellowstone River. Passing through the narrow defiles of the canyon south of Carbella, the railroad bed followed Yankee Jim's old toll road. Visitors stopping at Corwin Springs could luxuriate in the naturally heated swimming pool or venture to the OTO Ranch, the first dude ranch in Montana. (Goss Collection.)

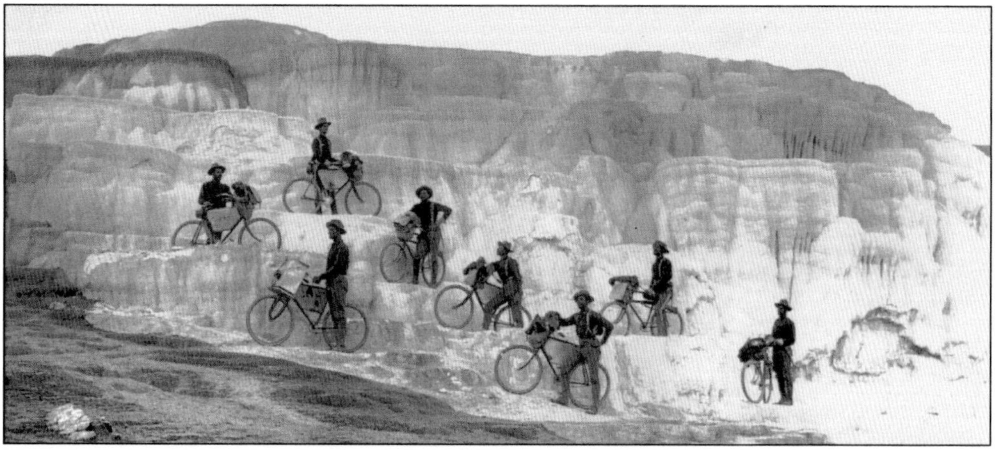

In an experiment to test the mettle of a bicycle corps against the continued reliance on horses for army transportation, Lt. J. A. Moss and eight black soldiers rode from Fort Missoula, Montana, to Mammoth Hot Springs in Yellowstone National Park in August 1896. Riding bicycles provided by Spaulding, Moss's wheeled infantry included Sergeant Green, Corporal Williams, Musician Brown, and Privates Johnson, Proctor, Haynes, Forman, and Finley. (Yellowstone National Park.)

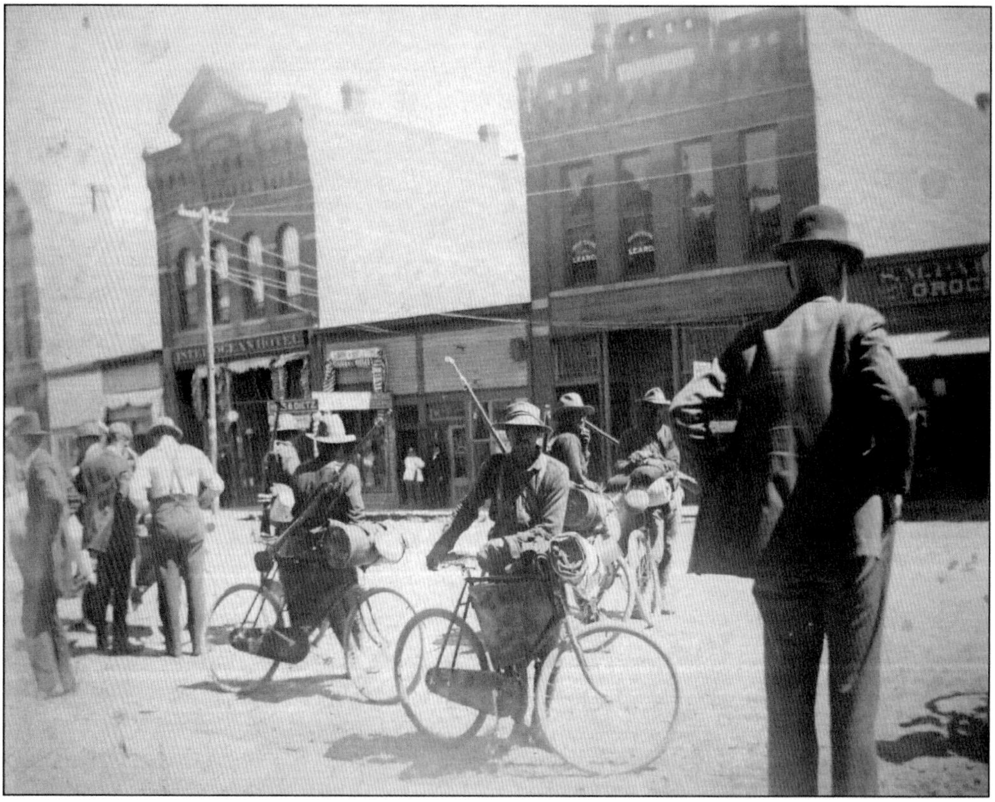

The ultimate test of Lieutenant Moss's bicycle corps began late June 1897 when he and 20 black troopers embarked on a 40-day, 2,000-mile trip from Fort Missoula, Montana, to St. Louis, Missouri. Captured in this image on Livingston's Main Street, the cyclists displayed the 77 pounds of gear carried by each soldier, which included rifles, ammunition, shelter tents, underclothes, cooking utensils, axes, ropes, tires, and bicycle repair kits. (Private collection.)

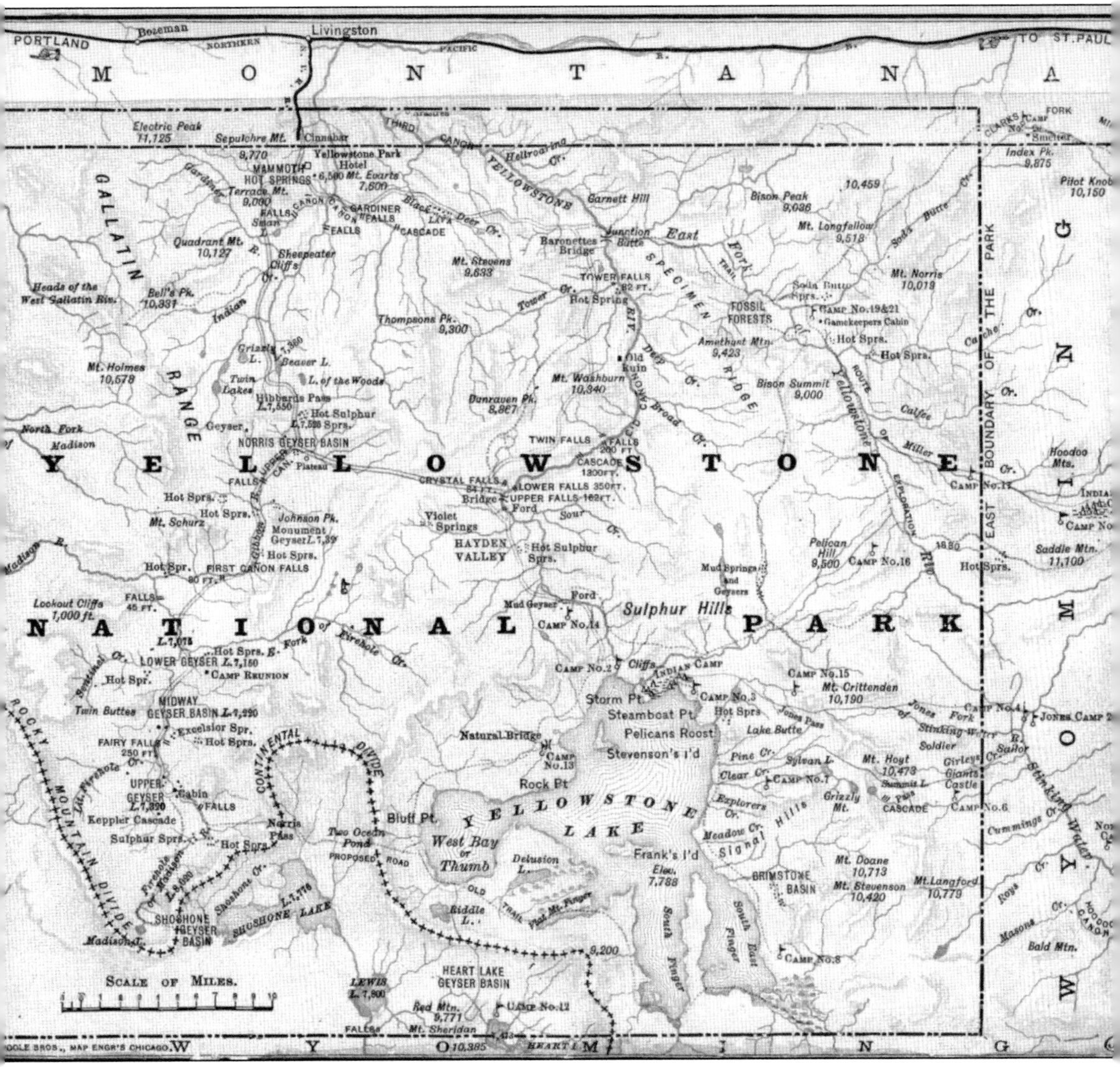

By the dawn of the 20th century, Yellowstone had become a premier western destination for thousands of American and European travelers. This 1888 map from the Northern Pacific Railroad's Wonderland series of brochures laid out principle features, accommodations, and the route of Yellowstone's grand tour. After a stop in Livingston, passengers boarded the Yellowstone Park Branch Line and traveled south through two rugged canyons as well as picturesque Paradise Valley. Arriving in Cinnabar from 1883 to 1902, and Gardiner from 1903 until the late 1950s, travelers alighted from the steaming iron horse and climbed aboard stagecoaches. With a crack of the whip over the heads of stamping and snorting steeds, the four- and six-horse teams with their equally raring-to-go passengers dashed into the "Wonderland of the West." (Watry Collection.)

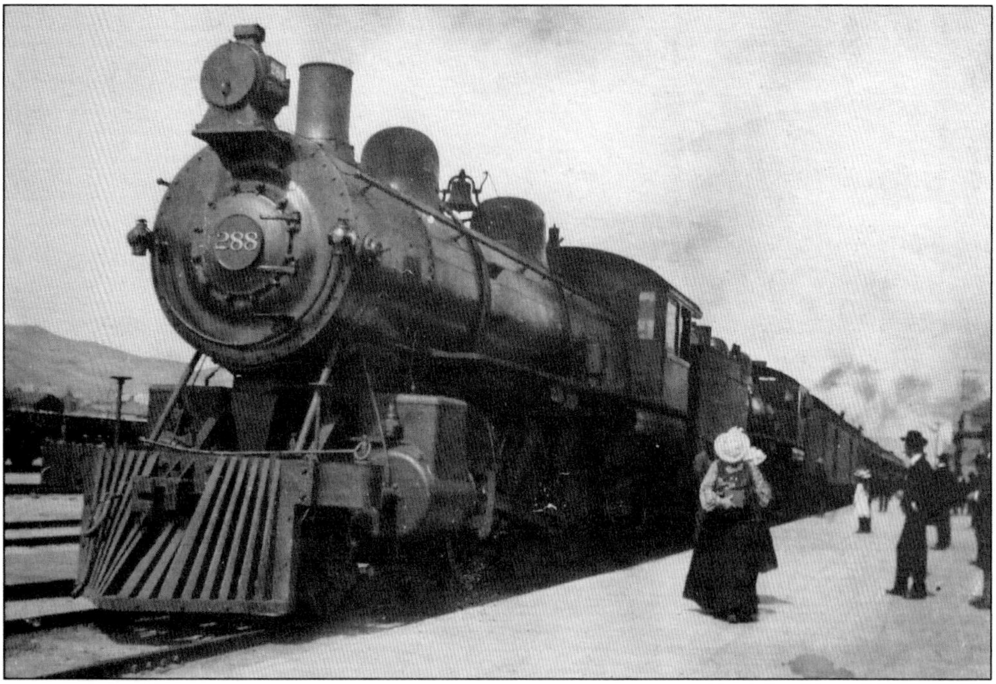

Dwarfed by the massive locomotive, these passengers on Livingston's depot platform in this 1890s image seemed to be awaiting the anticipated moment of departure. With the conductor's call of "All Aboard," and the melodious whistle that signaled their imminent farewell to Livingston, thousands of travelers such as these boarded the awaiting passenger cars and rode the rails to the NPRR's prized destination, Yellowstone National Park. (Private collection.)

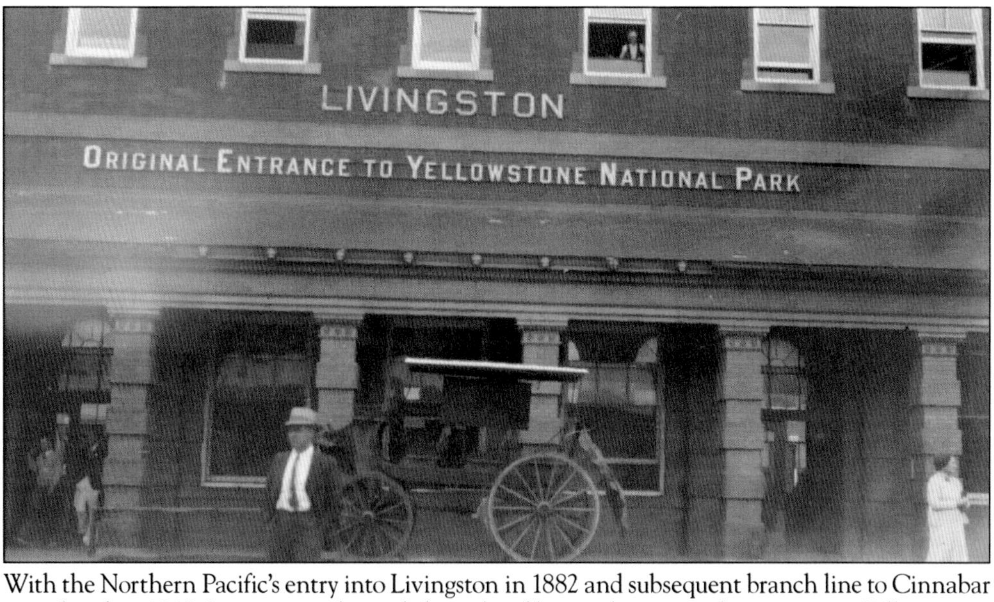

With the Northern Pacific's entry into Livingston in 1882 and subsequent branch line to Cinnabar completed in 1883, Livingston claimed the title of being the original entrance to Yellowstone. While intrepid travelers ventured on horseback, in their own wagons, on bicycles, and on foot via various routes to Yellowstone, it was 25 years before a competing railroad reached another park entrance. (Goss Collection.)

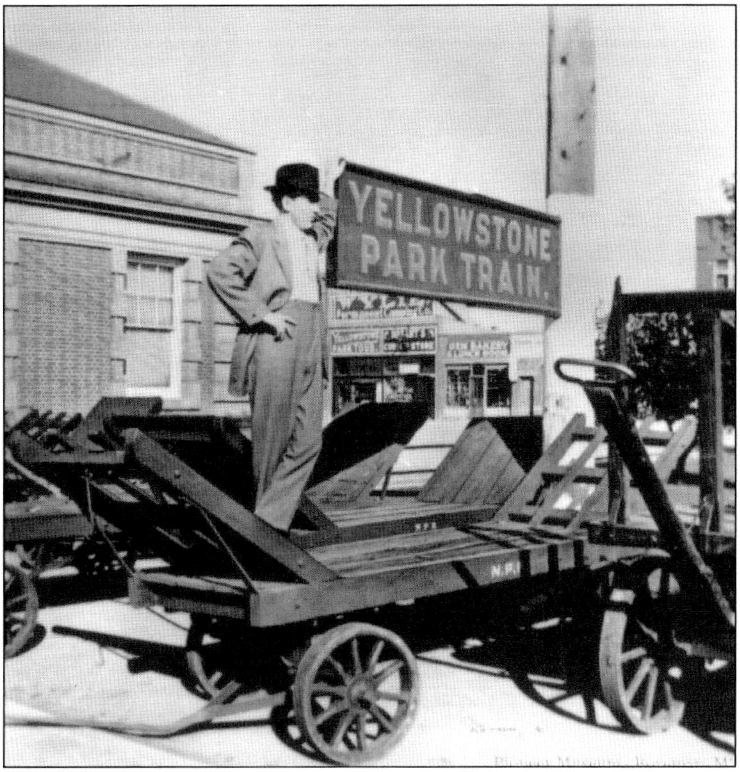

Dozens of hand-drawn baggage carts such as these lined Livingston's depot platform in readiness for the arrival or departure of the NPRR's Yellowstone Park Branch Line train. Visible in the background is the ticket office for the Wylie Permanent Camping Company that operated popular tent-style tours of Yellowstone. Livingston businessman A. W. Miles owned and operated the camping company from 1906 through the end of the 1916 season. (Pioneer Museum, Bozeman, Montana.)

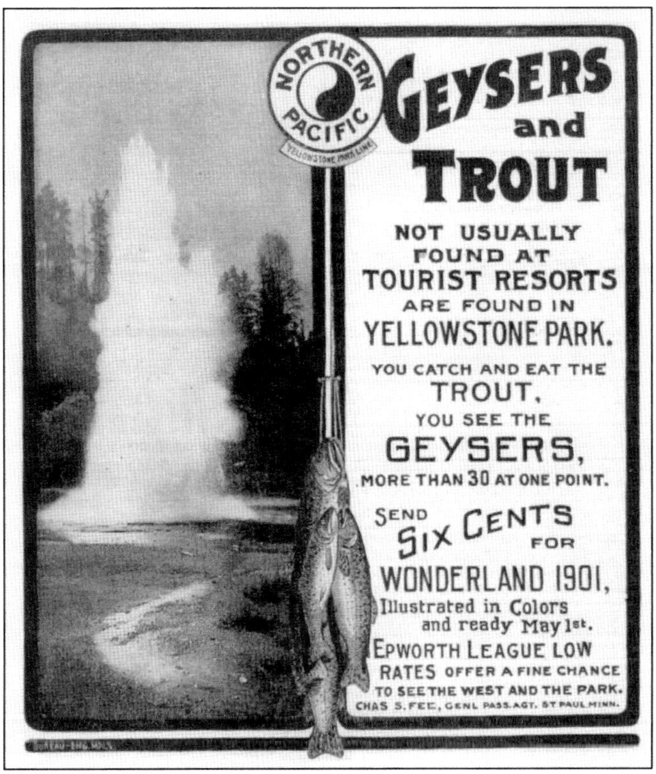

Appealing to the sportsman as well as the tourist, this 1901 NPRR Wonderland brochure represented general passenger agent Chas S. Fee's remarkable promotional efforts to hook the interest of potential travelers to Yellowstone. According to this advertisement, Yellowstone offered vacationers a place where they could not only catch sight of, but also cast for and consume, some of nature's wonders. (Watry Collection.)

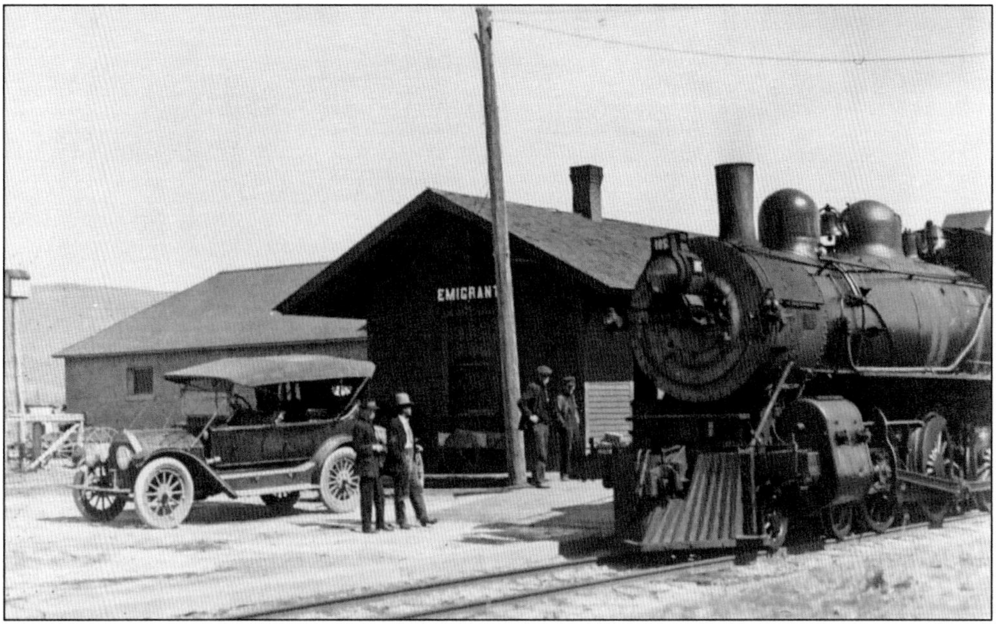

East of the Emigrant NPRR depot lies Emigrant Gulch, scene of the beginnings of this small community. Thomas Curry discovered gold in 1863, setting off a small gold rush. Yellowstone City was established in the fall of 1864, and although its future was short-lived, sporadic mining continued over the next century. Emigrant, also known as Fridley, was among several whistle-stops along the route to Yellowstone National Park. (Yellowstone Gateway Museum.)

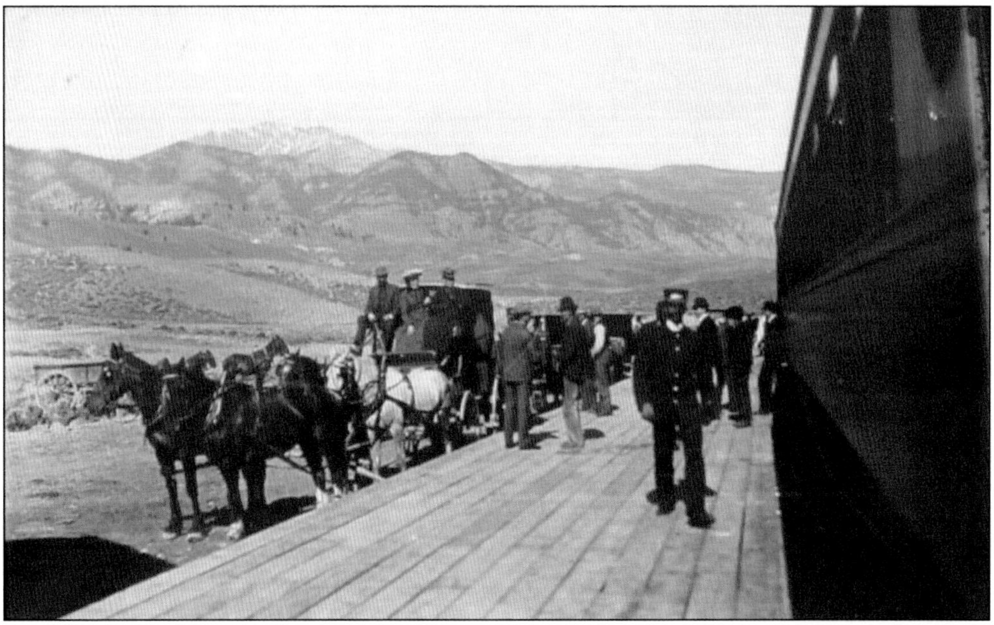

This rare L. A. Huffman image of passengers debarking from the train in Cinnabar, Montana, represents one of the scarce photographs of this hastily constructed town that existed from 1883 until 1903. Resolution of a land dispute in 1902 resumed the railroad's trek to Gardiner and tolled a death knell for Cinnabar. Occasional snow skiffs that outline foundations of long-gone buildings are ghostly reminders of this once busy hamlet. (Watry Collection.)

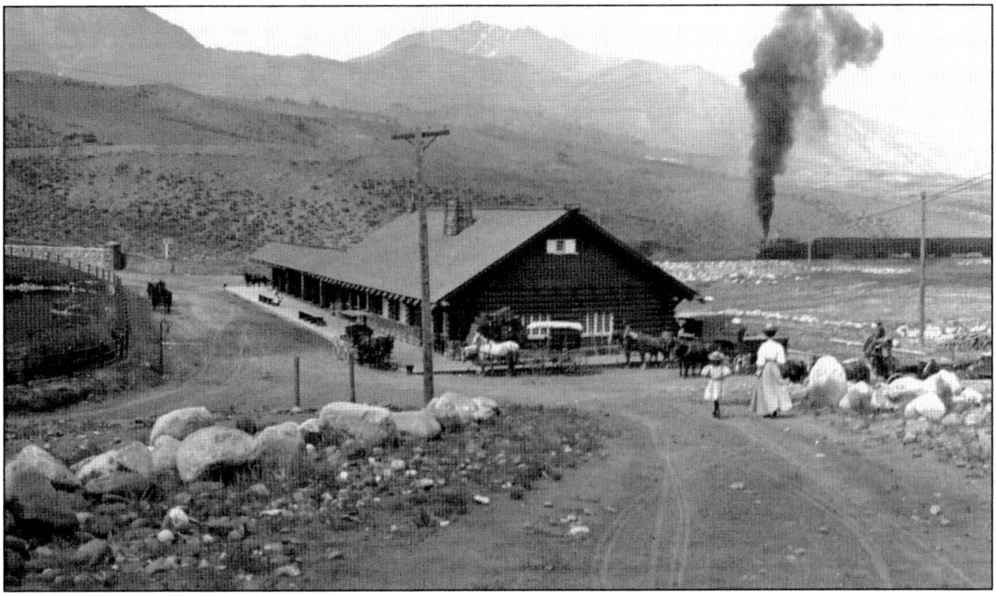

Grand adventures awaited Wonderland travelers in 1903 as smoke-belching locomotives chugged along the Yellowstone River amid the lofty heights of the Absaroka and Gallatin Mountains. Majestic Electric Peak, Sepulcher Mountain, and the newly constructed rustic log depot designed by famed architect Robert Reamer greeted visitors to Gardiner and Yellowstone. The depot welcomed visitors for 50 years until the closing of the railroad era brought about its demise in 1954. (Goss Collection.)

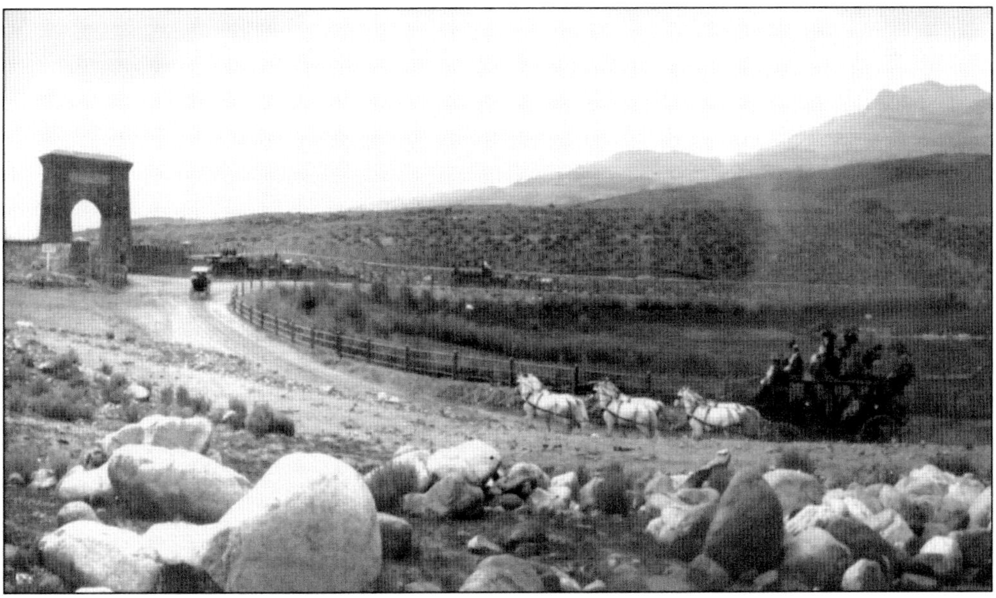

Departing Gardiner depot, travelers climbed aboard a 36-passenger, six-horse Tally-Ho stagecoach commanded by a "Knight of the Lash." Sporting monikers such as Buffalo Jim, Geyser Bob, and Happy Jack, these experienced jehus harnessed execrable language skills, yet treated their charges with regard and utmost courtesy. They expertly piloted passengers through the great stone arch dedicated by Theodore Roosevelt in April 1903, and thus began the journey to Yellowstone. (Goss Collection.)

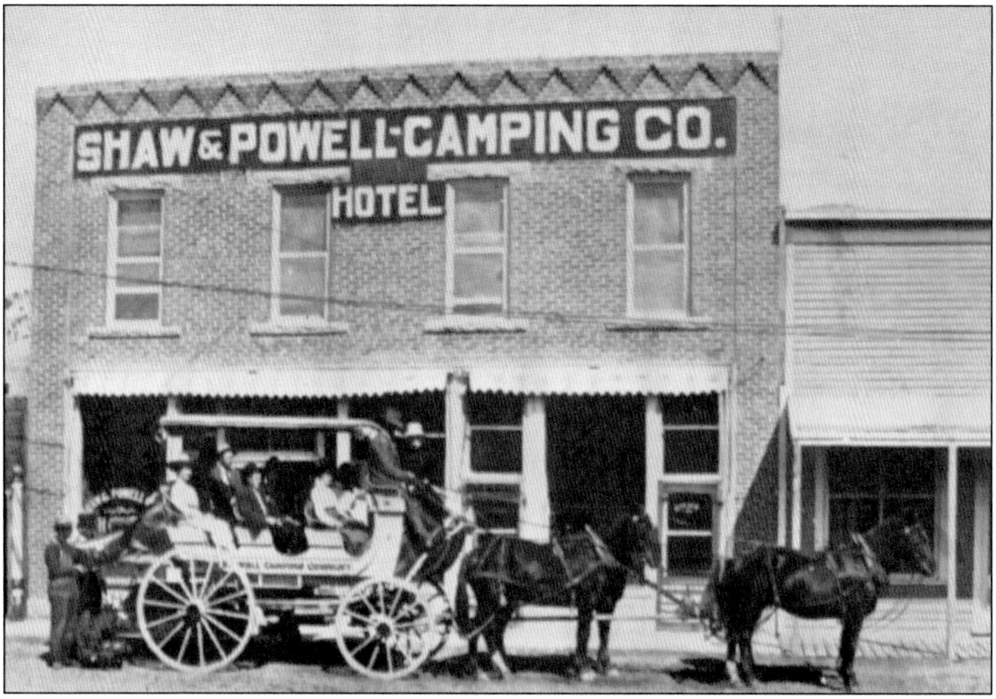

Headquartered in Livingston, the Shaw and Powell Camping company provided camping expeditions into Yellowstone Park from 1898 to 1916. The company was headed by members of the Shaw family that included Amos, Chester, Walter, Leo, and Jessie. This hotel was established in Gardiner for the convenience of their Yellowstone guests. (Yellowstone Gateway Museum.)

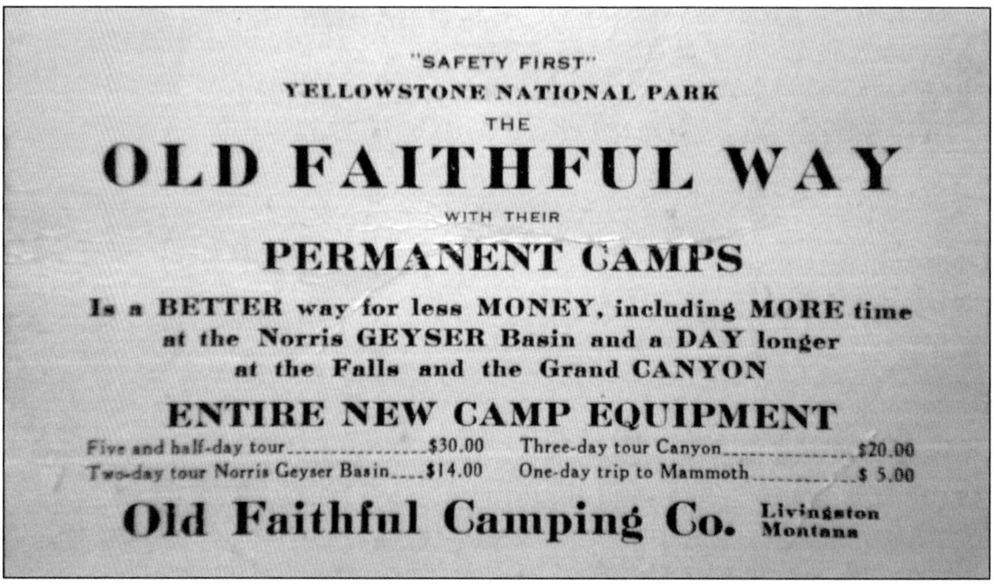

Brothers O. M. and W. N. Hefferlin of Livingston began operating portable tent camps in Yellowstone in 1910. Known as the Old Faithful Camping Company, they advertised themselves as the "Old Faithful Way." In 1915, they were authorized to operate four permanent camps and carried 1,692 tourists that year. The company was absorbed into the Yellowstone Park Camping Company in 1917 as a result of changes in park policy. (Yellowstone National Park Archives.)

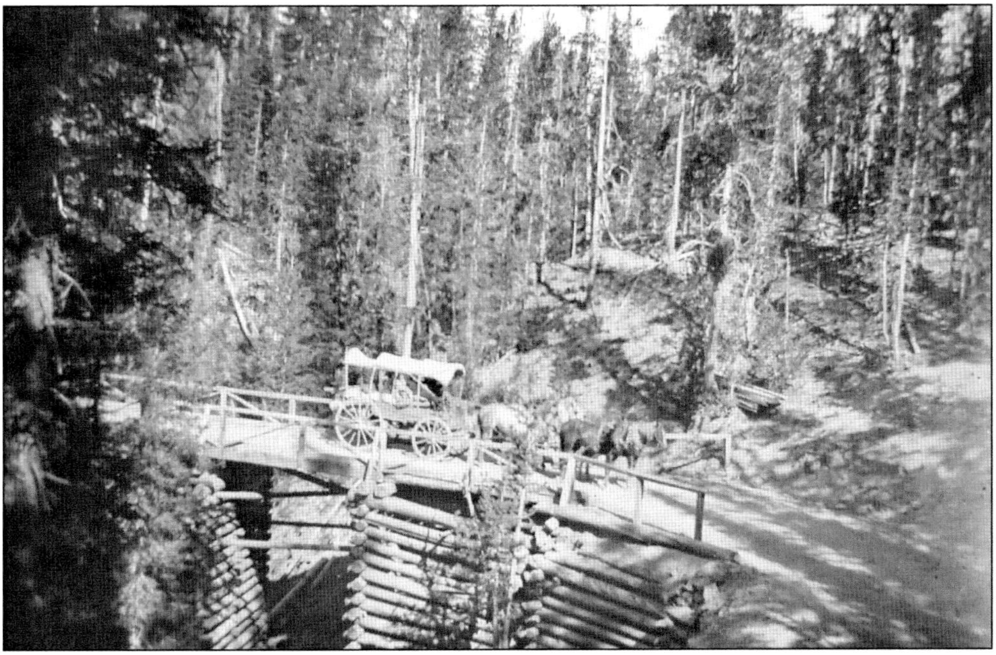

This view of Livingston businessman C. A. Talbot and his party traveling across the Continental Divide revealed the primitive conditions of Yellowstone's roads and bridges in August 1894. A remote wilderness with a limited snow-free season hampered efforts to construct substantial roads and bridges in the park until well into the 1900s. (Private collection.)

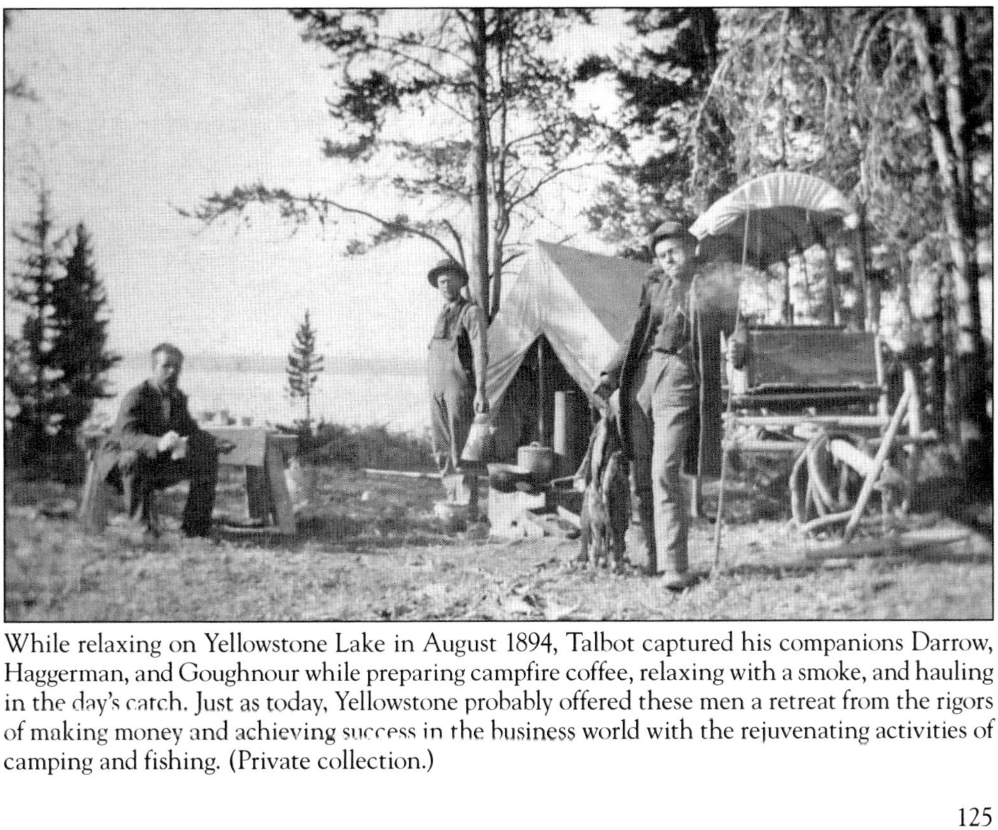

While relaxing on Yellowstone Lake in August 1894, Talbot captured his companions Darrow, Haggerman, and Goughnour while preparing campfire coffee, relaxing with a smoke, and hauling in the day's catch. Just as today, Yellowstone probably offered these men a retreat from the rigors of making money and achieving success in the business world with the rejuvenating activities of camping and fishing. (Private collection.)

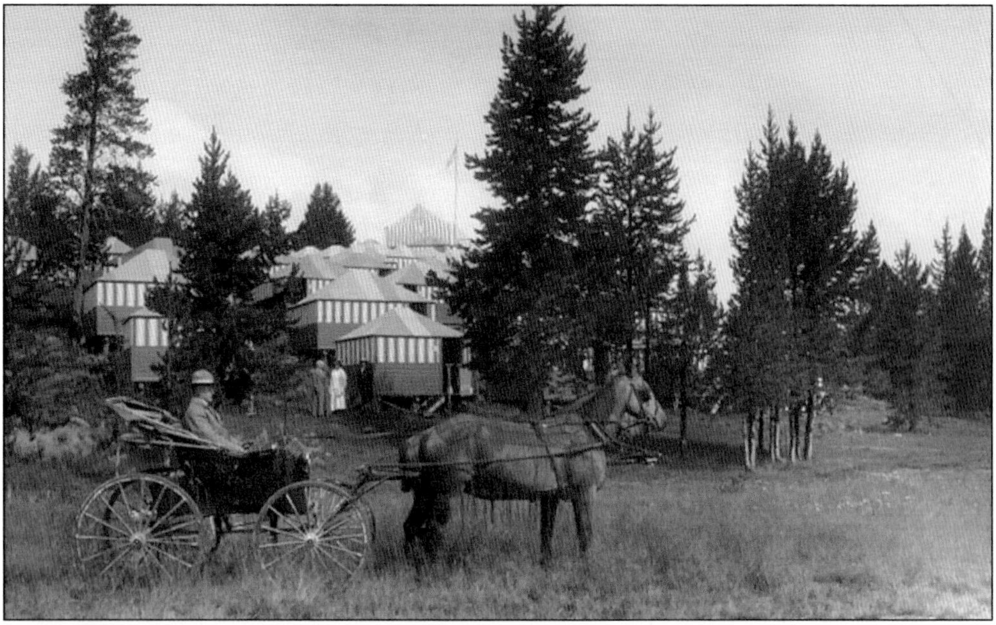

A. W. Miles, driving his one horse-surrey into Geyser Camp at Old Faithful in this 1915 image, seemed to be a Livingston businessman who invested in everything, including the Wylie Camping Company. Purchasing the camping company from William Wallace Wylie at the end of 1905, Miles obtained a 10-year lease from the Department of the Interior and proceeded to make considerable improvements to the popular camping outfit. (Watry Collection.)

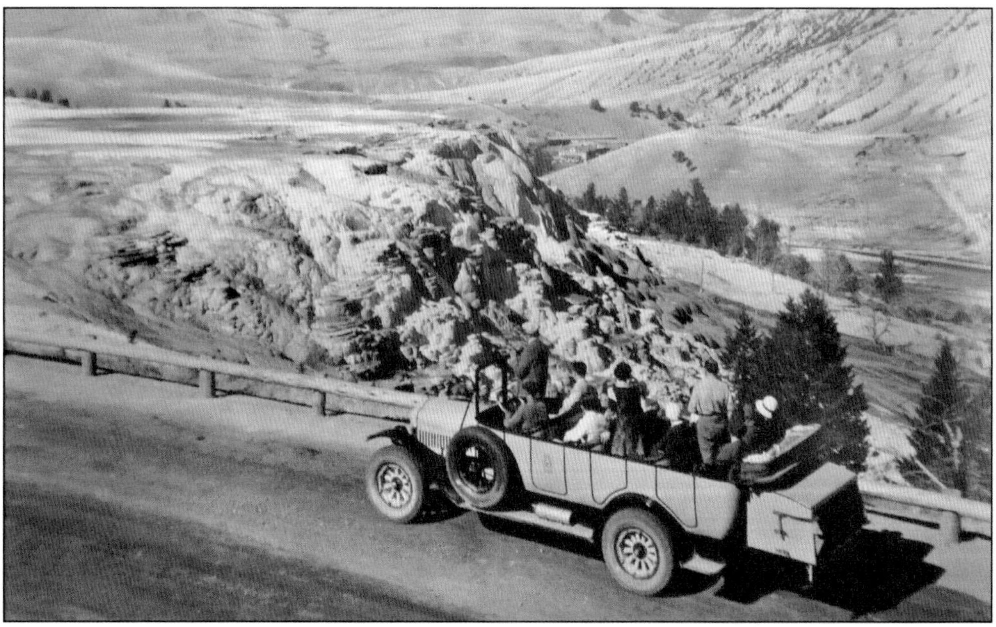

Until 1917, Yellowstone represented the last vestige of stagecoach transportation in America. That year, 117 White Motor Company auto stages took over Yellowstone's dusty trails to transport tourists from feature to feature. Park tours that previously lasted five and a half days were reduced to four and a half days with these motorized stages, and thus began the transition from the slow-paced grand tour of Yellowstone to swift modern excursion. (Yellowstone National Park.)

Bibliography

Anaconda Standard. Various issues. Anaconda, MT: The Anaconda Company.

Brekke, Jerry. *Our Time & Place*. Livingston, MT: Livingston Enterprise, 2003.

Centennial Scrapbook. Livingston, MT: Livingston Enterprise, 1982.

"The Growth of Livingston." *Rocky Mountain Magazine*. March 1902, Vol. IV, No. 1.

Illustrated History of the Yellowstone Valley. Spokane, WA: Western Historical Publishing Company, 1907.

Leeson, Michael A. *History of Montana, 1739–1885*. Chicago: Warner, Beers, and Company, 1885.

Livingston Enterprise Souvenir Edition, Park County, 1900. Livingston, MT: Livingston Publishing Company, 1900.

Park County Historical Society. *History of Park County, Montana 1984*. Dallas, TX: Taylor Publishing Company, 1984.

Polk, R. L. *R. L. Polk & Co.'s Livingston City Directory*. Helena, MT: R. L. Polk and Company of Montana, 1904, 1906, 1908, 1914, and 1918.

Progressive Men of the State of Montana. Chicago: Bowen and Company, 1902.

Sanders, Helen Fitzgerald. *A History of Montana*. Chicago and New York: Lewis Publishing Company, 1913.

Stout, Tom. *Montana, Its Story and Biography*. Chicago: American Historical Society, 1921.

The Livingston Enterprise. Various issues. Livingston, MT: Livingston Enterprise.

Van West, Carroll. *Capitalism on the Frontier: Billings and the Yellowstone Valley in the Nineteenth Century*. Lincoln, NE: University of Nebraska Press, 1993.

Whithorn, Bill and Doris. *Photo History of Livingston, Montana*. Livingston, MT: Park County News, 1966.

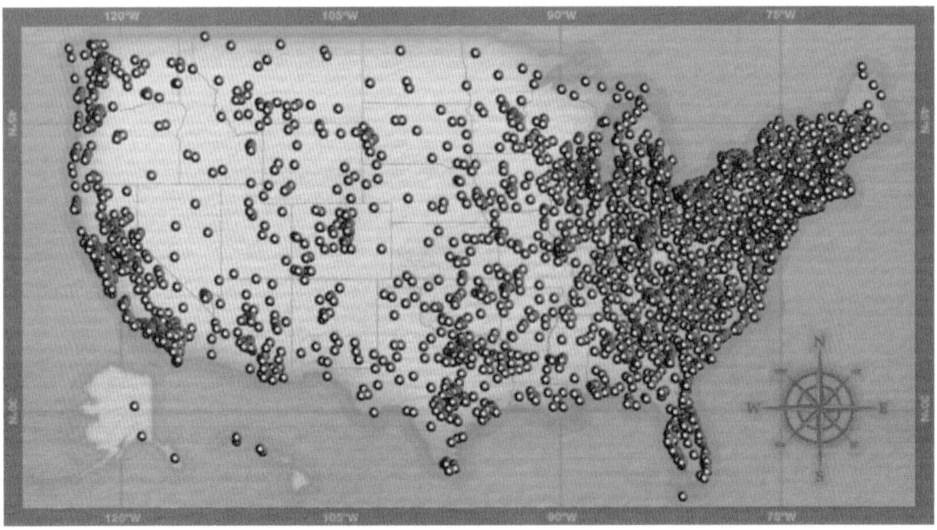